Formula One Uncovered

Formula One Uncovered

The Other Side of the Track

DERICK ALLSOP

HEADLINE

First published in 1998
by HEADLINE BOOK PUBLISHING

10 9 8 7 6 5 4 3 2 1

Cataloguing in Publication Data is available
from the British Library

ISBN 0 7472 2293 2

All photographs in this book are
copyright Formula One Pictures.

Typeset by
Letterpart Limited, Reigate, Surrey

Printed and bound in Great Britain by
Mackays of Chatham PLC, Chatham, Kent

HEADLINE BOOK PUBLISHING
A division of Hodder Headline PLC
338 Euston Road
London NW1 3BH

Contents

To colleagues past and present

Acknowledgements

I wish to thank the entire cast of the Forumla One show for providing me – directly or indirectly – with the material and inspiration to write this book. My sincere hope is that it serves as a tribute to their enduring skill, diligence and humanity. I would also like to thank members of my own team, especially Ian Marshall and Marion Paull, and Sue, Natalie and Kate Allsop.

Introduction

Near apoplectic commentaries and screaming headlines are as punctual as the first primrose, and tell us the same thing: it's Formula One time again. The perennial bloom of sport's most exotic show will mesmerise billions through a global media network. After a winter of seemingly interminable testing and talking, the 1998 World Championship comes out in Australia, then moves on through South America, leaving in its slipstream regulation controversy, conflict and cries of treachery.

At Melbourne, McLaren and one of their drivers, David Coulthard, are castigated when the Scotsman deliberately and overtly slows down, allowing his team-mate, Mika Hakkinen, to pass him and win the race. In Brazil, Hakkinen needs no one's help, dominating proceedings from start to finish, and Formula One is roundly condemned as a processional bore. In Argentina, Michael Schumacher puts the racing back into Grand Prix with a characteristically uncompromising overtaking manoeuvre which earns him victory and incurs the wrath of Coulthard, who complains of foul play. An authentic Championship, with all its phobias, foibles and fantasies, is on the road once more.

Next stop is Imola, home of the San Marino Grand Prix, first of the European races and, by common consent, the start of the season proper. The racing from now on is expected to reflect the true state of play. No longer will anyone be given the benefit of early year doubts or be allowed to hide behind those 'inevitable teething troubles'. The genuine title contenders have emerged, the pretenders have been exposed, and the no-hopers consigned to the forlorn struggle at the back of the grid.

There is another reason for this general sense of stability and order; it has nothing to do with the racing and everything to do with home comforts. Since all the teams are based in Europe, the journeys to races are shorter, there are no jetlag problems to contend with and surroundings are reassuringly familiar. Teams are able to move their cars and equipment from factory to circuit and back again by road in their own giant transporters, rather than having to crate everything to be sent by air. They also take along their own, purpose-built motorhomes instead of making do with cramped, spartan Portacabins. They park their vehicles and erect their awnings on designated plots in a designated Formula One paddock, a no-go area behind the pits for all but card-carrying drivers, officials and personnel. The nomadic tribe set up camp in this way more or less every other weekend of the summer, providing for themselves not only a workplace but also means of sustenance, shelter, companionship, gossip and all the other features of a village environment.

The exclusiveness of the Formula One paddock renders it all the more alluring to those who do not have the appropriate pass to gain entry. It takes on the aura and mystery of a forbidden fortress. At any Grand Prix, starry-eyed fans press their faces against the fencing or gather at the gate, hoping their vigil will be rewarded with a glimpse of their heroes or a clue to the machinations of the inner sanctum. The racing on the track is the tip of the iceberg. So much more of the action, intrigue and human interplay goes on behind the scenes, out of public sight and sound.

This is the story of the 1998 Formula One World Championship from inside the paddock. In many ways it is another story altogether. Here is a stage in itself, creating its own plots, dramas and characters largely unknown to the outside world. Until now.

1
Imola

GOD'S LITTLE GIFT

The simple motorway sign indicating entry to Emilia Romagna is as warm and assuring as any embrace. No disrespect to Lombardy, of course. Its great plain, nourished by the Po basin, is vital to Italy and the voracious appetite of the Italian people, but all those flat fields do become a tad tedious after a while. Once in this north-central region the senses are instantly excited. Here beckons the prospect of an earlier summer and the first rolling ascent of the Apennines. The hospitality is somehow more personal, the pasta unrivalled; and God gave this to Formula One.

In a way it is too much too soon, a spoiler for the rest of the season. Monaco has its obvious appeal, Spa has the greatest circuit of them all and Monza is the spiritual epicentre of motor racing, and yet nowhere packages all the emotional requirements quite like Imola.

The circuit here hosts Italy's other World Championship round, conveniently engineered under the banner of the San Marino Grand Prix. The tiny republic of San Marino is perched on a rock 50 miles south-east of Imola, inland from the hectic holiday resort of Rimini. San Marino has long been famed for stamps, more recently for its 'national' football team's eight-second goal against England, but perhaps above all now for its place on the Formula One calendar.

The case for two races in Italy is overwhelming. Motor racing is second only to football in the sporting culture and psyche here, and to Italians motor racing essentially means Ferrari. It is a phenomenon without parallel. The home of Ferrari is Maranello, a short blast up the road from the track dedicated to the memory of the Old Man's son, Dino, following his death. When the creator of the legend died, in 1988, they renamed it the Auto-dromo Enzo e Dino Ferrari.

At the motorway exit for Imola stands the Molino Rosso, the Red Mill, traditionally the Ferrari hotel for the race held in their heartland. It looks surprisingly modest, but then history has its own values. This entire weekend will be a monument to a national obsession. On the drive into the town the first evidence of red favours shares prominence with stacks of circuit directions: this way or that, according to pass, function and status. Formula One is organised like that.

There is a uniformity to this organisation yet outside the circuit, at least, all is authentically Italian: expressive, mildly to hopelessly chaotic, and loud. Even that seems soothingly reassur-ing. The weather, too, is a comforting agent. This Thursday afternoon is caressed by a gentle glow. It feels like Latin Europe for those arriving from the chilly outposts of the continent's northern lands. The trees and bushes are verdant and the old folk are shedding their top layers.

Young people wearing official bibs and an air of importance check passes along the route into the circuit towards the car parks. Drivers and high-ranking team officials are accorded places closest to the pits and paddock. The ever-expanding area beyond the Formula One paddock provides sites for the support-ing race teams and the digital TV compound which represents one of the most ambitious ventures in the ever-expanding commercial empire of Bernie Ecclestone, the man commonly referred to as Formula One's 'Ringmaster'.

Ecclestone, a former team owner, recognised the potential of the Grand Prix show, provided it was organised and marketed properly. As president of the Formula One Constructors' Asso-ciation, he ensured the organisation and the marketing, selling the package globally and taking his cut of the television fees. Digital TV, he is convinced, is the obvious next stage and he has gambled heavily on that conviction. To run the service he employs 260 people and to carry the equipment beyond Europe he lays on two jumbo jets. In Europe Ecclestone, like the teams, moves everything by road. His fleet of 18 silver-grey Renault trucks are now parked in slightly angled formation and in order according to their British registration plates. Alongside and beyond are sundry other vehicles. The whole setting up operation can take the best part of a week to complete.

Not so long ago this area was agricultural land; a vegetable patch and orchard still survive around a defiantly self-sufficient household. The juxtaposition is as bizarrely incongruous as it is inspiringly improbable.

Beyond the car parks, fruit trees and digital TV tent looms the final frontier. This is like coming to the last sheet of wrapping paper in pass the parcel. Beyond this high-tech turnstile lies the paddock, the dreamer's nirvana, forbidden territory to all but those with the appropriate pass around their necks. Even then, there can be anxiety, waiting for a machine to confirm the validity of the card. Eddie Jordan, one of the team owners, made several vain attempts to activate the turnstile on his 50th birthday and was eventually flashed the message: 'You're too old.' Contrary to popular belief, humour still has a place in the Formula One fraternity.

The confines of this paddock are determined not only by the pits, to the left, but also by the flow of the river, to the right, forming a wedge-shaped area. Garages and therefore parking spaces for transporters and motorhomes are allocated according to rankings at the end of the previous season, so naturally the top teams have based themselves at the nearer, spacious end and lower teams get the thin end of the wedge. Minardi, the other Italian team, who haven't scored a point in the past two seasons, are squeezed in at the top, at right angles to the rest and alongside Bridgestone, the newer of the two tyre companies. Goodyear, long established and long-time monopolists of the market, claim the privileged ground in what they say will be their last season.

Above the pits are hospitality suites, offices and the media centre. Above all that is the Paddock Club, a meticulously manicured and highly expensive corporate hospitality veranda, partitioned for individual sponsors. Beyond this block is the control tower, nerve centre of the racing operation.

By mid-afternoon the paddock is busier if still relatively relaxed. Most drivers and team members arrive at European races on the Thursday, the day before first practice. The majority have flown into Bologna, others to Milan, some, with private aircraft, to Forli. Gangs of mechanics, in team jackets, slacks and ties, trudge through the paddock dragging cases and bags. They have hotel reservations but how many hours' sleep they get for the next three nights depends on their workload. All-night rebuilds and repairs are not uncommon.

Drivers, team members and officials co-exist, not always easily, with the media and sponsors' guests. Already a familiar picture has emerged. When a driver ventures from his lair – a corner of the team motorhome or transporter – depending on his stature, he will run the gauntlet of the press corps or attract little more than a cursory word and a snap. Michael Schumacher is under constant siege. Not only is he acknowledged as the best driver in the world – some would say by a distance, some that he could even be the best of all time – but also he happens to be with Ferrari. A permanent guard of photographers watch the red motorhome and its accompanying activity. Schumacher rarely saunters in sight of the camera. He moves in straight lines, and rapidly, from motorhome to transporter to garage.

Jean Alesi, a French Sicilian and once the darling of the Ferrari fans, can take the air at will now he is a Sauber driver. But then he is a very different animal, his emotion seemingly charging off the public adulation. Mika Salo, a Finn, steps outside the awning of his team, Arrows, and chats with a couple of people. Jan Magnussen, a Dane, appears from his cover at Stewart and glances up and down the paddock. 'Looking for somewhere else to go,' someone suggests, cuttingly but apparently with good reason. Toranosuke Takagi, a young Japanese causing a stir with Tyrrell, flashes across view. 'He's catching the eye of the girls as well. Long hair, nice face.'

Back in the vicinity of Ferrari, Ulsterman Eddie Irvine, the team's number two driver, rests on a scooter and natters with engineers. Irvine's sister, Sonia, is never far away. Slim and blonde, she is his physio, organiser and, it appears, nursemaid.

Ecclestone is in conversation with Johnny Herbert's physio outside the Sauber motorhome yet such is his peripheral awareness he reaches out sideways to shake hands with someone else eager for a moment of his attention. Bernie, as he is commonly addressed in the paddock, still revels in being the hands-on boss of Formula One. Usually he has his hands full, a walkie-talkie in one, a mobile phone in the other. He is a tiny, dapper figure, in immaculately pressed white shirt and dark slacks. He is 67 and many here worry about the day he decides he cannot go on.

The marketing machinery established by Ecclestone is lubricated by publicity and at three o'clock the first of the weekend's official press conferences is held in the media centre. More than 600 journalists and some 1,000 television personnel are accredited for each of the 11 European rounds of the Championship. Today's line-up wins the approval of the press: Michael Schumacher, Jacques Villeneuve, David Coulthard and Jarno Trulli. An Italian driving for the Prost team, Trulli is granted the courtesy of inquiry about his season so far, but most interest is focused on Coulthard and Schumacher, the pair involved in the controversy in Argentina. They make a show of civility by shaking hands, but Coulthard still contends the German was unfairly aggressive in his overtaking manoeuvre. He seeks to rebut accusations he does not have the stuff of champions.

'I don't think my ability as a racer can be questioned,' the Scotsman says. 'Sometimes you come off better, sometimes worse. You don't base your opinion of a driver on one race. I'm comfortable with the way I race within the rules. I would never deliberately run anyone off the road or put them into the wall. But that doesn't mean I won't squeeze them as far as I think is safe. That's fundamental to racing.' Pressed to say whether he will react differently if Schumacher muscles inside him again, Coulthard smiles and replies: 'Yes, next time I'll do something different.' Schumacher, sitting a few feet away, smirks.

Villeneuve, the defending world champion, has also come under attack from the media. He is deemed to have made an inept start to the season for a Williams team patently in need of forceful leadership. The Canadian sinks low in his seat, barely visible but for his bleached hair. Right now he might prefer anonymity. He responds to the criticism.

'I don't think it's fair but it happens all the time. You're only as good as your last race and people forget the other twenty or thirty races and all the pressure you're fighting under.'

Down in the paddock, the previous champion, Damon Hill, is another target for the media inquisition. The Englishman has made scant impact in his first three races for Jordan. He has so far failed to out-qualify his team-mate, Ralf Schumacher, the younger brother of Michael, and has yet to register a point. To Hill's relief, 22-year-old Schumacher has yet to finish a race.

Hill's detractors – and he has many in the paddock, chief among them Michael Schumacher – question his pace and now his motivation. They also maintain he is moody. Those closer to him tell you he is a thoroughly decent, intelligent, sensitive man with an alert sense of fun. It could be his 'moodiness' is a product of shyness. Certainly he does not always look comfortable under public or media scrutiny. He is a mite uneasy now, confronting a group of British journalists around a table outside one of the Jordan motorhomes. He is, however, articulate and talks a good interview.

'Ralf has impressed me,' he admits. 'I heard all sorts of rumours and reports about him before I joined the team but I was determined to take as I found and he's a very good team-mate. He's very quick and that's a challenge for me. His pace is without question and that's good for me. I need a spur, that motivation. As a driver you're in it to pit yourself against the best talent. I'm surprised I've been behind him in the three qualifying sessions so far and I wouldn't want that to continue too long.'

That chore over, Hill has something else to attend to before he can retreat for the evening. He has a modelling engagement – in the middle of the paddock. The photo-shoot prompts suitably irreverent comments from passing team members. 'Must be for *Playboy*,' one reckons. 'It's for his collection,' interjects another, straight-faced. Hill effects various poses, showing jackets and T-shirts, standing and sitting on a scooter. He is hugely grateful to be told by the photographer 'that's it' and gives him no opportunity to change his mind.

The sun is still warm as it falls in the early evening sky. Some will take refuge in Imola, others adjourn to towns and villages up to 50 miles away. Those heading up the hill on the other side of the circuit, between the vines and the cypress trees, to the spa resort of Riolo Terme, believe they have found heaven.

By 8.30 on the Friday morning the sun is already promising another idyllic day. This is the first day of business proper. Practice starts at 11 and goes on until midday. A further one-hour session begins at one. The times recorded today are unofficial in the sense that they do not count towards determining grid positions. Teams concentrate on finding a good set-up for Sunday's race.

Mechanics and engineers have begun work on preparing the cars and planning their schedule. Some are at breakfast. This may be the middle of Italy but the unmistakable smell of the traditional English breakfast wafts through the paddock. Of the 11 teams, two are based in Italy, one in France, one in Switzerland and the rest in Britain.

A fry-up tends to be off-limits for drivers, even the British. Muesli and bananas – not necessarily together – are common fare. The drivers often take their first meal of the day with their first technical meeting. They confront the inevitable photographic reception committee as they arrive in the paddock and make for their respective camps.

Michael Schumacher, his wife Corinna and entourage try to bypass the obligatory turnstile in a Ferrari people carrier but, to their dismay, are ordered off at the vehicle entrance and made to go the way of everybody else. Even the combined power of Schumacher and Ferrari is repelled this time. 'Quite right too,' mutter onlookers. Not content with that, one witness offers the opinion: 'Corinna's looking rough these days. I think Frentzen got the better of that deal.' Laughter among his colleagues. Corinna Betsch was the girlfriend of Heinz-Harald Frentzen before she fell for Schumacher. Frentzen's current lady is reckoned by one seasoned observer of these matters to be 'the best looker in the paddock'.

Damon Hill enters the paddock with no fuss or commotion, huge feet striding out, familiar serious expression shaded by the equally familiar London Rowing Club cap. Come 9.30 drivers are still rolling in. Johnny Herbert is among the latecomers, scuttling between the knots of people with suitable haste. He is unshaven, takes a bit of ribbing and is typically jovial. He'll have time for a chat after his breakfast/meeting, he promises.

A British driver from a bygone era has the cameras trained on him. John Surtees, the only world champion on two wheels and four, is here to give the gallery a glimpse of a classic Mercedes and, doubtless, enjoy the attention. He won his four-wheel title in 1964, driving a Ferrari, and the bond with Italy has endured the passing decades. Suddenly Schumacher, still dressed in dark civvies, makes a beeline for the motorhome and a photographer stumbles backwards in his anxiety for yet another angle on the great man.

Schumacher's sportsmanship may be in question after a series of skirmishes over the years, but his pre-eminence as a driver remains unchallenged by all but the blindingly bigoted. Hill's reputation as a sportsman is unblemished, but as a racer . . . The debate continues and Eddie Jordan, an ebullient, loquacious Dubliner who is reported to be paying Hill £4.5 million for his services this year, is a worried man.

> I'm seriously worried. Even as we speak he's in there having a one to one with Gary Anderson [the team's technical director]. Gary is telling Damon he owes it to himself, his fans, everyone, to show what he can do. It's not about money. This is about wanting to perform as you can. It is not a question of kicking backsides because if there is any kicking of backsides to be done that would be my job. If Ralf continues to out-qualify Damon, and gets it together in the races and runs ahead of Damon continu-ally, I would want to know why. Damon needs things around him to be in good shape before he can show his

true ability. That's my problem and my job. He's got to do better and so have we. We've got to give him a better car and there's no doubt Damon can help make the car better.

Damon's got to be saying to himself. 'How can I let a twenty-two-year-old blow me off?' I would expect Damon to be quicker than Ralf based on his experience, knowledge of the circuits, set-up and so on. Damon has certainly fired up Ralf. They get on extremely well but Michael is no doubt telling Ralf not to let Damon out-qualify him. From here on in I expect a significant improvement.

One of Jordan's lieutenants doubts Hill will improve his pace sufficiently to contain the precocious Schumacher. 'I can't see that he will ever be faster than Ralf.' The sniggers ripple through the camp and along the row of motorhomes. The competitive edge in this village sharpens the emotions. Hill's discomfort is relished by some because he is perceived as a driver of unexceptional talent who found himself in the right car – the Williams – at the right time and has shamelessly cashed in. After being shown the door by Williams he joined the lowly Arrows team for around £4.5 million and was publicly admonished mid-season by his boss, Tom Walkinshaw, who questioned his application. Now his critics say it is a case of *déjà vu*.

Hill is repeatedly questioned about his motivation and here he reiterates: 'I'm just as motivated as ever.' He does, however, add: 'It's just that the position is different. Your spirits are lifted when you're running at the front because victory is in your grasp and you can't manufacture that.'

Johnny Herbert has consistently stated he believes he is quicker than Hill and would prove it, given the equipment, a conviction borne of racing experience before they graduated to Formula One. Herbert is just about the most popular driver in Grand Prix racing: small, smiling, mischievous, candid, unaffected and uncomplicated. He still walks with a slight limp, the legacy of a horrific crash during a Formula 3000 race in 1988. Many feel he has never had the break he deserves. He won two races with Benetton in 1995, although largely by default and consequently he received little credit, especially as his team-mate, Michael Schumacher, won the Championship. Some say that season exposed his weaknesses: a lack of application and intelligence. Now he drives for the modest Sauber team and still, at the age of 33, craves that elusive 'chance'. Watching Hill and Coulthard heightens the frustration. He sits in his race-suit, munching a banana and chewing over the plight of his compatriots.

Damon is damaging his reputation, and those people who never really rated him all that highly in the first place are beginning to say 'I told you so'. Everyone knows the Williams was two seconds a lap quicker than the others, and although Damon did a good job in winning the Championship people have always had their doubts about his speed. Now he's being outpaced by an inexperienced team-mate and it's not good for him, or his reputation. Jordan expected better things of him and if it goes on like this I don't think they will want him next year.

You just sense certain things with Damon. He has been saying some very odd things in press articles. He is still um-ing and aah-ing about Michael and things that have happened between them in the past. You need to put that to one side and get on with it. I've had my problems with Michael, having been with him at Benetton, but you have to be positive and look ahead. The other thing about Damon is that he is so relaxed. In fact he's so relaxed he's almost horizontal. Motivation can obviously be a problem when you've been world champion and done well out of the sport financially. I don't know whether Damon has got a motivation problem, but I do know that as a world champion he will be expected to produce certain standards and at the moment he is not doing that.

Herbert does, however, have rather more sympathy for Coulthard, suspecting there is more to the McLaren conundrum than meets the eye, yet still warns the Scot he must assert himself more forcibly on the track and off it. They all have their pride and self-belief. If they didn't they would have no place at this level. A steely determination to promote his own cause lurks beneath Herbert's amiable countenance.

David needs to be harder, both in his racing and within the team. I have learned that from experience. Everyone can see what is required on the circuit but may not necessarily know the story of what goes on behind the scenes. For some time there have been suggestions of favouritism towards Mika at McLaren and that could make things very difficult for David. It happens in Formula One. It happened to me when I was with Michael at Benetton. Although I won two races that season I know I didn't get fair treatment and it harmed my career. I won't allow myself to be put in that situation again.

People tell me I am driving better than ever and I believe I am. I am outpacing Jean [his team-mate, Alesi] and everybody has always said how quick he is. I've got plenty of racing left in me and both Damon and Nigel Mansell were much older than I am when they won the Championship. All I can do is make the best of what I have got now and convince a top team that I am their man.

With that he hurries to his garage, his physio hard on his heels, clutching a bottle of some energising drink Herbert will presumably be required to empty before practice – barely 20 minutes away – to keep up his fluid levels. Schumacher, now in red overalls, makes for his car, a film crew recording any and every flicker of the eyelashes. Between the two one-hour sessions, and again after, the ritual monitoring of Schumacher is unrelenting. He has finished the day third fastest, behind Hakkinen and Coulthard, and a scrum of reporters wants his reaction. He says he is a little disappointed and looks downcast, which will fuel stories he is likely to leave Ferrari for McLaren at the end of the season. Ralf Schumacher is again faster than Hill, while Herbert is well down the order at 15.

Up and down the paddock people with no apparent work to do amble in the sunshine, hands clasped behind their backs, as they would in any Italian town or village. They all have swivel heads, missing nothing and no one. Irvine is out in the open again, relatively undisturbed. He has had a prickly relationship with the Italian press ever since he joined the team and dismissed the media as knowing 'nothing about motor racing'. He sneers contemptuously at any challenge to his judgement.

Giancarlo Fisichella was hailed as Italy's long-awaited star last year only to be put through the mill this season by his Benetton team-mate, Alexander Wurz of Austria. Still, Fisichella being approached by a curvy creature with short-cropped blonde hair is deemed photogenic and soon the pair are surrounded. Norbert Haug, Mercedes' racing chief, would never claim to be photogenic but his familiar, portly figure is very much to the fore this season.

Other team officials seek shade and a degree of privacy, leaning by the side of transporters and chewing the fat. Already there is much fat to chew, including an exposé by a former Benetton mechanic of the 'real' Gerhard Berger and Jean Alesi, partners at the team in 1996 and 1997. The unmasking of Berger, a much-liked and respected driver, is particularly startling. He is denounced for his incompetence and a catalogue of whinges and excuses.

It is an irresistible topic of conversation in this community and leads to more revelations about the supposedly easy-going Austrian. Berger admitted that attempting to keep pace with Ayrton Senna during their time together at McLaren screwed him in the head and that he regained his sanity only when he left the team. More recently, however, a medical in Japan discovered traces of ulcers he suffered during his ordeal alongside the Brazilian. Someone else recalls when Berger's temper snapped and he reduced Benetton's press officer to tears.

A few unpleasant clouds shroud the first light of Saturday but by the time the paddock is bustling with life the sun is piercing its way through. The build-up of traffic on the approach roads is reflected by the additional sense of urgency at the circuit. One and a half hours of practice, with a half-hour break, starts at nine o'clock, one hour of qualifying gets under way at one o'clock. It is a big day of business and the shift up the gears is discernible.

The scrum outside the Ferrari awning is agitated, photographers and film crews on tip-toe, straining for a shot. Presumably of Schumacher? Or perhaps of Luca di Montezemolo, the president? The crowd parts and out comes Niki Lauda, wearing the trademark red cap, jacket and jeans. The Austrian, who almost died in a Ferrari after winning the first of his three world titles and is now a consultant to the team, even dresses his airline crew in jeans.

Schumacher apart, the quickest man across the paddock tarmac has to be Alain Prost, four times world champion and now commander of his own team. The Italian media have Ferrari, the French have Prost, and the chase is almost as intense. The tiny figure is swallowed up but drags the pack along with him. Coulthard cuts an altogether different figure. Tall, cool, overalls unzipped down to his waist, he calmly sips a drink as he strolls to work. Schumacher, helmet in hand, has cries of 'Schumi, Schumi' raining down on him from a balcony above. His eyes remain focused on the back of the garage and he is lost from view.

The two-hour lunch-break gives the paddock guests ample time to saunter and star-gaze, as well as partake of the hospitality. They tip-toe through rivers of soapy water, running from the piles of wheels being washed by mechanics. The Italians among the paddock set – all shades, swagger and chins pointing skywards – recognise someone in the distance worth checking out, clearly a purely national celeb because only the Italians know him. One Italian known to everyone here is Flavio Briatore, former managing director of the Benetton team. The rumour mill is putting out the story he could be returning to Formula One with Ferrari. After all, sporting director Jean Todt's contract expires in the summer. Briatore says: 'I enjoy what I am doing. Nothing.' Di Montezemolo's comment is quite brilliant: 'Yes, and I will have

Ronaldo driving the car instead of Schumacher!'

Schumacher's manager, Willi Weber, stands outside the Ferrari compound, arms folded, wearing team colours and his perma-smile. So he might. Twenty per cent of Schumacher would make anyone smug. Mind you, don't ask him about his dog, someone advises with dubious sensitivity. Apparently Weber was walking his Chihuahua, both minding their own business, when an unleashed German Shepherd pounced with inevitably sad consequences. Willi is now said to be suing the owner of the Alsatian for the loss of his little friend. You cannot help thinking life would be less traumatic with a pet like Hakkinen's. The Championship leader has a tortoise.

The man who has guided Hakkinen into a potentially Championship-winning situation is Keke Rosberg, Finland's only winner of the title, in 1982. He has presumably come straight from his homeland. How else can you explain the heavy three-quarter length coat? The temperature now is in the mid-twenties centigrade. But then Keke was always wont to do his own thing. He was a smoker throughout his halcyon days and the tale of how he put out a cigarette on the sole of his shoe before nonchalantly climbing into his racing car has passed into racing lore.

The Winfield (sponsor of Williams) motorhome is always a popular watering hole. It is run by a crazed, middle-aged Austrian restaurateur called Karl-Heinz who lets off steam by impersonating Hitler and firing a homemade bazooka from the roof. Niki Lauda is a regular visitor. So is Prof Sid Watkins, Formula One's resident doctor, and so is Bernie Ecclestone. Today he has also brought along Mrs Ecclestone and two Misses Ecclestone.

The *Sunday Times'* recent and ever-alluring feature on Britain's richest people has Bernie up to number six, with a personal wealth of £1,500 million, whatever that means. Does that make him a happy man? Apparently not; well not at the moment, anyway. Pictures of the Ecclestones have unavoidably portrayed them as the odd couple – he of pensionable age, 5ft 3ins, large glasses; she, his second wife, Slavica, 30 something, Croatian, 6ft, a former model. But it is a recently circulated set of pictures from her earlier, 'professional' career and allegations she was a spy in the Croatian secret service that have upset Bernie and got him threatening revelations and political repercussions that will hit Croatia like a 'bombshell'. He has taken the case to the courts.

Most thoughts are now on qualifying, the 60 minute session in which each driver has 12 laps to claim his position on tomorrow's starting grid. Those who are not trackside, working in the pits or in the media centre, watch on monitors in the motorhomes and hospitality areas. Those equipped with Bernie's digital TV have a variety of pictures as well as a screen which registers the drivers' lap times and places.

The shake-up is much as expected. The only three drivers in the frame are the McLaren pair and Schumacher. Even the great man cannot split Coulthard and Hakkinen this afternoon, the Scotsman taking pole a tenth of a second ahead of his team-mate. The leading Ferrari is four-tenths adrift. Irvine is fourth fastest and Hill seventh, two places in front of Ralf Schumacher. The relief is tangible.

The first three are brought before the media for the formal interview, then individually they face informal, if not chaotic, interrogations in a corridor, at the back of a garage or on the steps of a transporter.

'I feel it's my turn for a win,' Coulthard says with a dozen microphones poking in his face. 'I want to see my name up there.'

Finnish interest focuses on Hakkinen, German and Italian squads move in on Schumacher. Again di Montezemolo is quizzed about Schumacher's future. He confirms Ferrari have made him an offer for life and Schumacher states he has no intention of jumping ship. Weber is tantalisingly non-committal. His man, it is said, has a clause in his contract enabling him to leave the team at the end of the year if the Championship again eludes them. All in all, there is sufficient material to keep the presses rolling.

Along the row of motorhomes, television sets are tuned in to the channel showing the Tottenham–Newcastle Premiership match live from White Hart Lane. Spurs fans, haunted by the spectre of relegation, are drawn to the screens in clusters and trepidation. Others huddled around a bottle of wine in the Ford haven are pondering the fate of a team closer to home.

Jackie Stewart's return to Formula One as a team principal at the beginning of last season, in partnership with Ford, was accompanied by an inevitable fanfare. Stewart, three times world champion driver, painstakingly played down expectations in the short term but a second place for Rubens Barrichello at Monaco gave the team a priceless early dividend. That form was not maintained and the opening three races of this season have fuelled stories of disenchantment at Ford and within Stewart. Paddock gossip tells of spats between Stewart and his technical director, Alan Jenkins. Jan Magnussen, who narrowly avoided the sack last season, could soon lose his drive to Jos Verstappen. Most round this table believe it will happen before the next race. Heads suddenly swing towards the screen as the Spurs masochists hail a rare lead, but just as quickly turn back to the Brolio.

Beneath the Winfield canopy there are concerns about Frank Williams, who has not travelled to this race. He has been a quadraplegic since a car crash in 1986, but rarely misses a Grand Prix.

'He's got a bladder infection,' one of the better-informed sources says. 'It seems to be affecting Patrick [Head, technical director of the Williams team]. He's been giving the team hell. I think he's really worried about Frank.' Another informed voice pipes up: 'They deserve hell the way they've performed this season. The drivers especially. Mind you, Patrick's not exactly covering himself in glory at the moment.'

Williams' dip and McLaren's revival have coincided with the switch from the former to the latter of Adrian Newey, a highly regarded designer and aerodynamicist. He joined McLaren on a contract said to be worth £2 million a year, after an acrimonious separation from Williams.

Jean Alesi has lived well above the breadline for some years yet still hungers for the chance to prove he is the fastest driver in the world. His Sauber is palpably no vehicle for such ambition and, in a fit of characteristic pique, he calls his old partner, the retired and exiled Gerhard Berger, pleading with him to come back and help out rather than sitting there doing nothing. Berger is disinclined to interrupt his life of leisure just now and advises a visit to Dr Karl-Heinz, who will be sure to dispense a medicinal shot of schnapps. Alesi troops off to the surgery but rejects the schnapps, opting instead for apfel strudel.

Berger always had a mischievous faith in Karl-Heinz's potion. He recommended the same remedy when Senna came off the track in Japan in 1993, raging over the antics of Irvine, a driver who had just made his Formula One debut. Senna took on board a little more than he could handle and went off in search of Irvine, Berger chuckling in anticipation of the inevitable. Senna confronted Irvine and gave him his advice on racing etiquette. Irvine was unmoved and unrepentant and Senna, in exasperation, threw a punch. 'He showed me no respect,' he stated in mitigation. Berger doubled up in laughter.

A roar from in front of the screen at this end of the paddock greets a second goal for Spurs. Those merely promenading in the early evening sun are equally content. Mechanics are at work in the garages, stripping, checking and rebuilding the cars; engineers and drivers are wrestling with sheaves of technical information. All is calm, eerily so. Tomorrow is race day.

Schumacher prays for rain to negate McLaren's technical advantage, but the church bells ring in another glorious day. While God may be a Ferrari fan, the German will have to perform his own miracles. Down in the old town centre, a mere five- or ten-minute walk from the track – depending on your grip and downforce, as they say hereabouts – cyclists of every age snake through the throng of race fans who have arrived by train. In the main square old women talk noisily and old men lean on a barrier, silently peering at a collection of vintage cars.

At Mass the priest uses the analogy of the race and the drivers' endeavours to make the top of the podium to capture man's struggle through life. Four years ago he asked his congregation to pray for the repose of the soul of Roland Ratzenberger, the Austrian driver killed in practice on the Saturday, and for the safety of those who would line up on the grid that Sunday afternoon. Ayrton Senna, the greatest driver of his generation, died after his Williams smashed into the wall at Tamburello curve. The tragedies still hurt but the passing years do ease the pain. No one enjoys recalling that black weekend, so in the main no one does and Imola smiles again.

The atmosphere this morning is in keeping with the weather. There is a warmth though none of the oppressive passion sometimes evident at Monza. The fans here seem a gentler, more phlegmatic breed. Even the gangs of Germans, who drink and sing to Schumacher's cause across the continent, appear to have had their hard edges softened. Those arriving now presumably have grandstand seats. The great, fabled hill overlooking the last sector of the track is already full, a swaying mass of humanity in red. It is one of the most stirring sights in sport.

Inside the paddock the teams are preparing for the final practice session, the half-hour's 'warm-up' which should ensure the cars are ready for the race. Everybody appears a bit more intense. It feels more intense. Schumacher always manages to look self-assured and intense at the same time. He crosses the paddock followed by a woman dragging the hand of a small child dressed in a red jumpsuit. The child is coaxed into waving and blowing a kiss at Schumacher, who for once betrays a hint of unease.

Wurz makes his way to the pits almost unnoticed. Perhaps that's why he wears odd shoes, a blue one on his right foot, a red one on his left. It is, in fact, a superstition that goes back to 1992, when he shared a room with a particularly untidy friend and could not find a matching pair of shoes on race day. He had to make do with what he could come up with and . . . yes, that was a blue one and a red one and . . . yes, he won the race. Coulthard is sipping a drink. Hakkinen is patently not thirsty but a Finnish photographer will probably require a glass of something strong and cold after performing a remarkable slalom, in reverse, to snap a stubbornly uncooperative future Mrs Hakkinen.

Warm-up over, the next action for the Grand Prix drivers is the race itself – four hours from now. Formula One knows how to spin out the drama. Time to catch up on the gossip and the stars. Someone was amused to see Irvine at dinner with his sister and their parents, Edmund and Kathleen. Now, Irvine likes to be seen as a bit of a lad but he looked more like Harry Enfield's Kevin as Mum directed him through his meal, and still more so slumped in the back seat of the car next to Mum, while upright Sonia drove, with Dad next to her. 'It's not fair,' you could hear him protesting.

Next on the agenda is the drivers' briefing, where they are reminded of the decorum required when the race starts. Coulthard stops to shake hands with Stewart, once his mentor. 'Well done,' Stewart says, this being his first opportunity to congratulate his compatriot on his pole position.

The drivers are paraded around the circuit on the back of a truck to prove to all those who will never get anywhere near the paddock that there really are human beings inside those helmets.

Another former driver, Martin Brundle, is Coulthard's current managerial mentor, as well as being Murray Walker's much-acclaimed side-kick in the ITV commentary box.

'David's got to win today,' Brundle says, standing in the heat of the paddock. 'And he knows it.' Brundle discounts any notion the team will rein in Hakkinen as pay-back for Melbourne and defends his man's submission in that opening Grand Prix. 'He could have been fired if he hadn't done what he did. This could be the dominant team for two or three years. He'd be foolish to upset them.'

Hakkinen wanders along with the carefree air of any Sunday stroller. Isn't he worried about Coulthard's pace?

'No. The only thing I'm worried about is the oil they dropped at the first corner in that last race. In fact it goes on for four or five corners. All they've done is put down white powder,' he adds with disdain.

The thought crosses the mind it might make for some fun. Perhaps he might not think so but what about all those paying customers? Herbie Blash, a small, chubby, affable figure who has been a fixture on the scene for a generation and now has the label 'FIA observer' reckons there are 180,000 of them out there. He is approached by a member of a team clutching the rule book and seeking clarification on where, precisely, racing resumes following the intervention of the safety car. At the line at the green light, they agree. The team member departs satisfied and Blash winces.

'I just say yes. It's the best way,' says the self-effacing Blash, who has encouraging news of Frank Williams. 'I was with Patrick last night, getting quietly smashed and telling him his car was crap, the colour scheme, everything, when he gave me his phone and said, "There's somebody here wants to speak to you. Tell him." It was Frank. So I did. He wasn't bad at all. Just missing this. If you think about it, this is everything to him. What else has he got? He's better off at the races than being stuck at home.'

Blash is reminded of Ken Tyrrell, who sold his team for the kind of money you dare not dream about but fell out with the new owner, Craig Pollock, and no longer comes to the races. Tyrrell recently remarked he scarcely knew any of his neighbours. His friends were here, in the Formula One paddock. He and his wife, Nora, had made it an extension of their family.

'To be honest, it's really the same for me and a lot of others here,' Blash confesses. 'When you think about it, the mechanics are living and working together all hours of the day, virtually three hundred and sixty-five days a year. These are their friends and family. It sounds corny but it's true.'

One of the newer members of the family is David Richards, a highly successful leader and businessman in other areas of the sport, who took over from Briatore at Benetton. According to the rank and file: 'He's liked by the crew, he's obviously good at his job and he's not interested in getting involved in all the politics. He can no doubt be a hard man when he has to be, but that's fair enough.'

The paddock has its usual mix of 'name' guests to fill the gaps between the action. 'Mad' Max Biaggi, the Italian 500cc motorcycle idol, causes due fuss, especially when he meets Surtees. Ken Clarke, the former British chancellor, is a more acquired taste. The ubiquitous Surtees bumps into Stewart and the pair not only pose side by side for pictures but actually embrace. That has one veteran observer choking: 'There was a time when Surtees couldn't stand Stewart.' This historic moment is likened to a Bill Clinton–Saddam Hussein love match.

Not all old drivers are guaranteed automatic entry to the

paddock. Bruno Giacomelli, an Italian who made his Grand Prix debut with McLaren and once had pole position, comes up against a local jobsworth who will not budge until he sees a paddock pass. The crestfallen Giacomelli is turned away with scores of others 'trying it on'.

It really must be time for the Grand Prix now. Coulthard is off to the perfect start, Hakkinen is briefly threatened by the tenacious Schumacher but the McLaren fends off the Ferrari. After the excitement of Argentina, it's as you were at Imola. Already the caterers are packing up, keeping an eye on the television screen. They stop as Hakkinen slows and pulls into the pits to retire. The Ford camp are exasperated as they learn their cars have hit each other. Hill has also had a bump but is on a charge after repairs. Herbert stops, thinking he has a broken suspension and abandons his car. He has only a puncture.

Coulthard is comfortably ahead of Schumacher when McLaren's boss Ron Dennis is pictured anxiously walking back and forth between the pit wall and garage. Unbeknown to Coulthard, Hakkinen's gearbox failed and now his own is overheating. Dennis orders a controlled pace, which enables the rampant Schumacher to close the gap and whip the *tifosi* into a state of frenzy. It is a flamboyant show and, as he suspects, a forlorn one. Coulthard has enough in hand to win by 4.5 seconds. Irvine, after seeing off Villeneuve with a quicker pit stop, is third.

They go through their ritual sequence of national anthem, champagne spraying, media interviews. The unofficial interviews seem unending and Coulthard cooperates with the composure he displayed on the track. He might now be forgiven a venomous, or at least gloating, response to his critics, yet maintains a dignified demeanour throughout.

'To be 13 points behind Mika before this race was an uncomfortable gap,' he says. 'Mika still has the advantage but I can feel more comfortable. This is a great kick-start to the European season. It is a boost in terms of the Championship and stopping the rumour mill. There's no point thinking about the past. To be honest it was easy, but then I don't want to make it look exciting. I want to win Grands Prix.'

Coulthard has moved three points ahead of Schumacher into second place in the Championship, three points behind Hakkinen. Dennis, standing in the back doorway of the McLaren garage, has a paternal air about him as he says: 'We are completely happy for either driver to win. A little suggestion of internal friction within a Grand Prix team is very newsworthy, but really there isn't any here. Mika is disappointed but only because he didn't finish a race and not because David won. We are a team first. It's not complex.'

The race winner gets changed as the beer flows and rock music booms from the McLaren–Mercedes compound. All about them teams are stacking tables, chairs and wooden floors, loading cars and equipment into trucks and saying their goodbyes. Most drivers and senior team officials are long gone, but Coulthard answers another round of questions about his self-belief and Haug, never one to miss a party, lingers and talks of his faith in the Scotsman.

'I'm happy for him,' Haug says. 'He's taken a lot of criticism recently and it's not right. It was very unfair. I knew he would respond well. He's that kind of guy. There was a lot of pressure. It shows we made the right decision last year when we had to choose one or both drivers. We decided to stick with David and he's proved us absolutely correct. He has a big future. He's not at all arrogant and is always willing to learn. You can have fun with him.'

The fun is over for another race weekend. A strange sadness envelops the paddock as the camp is dismantled and the circus moves out. The great hill, where the Ferrari flags – and a lone, defiant cross of St Andrew – waved a few hours earlier is now a mountain of trash. Coulthard can be forgiven for thinking the doubts and jibes about him have been discarded up there too.

And still the sun shines and the dinner table beckons. This is, indeed, God's gift to the tour.

2

Barcelona

KINGS AND QUEENS

Just as Imola invigorates the soul, so Barcelona has an unerring knack of dulling the mind. Perhaps that is partially because familiarity breeds contempt. The Circuit de Catalunya has been a second home for many of the drivers and crews over the winter and they have been down here in force again for testing since the San Marino Grand Prix.

There is more to it than that, however. While Barcelona itself may be one of the stimulating citadels of Europe, the neighbourhood where they laid the track for the Spanish Grand Prix, half an hour's drive north-east, is a prime example of man's propensity for raping the countryside. Housing blocks and factories have been daubed on the landscape like graffiti. The hills and green valleys must have made this a beautiful corner of Spain before the post-War quick-fit developers were let loose on it.

The atmosphere here has traditionally been as dour as the backdrop. The circuit itself, by modern, sterile standards, is not at all bad. The facilities and access are good, the climate usually clement, hence its attraction as a winter-testing venue. Now, on this second weekend of May, the race beckons and enthusiasm for the event may need a kick-start.

Those interminable queues for hire cars at the airport scarcely help, although the first spike of wicked humour brings the troops to life. Jan Magnussen, the driver who would have lost his job with Stewart if they had been able to agree a deal with Jos Verstappen, spots an empty car-hire desk and steers his luggage towards it – smart move, or so it seems. Several minutes on and he is still there. 'Jackie Stewart's told them not to let him have one,' someone mutters and giggles attack the adjacent line.

The Catalan notion of separatism is apparent in the dual-language signs which guide the fleet of hire cars around the city and along the motorway towards France. The weather is warm, the going easy, but that is scant consolation for the cement works and junk yard the Formula One troubadours confront on the approach road to their next performance. It can be worse still if the wind takes a pernicious turn from the direction of the abattoir.

This early Thursday afternoon the hills are almost hidden behind a heat haze. One year the peaks were snow-covered, but summer has arrived and the forecast for the weekend promises almost unbroken sunshine. A few fans, ambling outside the perimeter wall, are dressed in shorts and armed with sun-cream. For the workers, the paddock turnstiles are activated to musical accompaniment. 'It'll take more than that to jazz up this place,' groans a cynical commentator.

The bells do not chime, however, for a couple of the tour's regular journalists and, after much toing and froing, Bernie's stern-faced henchman furnishes them with temporary passes. Bernie is doubtless surveying their discomfort from behind the darkened windows of his bus, positioned at the end of the row of team transporters. Just one of his little jokes.

'We need more fun. It's much too serious around here,' the henchman declares as his mask slips.

David Coulthard is constantly being told to lighten up but he makes no discernible attempt to do so at the day's official press conference until he is asked if there is any prospect of his becoming Michael Schumacher's team-mate.

'I hope not,' he replies. Schumacher's current partner, Eddie Irvine, says that if the German leaves Ferrari he will relish the chance to earn his status. 'Let the stop-watch decide who's number one.'

Heinz-Harald Frentzen, the undertaker's son with the deep-lying humour, was one of those who called for the ban on tower wings – the antennae that made Grand Prix drivers look like easy riders – on safety grounds. He now expands: 'They could fall into the car and damage your properties!'

The absence of a Spanish driver has always been cited as a major reason for a limited local interest in this event and Esteban Tuero, the young Argentine with Minardi, completes the conference line-up as a token gesture to the Spanish-speaking market.

Coulthard continues his round of duties at a less formal meeting with the British press corps, grouped around a table under the awning of the McLaren motorhome.

'I don't enjoy that,' he says, tossing his head in the direction of the FIA press-conference room. 'I don't want to be there and I don't pretend otherwise. It's like being in a box. What you see with me is how I feel. It's the same on the podium. I don't have to be jumping around to feel happy. People are always going on at me to smile more, even my family. But I don't see the point in putting on an act. We're all different.'

The man from BBC Radio Five Live provokes another sense of humour fade when he asks Coulthard what it is that makes Schumacher a cut above the rest. The Scotsman cannot suppress his irritation over the implication.

'Thank you for making me feel like a second-rate driver,' he says, bitterly, even if he manages a conciliatory smile.

'I'm sorry, let me put that question another way.'

'I think you should.' Red faces both sides of the microphone.

Coulthard, in common with a number of his peers, cannot bring himself to admit another driver is better. It is part of a driver's protective mechanism. Sometimes they are laughed off for their foolish pride but then when Irvine eulogises Schumacher he is ridiculed; not that he cares. He has his bank account to comfort him.

It is put to Coulthard his temperament might give him the advantage over his team-mate, Mika Hakkinen, in the Championship. He agrees. He also reckons living in Monaco spares him the pressures of expectations back home.

'I can blend in the background, do my shopping. Nobody notices you because there are so many celebrities there. I'm probably more of a star spotter than anyone.' He is equally at home on the circuit here. 'I probably know it better than Silverstone.'

All are agreed McLaren are unlikely to be hospitable this weekend. They posted ominous times in testing, another contributory factor to the low-key feeling along the thoroughfare between the rows of trucks and motorhomes. A bewitching girl, wearing a flowered sari-style outfit, walks up and down, never stopping, never talking. Damon Hill marches in wearing his business-like look; no modelling this time. He is accompanied by his wife, Georgie. Benetton have the modelling assignment here, and a crew drag their equipment along the tarmac.

The word is Frank Williams has arrived for this race. His wheelchair is positioned by his male nurse in the far corner of the Williams camp, which is in the far corner of the paddock. You get the impression he prefers to be as remote as possible.

'Good to see you back, Frank. We were worried about you.'

'No, it was nothing really. I'm fine.' He doesn't look it. He is thinner, paler.

Eddie Jordan is not one to hide his light under a bushel. His team have a central pitch, and an appropriately loud yellow livery. The more familiar gold of sponsors Benson and Hedges does not work on television. Parked outside the twin motorhomes are three scooters, also in the sponsor's racing colours. One has Damon stamped on it, another Ralf, the third Eddie. Ferrari's vivid red is scarcely necessary to attract attention, although they and Schumacher are doubtless relishing a quieter weekend here.

Every pit revs, taps and rattles to the sound of mechanics at work. As on every factory floor, the banter is sharp. Arsenal fans have come out of the woodwork of late with cutting remarks for those of Manchester United or Spurs persuasion. United fans have gone to ground. With a bit of luck they'll all be back in their hotels, washed and changed in time for a few beers tonight.

Spaniards are more concerned about their nominated World Cup squad than the Grand Prix, and the sports media here is wall to wall with analysis and comment. Congestion on the motorway system between Barcelona and the circuit might suggest healthy interest in practice day but this turns out to be normal rush-hour traffic. The track is a relatively tranquil oasis in the heart of this sprawling industrial estate.

It is 8.15 and the paddock stirs in cool shade. Anoraks and sweaters are still in evidence. A hot breakfast is equally appreciated and Ford is a popular diner. The ongoing traumas of the Stewart Ford team remain similarly irresistible conversation fodder. The whispers from inside Ford reflect a sense of betrayal that Stewart appear to be dumping undue blame on their doorstep. Ford are less than ecstatic about their partners' performances, but choose not to go public with their sentiments.

Stewart, too, have scooters, in white and the team's tartan, standing idle. Jackie Stewart looks as if he needed a ride through the paddock, arriving with arms full of baggage. The familiar, jaunty step has become a weary trudge of late. The observation that 'he is ageing with every race' meets with solemn agreement among a group stationed by one of the trucks. The tartan trousers and cap seem to emphasise his discomfiture. When at last he reaches base and drops the assorted bags, Stewart produces a smile, a round of handshakes and the usual warm greeting. Whatever he is feeling inside, he has no intention of presenting anything other than his trademark demeanour. He is content to sit and give his version and explanation of events so far.

There's no doom and gloom from our point of view. I have absolutely no regrets about going through with this. The most difficult part was putting it all together, financially. I've been through ups and downs as a driver and this is no different. As a driver I had a good first year and people said I was the new golden boy of Formula One. Then I had a car that wasn't so good and things didn't go well for me before I had my halcyon days. But then I lost a lot of my friends, killed on the track. Those were the really hard days.

I'm not saying this isn't tough, but it's nothing I didn't expect. I always said it would be a five-year programme, and that you wouldn't see us deliver until the fourth or fifth years. I knew when we came in last year that people would be looking for us to fail. You always get that and it doesn't concern me. It was the same when we formed Paul Stewart Racing, ten years ago. That team has won twelve championships and a hundred and twenty-two races. People expect us to do well partly because of my name and what I've done in the past. But I'm not a person who looks over his shoulder. We're in the business of today and tomorrow, not yesterday.

Stewart confirms he had talks with Verstappen's manager but was not disposed to meet his range of demands. Now he is imploring Magnussen, the driver he dubbed 'the next Ayrton Senna' following his 1994 British Formula Three Championship success, to prove he can apply his talents to the ultimate motor-racing challenge.

'The problem with Jan is that he is over-driving,' Stewart says. 'I took him to Oulton Park for three days last year to help him out of the problem and on the third day he drove superbly. But he's had very little driving, very little testing during the winter and . . . But having said that, Rubens hasn't had much driving either.'

Magnussen has been told his position will be reviewed race by race, which might not inspire him with confidence. But then the team are baffled by what they consider a lack of application and dedication to his career.

'Jan has the chance to make the job his own,' Stewart adds.

The Dane is sitting two tables away, giving his side of the story and clearly not enjoying the burden placed on him.

'It gives me extra pressure knowing I can lose my job,' he says. 'But I've just got to get my head down and try not to think about it too much. I think it would be unfair if he kicked me out before I had the chance to show what I can do.'

Stewart, meanwhile, denies Alan Jenkins' job is in jeopardy, although he does state the late delivery of the car was the responsibility of the technical director, and that the team have been forced to play catch-up. He also reiterates problems with the engine have further inhibited the development programme. Come next month, he says, when the test team is in place and the new factory is officially opened, his charges will be able to compete on a level playing field.

'We have the resources and facilities, we have the team, we have the people. But there is no magic about this business. We've got to work at it and get it right.'

He is off to work now, to check on the team's schedule for the first practice session. Back along the row at Jordan, Ian Phillips, the team's gregarious commercial man, is doing his best to vitalise proceedings with his sardonic banter.

'Trouble is,' he says, drawing on his sponsor's product, as any good commercial man would, 'it's so flat here. It's not got any atmosphere.'

Jordan's senior driver, Damon Hill, makes his contribution to the hype by giving the British press an angle on Coulthard. Has his former Williams team-mate got what it takes to be world champion, he is asked. Hill is aware of what is required and goes along with it.

> Absolutely, he has. He's got an excellent chance of cracking it. As we stand here right now, I would put my money on David rather than Mika. David has tilted it psychologically. Massively. That result at Imola will have been a huge blow to Mika. After the first two races Mika must have thought it was easy. Everything was looking hunky-dory for him. He must have thought he had it in the bag. But then David was the quicker in Argentina, and won easily at Imola.
>
> David has learned a lot since we were together. He's matured as a person and a driver. Everything is there for him. He just has to keep his head. I just hope David enjoys the experience this season and doesn't get too tied up in McLaren speak. He's got a lot of personality, and so has Mika. The problem there, you sense, is that the drivers have to toe the party, or corporate, line. For the sponsors. They should forget what they are told to say and just be themselves.

Hill, who had unproductive talks with McLaren last summer, palpably wanted to get that off his chest. Corporate McLaren have the car he would dearly wish to be driving and he resents the way they conducted their negotiations with him. He insists he was never made a realistic offer, they contend they re-signed the drivers they wanted. Hill's 14th place today soothes nothing.

The entire Benetton camp express relief they have Wurz and Fisichella after Berger and Alesi, the drivers accused of dismantling a winning team in record time. Pat Symonds, the team's unobtrusive technical director ruefully confirms they have damaged a lot of cars and made a lot of parts this season, yet is highly delighted to have them on board. He admits he is surprised Wurz has been the quicker of the two, but is at pains to stress Fisichella 'hasn't had things go his way'. On his way out of the circuit, the Italian finds plenty of consoling attention and gratefully laps it up.

A driver from another era has turned up in the paddock – Derek Warwick, an Englishman who had a knack of joining the right team at the wrong time. He now runs and drives for his own team in the British Touring Car Championship, and has other long-established business interests. He is here as part of the ITV team and will chip in his comments at this race, as well as sitting in for Martin Brundle in Canada while Murray Walker's regular co-commentator competes at Le Mans. Warwick is agitated after looking in on one of his old teams, Arrows, and old boss, Jackie Oliver.

I go in there and say, 'Hello,' and Oliver says, 'What the hell are you letting yourself in for?' I do a double-take and say, 'I'll start again. Hello . . .' and again he says, 'What are you letting yourself in for, competing with Martin Brundle?' I tell him I'm not competing with Martin Brundle. I have no desire to and no intention of competing with Brundle. But that's typical, isn't it? Typical Oliver, anyway.

To be honest, now I'm here I wish I'd not said I'd do it. I wish I'd not come. Not because of the TV thing or anything but because it makes me realise what I'm missing. Just the noise gets you going. Oh, I'm not kidding myself I could still be doing it, because I know I couldn't. But even so. I've not been to a Grand Prix since Silverstone '97. It's good to see a lot of old friends and in many ways it's not changed. But there are a lot of new faces among the mechanics and obviously the drivers always seem to get younger.

They all seem so serious about it but then in fairness they have to be. They have to be trained athletes and they have to spend hours in briefing going over data. How can they go out and have a few beers and laughs? Even in touring cars now it's all technical data. But whether the drivers are better today is a different matter. I mean, who after Schumacher would a team boss really want? Tell me. No one else stands out.

Warwick should be good value on TV. He's enthusiastic, not afraid to say what he thinks and a lot of fun. Things could be looking up for the race, as well. The forecaster says rain will cross the Iberian peninsula over the weekend and just might reach these parts by Sunday afternoon. The consensus is that only rain or the cavalry can save another Grand Prix from annihilation by McLaren.

Tyrrell's new boss, Craig Pollock, is looking beyond Sunday and beyond this season, to the introduction of what will be to all intents and purposes a new team with, he hopes, a new name. Pollock, a Scotsman who came into Formula One as Jacques Villeneuve's manager, has embarked on this ambitious venture in partnership with British American Tobacco and Reynard. He is developing a new factory and plans to employ 220 people. But doesn't he feel a tinge of sadness that Ken Tyrrell, having sold control of the team, felt obliged to sever his links totally when Pollock signed Ricardo Rosset for the money he brought to the team rather than Jos Verstappen? Now Pollock looks, frankly, a bit of a smoothie – perma-tan, cool, no histrionics – so you might expect a bit of a smoothie response. Instead he is straight, unequivocal.

No, I don't feel any sadness. Ken had a good, long life in motor racing. He's getting out with a good deal. Yes, I've got some egg on my face because Rosset is having a hard time of it, but the people in the team are being paid and they are happy about that. If Ken was so concerned why didn't he take twenty-five million dollars instead of thirty million and help pay the staff? We needed the money Rosset brought in. I had to mortgage everything to put this deal together. When it was done I rang my wife and said we don't even own the dogs.

It's tough in many ways. When you're in negotiations with people like Frank and Bernie you think you'll go straight in at the target, but they come at you from all angles. You feel as though you have been slapped around the face. It seems it's something you have to go through, so you hold up your hands and say, 'Okay'.

BAT have committed themselves to a long-term contract as part of the deal with Pollock and you might expect their man to be an unsentimental, hard-headed go-getter. Instead Tom Moser, a Canadian now based in England, confesses his sorrow over Tyrrell's retreat.

'I got to know Ken quite well, and his wife, and I like them both,' he says softly, as if making an act of contrition. 'They are really nice people. It was all very emotional for him. He talked about it being like saying goodbye to White Hart Lane for the last time. I didn't know what he meant until it was explained to me about Tottenham and Ken's love for the team.' Moser is learning a few things about the English football scene. A few months ago his wife was telling him about this 'very nice' man she had met.

'She said she didn't know what he did. He didn't seem to work. Then we were watching the England World Cup game in Italy and she says, "There he is, that's the guy I was telling you about." It was Glenn Hoddle.'

Ken Tyrrell and his wife Nora had been part of the paddock cast for 30 years. Jackie Stewart won three World Championships – in 1969, 1971 and 1973 – under Tyrrell's stewardship. But the team last won a race in 1983 and in recent seasons have been consigned to the back end of the grid. Stories have circulated of sponsors' dissatisfaction with his son, Bob, and his commercial direction. Last year team members gave a frank assessment of the food being dished up to them when they pinned a plate, with a meal stuck to it, on the notice board.

Saturday morning is a delight. Mist shrouds the valleys, leaving only the virgin hilltops on view. It is, however fleetingly, nature's glorious revenge. No sign of rain clouds yet, the sky is crystal clear. It is going to be another warm day. The butts of Bernie's turnstile joke are fully operational again and peaceful order reigns in the paddock. Hakkinen goes to work, calm and unhindered, as if he might be heading for the office. Ron Dennis strolls up at 8.45, 15 minutes before practice. No need for him to rush to the office; everything is in place and it shows on his face.

Little groups dot the paddock thoroughfare, reluctant to break up and go about their business. Even Alain Prost, a habitual fidgeter and nail-nibbler, looks relaxed here. He is down to a mere canter. One of his drivers, Olivier Panis, succumbs to the first signs of urgency, running from motorhome to pit with just a hint of a limp, the legacy of a big accident in Canada last year.

Tyrrell's truck and motorhome stand out from the rest because of their space-age design; a sign of things to come, perhaps. No sign of Warwick yet, though. By all accounts he enjoyed himself at a birthday party for another member of the ITV team last night. He is due at rehearsals in half an hour and his colleagues are a little anxious.

The noise of whining engines disappearing down the main straight announces that practice is under way, but those who can afford the luxury linger in the paddock sunshine. Those busy in the motorhomes glance at the screens when somebody says Coulthard is in the gravel. The distraction is brief. Half-time in morning practice is the signal for more people to bask in the sun. Is *anyone* interested in what's going on out there?

Dennis misses the start of the second half and is clearly not perturbed. Everything is still in place for his team. Everything seems to have been displaced at Williams and Frank Williams, his wife Ginny standing behind him, monitors the times in the pits. His expression could be described as glum but it is like that when his cars are leading races. At the end of the session he is wheeled back to his sanctuary at the motorhome.

A pleasant breeze takes the sting out of the midday sun and suddenly the paddock has come alive. Among those settling down for lunch at Arrows are Adam Faith, pop star turned actor and a long-time mucker of Ecclestone, and a couple of scriptwriters, trawling for material to adapt into a forthcoming TV production. Faith, tiny and craggy-faced, could be a dead ringer for Bernie, but apparently he is to be a team boss. There again, that's how Bernie started out in Formula One. Faith and his men are milking Tom Walkinshaw, who took control of Arrows from Jackie Oliver. They have also talked to the likes of Frank Williams and Ron Dennis, and asked to meet 'an unsuccessful team owner, like Jackie Stewart' – more mirth at wee Jackie's expense.

Attention is diverted from Walkinshaw's table to a leggy creature entering Arrows' adjacent hospitality area. She is wearing a micro skirt, a minimal bodice, and closer scrutiny reveals she is not in the first flush of youth. She makes her way to the doorway of the motorhome itself and wants to know, 'Who is that gorgeous man? Is it your driver?' The answer is in the affirmative and she moves in, displaying her wares. The driver, Finland's Mika Salo, scurries out of the bus for safety. Flustered but still in one piece, he smoothes down his blond hair and gulps: 'I couldn't believe it. She, she . . . And now I'm supposed to get in the car and drive!' The leggy creature wanders off, a wry grin on her face, doubtless to disport elsewhere.

Qualifying is nothing like as exciting. McLaren are first and second, of course, Hakkinen lapping seven-tenths of a second faster than Coulthard. Schumacher is third. For some reason Salo is below par, struggling to 17th place on the grid. Magnussen is 18th. Rosset's time is outside the cut, 107 per cent of the pole time, and he will miss the race. You cannot help wondering what Ken Tyrrell is thinking, back home.

Coulthard is already thinking this race could be beyond him. 'I've not got my act together this weekend . . . I came here feeling confident but I lost some ground in practice and I've never been able to make it up . . . It's down to confidence on the track and I've not been able to attack the corners with the same speed that Mika has . . . I believe I've still got a chance to go for a win . . . But I won't take any unnecessary risks . . . Second place wouldn't be a disaster . . . This is just one race . . . He'll be quicker at some circuits, I'll be quicker at others . . .'

He looks and sounds like a man settling for second place, while Schumacher makes no bones about it, third is the best he can realistically aspire to. Hakkinen is restrained in his comments at large, but to Finland's viewers he declares with a voracious grin: 'Nobody can catch us tomorrow.'

The screaming of Formula 3000 cars cannot disturb the concentration of the dedicated Formula One paddock cruisers. A posse of autograph hunters closes in on Hill as he chats to guests at Jordan. Another focal point, this time for journalists, is the silver-grey McLaren–Mercedes compound, where the man with the microphone sounds like a seaside bingo caller. It is, in fact, Ron Dennis disclosing details of Hakkinen's gearbox failure at Imola. It was caused by a rogue bearing, part of a faulty batch that cheated the security and quality-control systems.

'It's the first time I've experienced anything like this in thirty years in the business,' he says.

Further along the paddock, past the yellow of Jordan and the blue of Prost, is the somewhat garish violet, turquoise, strawberry and custard of Sauber, where Alesi and Herbert are having their regular Saturday afternoon talk-in with the press. Herbert has a mixed gathering of national newspaper, agency, specialist and non-specialist magazine journalists, and answers every question in a manner that convinces you he is the absolute genuine article: no edge, no arrogance, no deceit. As he talks, a pukka mug of English tea arrives from over his shoulder, delivered by Mum – not his mum, but everyone's surrogate mum, Di Spires, who is actually Ford's caterer yet still looks after her prodigal sons, especially her favourites.

A woman reporter wants to know what Herbert makes of 'this whole circus, the things going on away from the track – such as this'. 'I accept it as part of the job,' he says. 'This is not really a distraction. The driving part of the job and the briefing have been done. I don't mind this.'

'Do you socialise with other drivers?'

'I don't actually see the other drivers that much in Monaco, even though there are a few of us living there. We always seem to miss each other. But there are some you wouldn't want to socialise with, anyway!'

'Will you have an advantage racing at Monaco, your "home" track?'

'The school run doesn't go that way so there's not so much of an advantage living there. But I really enjoy qualifying at Monaco. You know you have to be so precise because the barriers are so close. If you kiss the barrier you know you have done it as well as you can. Spa is probably my favourite circuit, but Monaco is a different challenge and in qualifying it's the biggest challenge. When the Grand Prix is not on it's quite normal. It's quiet. It's a sacrifice going there to save your money [tax]. Our two daughters are settled but my wife still finds it difficult; I'm away so much.'

Down at Williams, Frank is having one of his periodic sessions in a stand-up harness. He is talking to Niki Lauda and both probably appreciate the eye-level contact. Members of the fraternity make a point of popping in here for a chat with Frank. Salo is relieved to be chatting in familiar company. He is exchanging juke-box intelligence with Herbie Blash.

'You must get remote control,' Herbie urges him. 'I've always had juke boxes. Love them.'

Music fills the air deep into the paddock evening. Mercedes are entertaining and a senior representative of the British press, a rocker manqué, is regaling his German hosts with his time-honoured and honed repertoire. Norbert Haug, another ageing rocker, is lapping it up. Things are a little more sedate at Stewart, where the chief guest restrains any inclination to ape Chuck Berry. But, then, he is the King of Spain. Jackie Stewart may be an 'unsuccessful team owner', but he certainly knows how to pull a name and they don't come any bigger in these parts than Juan Carlos.

A dinner party for a German contingent is being given by one of Williams' sponsors at a posh restaurant in Barcelona. A group turn up with a television set and speakers, which they plonk in the middle of their table. No offence, but they really have to see their man in the Eurovision Song Contest. This surreal scenario is complete when the vocal 'Jeux Sans Frontières' is won by an Israeli transvestite.

Another fine morning ushers in race day. McLaren can start making more room in the trophy cabinet, early paddock dwellers concur. A man in a grey FOCA TV anorak, armed with a long-handled brush, is cleaning the windows of Bernie's bus. He has some important visitors today, but then Bernie always insists on impeccable presentation.

Kings and queens are high on the conversation agenda up and down the paddock; so is mainland Europe's Mother's Day. 'Good day for Schuey's dad to bring his bird to the track,' someone reckons. Rolf Schumacher, having shunted his wife into the matrimonial gravel trap, is walking out with his new lady friend – an auburn-haired, younger model – this weekend, presumably with the boys' approval if not their overwhelming enthusiasm.

Laughs are in short supply at Williams, and technical director Patrick Head looks none too amused to be changed into his Winfield red shirt, with all the other sponsorship logos and bits and pieces, in time for warm-up. 'Bit too loud for my taste,' he says, managing a smirk. Much of this season is proving unpalatable for the man who has accompanied Frank Williams through the highs and lows of the team's Formula One adventure. This is definitely a low, as the grid positions testify: Villeneuve 10th, Frentzen 13th.

Warm-up does nothing to lift the spirits. Team members seem to be going about their work on automatic pilot. Someone emerges from the garage with what look like two surfboards. They are skid blocks, which are fixed beneath the cars. Tyres are stacked in warmers and their pressures checked. There is constant movement up and down the steps at the back of the transporters. And yet you sense they know they are going nowhere; not today. A heavy stands on the door, his function seemingly rendered redundant.

Head appears from the garage, the burden almost bending him over. Some say that when he is serious he looks like Meatloaf. You can see the resemblance now. Williams' plight has forced much of the 'front man' duty on to Head and mostly he accepts it with good humour and candour. He musters a little of the former and much of the latter as he leans against a wall, assesses the team's demise and considers what is to be done.

'It's more than a bit of a dip,' he concedes. 'There is an upslope on the other side. It's hard to take but I worked out many, many years ago that throwing the toys out of the pram is not the way to put it right. I don't tend to have great smiles across my face in practice sessions these days, but all you can do is keep your head down and keep working at it.'

But isn't it true you have had the motorhome reverberating to your explosions?

'I'm not aware of that. I'm told that I often don't need a radio to be heard from one side of the paddock to the other, but I don't think there's been any particular explosions in the motorhome.'

Paddock pundits list the reasons for Williams' current position as the loss of Renault works backing; sticking with Goodyear instead of switching to Bridgestone; the defection of Adrian Newey to McLaren; over-diversification of racing projects; the limited development acumen of Villeneuve and Frentzen. Head acknowledges there could be many contributory factors but makes no attempt to shirk his responsibility. He also admits he has no ready solution.

'At the moment the car is not very good and the grid positions reflect that. I'd like to be able to say I know totally why, but I can't. We have some fairly serious clues and we're in the process of making some new parts to put right the deficiencies we see are there but, like a lot of these engineering parts, they take time to produce.'

The changes are concentrated on the rear suspension and

aerodynamics, and are, Head believes, fundamental to the team's prospects of recovery. He is loath to complain about the Mecachrome/Renault engines, which Williams will use again next year before launching their alliance with BMW, although he says Bridgestone rubber is giving Benetton a significant advantage here.

'If the engine is a part of the deficiency it is a very small part of it, so I'll start worrying about that when I think we've put right our part of it.'

So does that point an accusing finger at the drivers?

'You have the drivers you have and to spend time wishing you had Alain Prost or someone is not very productive. It's irrelevant. I don't really have any argument with either of the drivers. I think they are both trying their best. I've come across drivers in my time who I think have a better knowledge and a better understanding of vehicle dynamics than either Jacques or Heinz-Harald, but if we gave them the equipment they'd be up there.'

According to the latest bush-radio news, Gerhard Berger has been acting as an intermediary to bring together Williams and Michael Schumacher for negotiations, but Head contends there is no substance to the story.

I don't know anything about it. Frank would have to look to the bottom of his piggy bank. I don't think it's a realistic proposition. I don't think Michael would be interested in coming to a team without a works engine and preparing to start with a completely new engine. Ultimately the problem we have is with the car and putting another driver into the car wouldn't make an awful lot of differ-ence. Michael is very good in that he's developed this aura around him of being able to lift a car, wherever it is, to a higher level and it's a great reputation to have, particu-larly when you're negotiating contracts. But it's not crossed my mind. It's like thinking, 'I wish I'd got a different engine.' Why waste time on it?

We've had some difficult times in the past, even last

year, when we had some bloody awful races. But everybody in the team is very professional, very competitive,
and they'll put a hundred per cent into their jobs until we
engineers press the right buttons. They're not happy
about what's happening at the moment and I'm not happy.
I'm pretty hacked off we're not at the front, although I'm
not sure whether that's the right motivation. People have
a fanciful notion of how quickly you can get these things
right. There's no magic. It's mostly hard work.

While the teams work on, paddock eyes focus on the tall,
distinguished figure arriving at Bernie's bus. King Juan Carlos,
wearing his pass, looks far more comfortable in this environment
than, say, your British Royal. Juan Antonio Samaranch, the
Olympics supremo, is another on Bernie's guestlist. And still
Bernie finds time to meet a representative of India's bid for a
Grand Prix and fix it for a young Spanish driver to meet
Schumacher. The wannabe champion is delirious.

A man with football's World Cup on his mind, Real Madrid's
Brazilian, Roberto Carlos, moves more quietly, almost self-
consciously, through the paddock with his lady. He produces the
sort of power with his left foot that Grand Prix drivers seek with
their right. Anthony Quinn, the veteran actor, has a walk-on part
today. Monarchs, mega-stars, they all feel the compulsion to be
here and to be seen here.

Head finds time in his work schedule for a spot of lunch. For
afters he requests 'something sweet and mushy', giving the diet a
sidestep. He may take an entire race weekend off in a fortnight to
be with his wife, who is due to give birth to their first child.

'People keep telling me I should be there for splashdown,
though I'm not sure I'd be able to cope with that. It's a boy. We're
going to call him Luke.'

Theirs is a poignant love story. Both Head and Betise
Assumpcao had been married before and their romance developed
out of the most tragic of circumstances. Betise, a vivacious,
voluble Brazilian, was employed by Ayrton Senna as his personal
press officer. Senna was killed at the 1994 San Marino Grand

Prix, driving a Williams created by Head and his design team. Patrick and Betise are teased their baby will need healthy lungs to make himself heard in the Head household.

Villeneuve is hovering and chatting nearby until he is dragged away by a team official with a glare that says 'you've got a race to drive'. Head moves to the far table of the hospitality area to sit with Frank Williams. Ron Dennis, too, joins Williams and they are deep in conversation. The pair have held out against elements of the Concorde Agreement, Formula One's constitution, in particular the carve-up of income from television rights, and the common cause has brought the old rivals close.

Dennis' former partner and designer, John Barnard, is making his way to the pits, silently, head bowed. His work at McLaren, and later at Ferrari, was widely acclaimed for its innovation. Now he is attempting to make a winning car for Arrows and prefers to do so with minimum attention. Dennis and Barnard were once bracketed with Williams and Head. They were even room-mates, although it is said that became an unworkable arrangement because they each wanted an hour and a half in the bathroom to get ready for work. Barnard may be quiet, an almost anonymous figure, most of the time, but he has a reputation for outbursts that make Head's rockets sound like whimpers.

The growl of engines signals pre-race preliminaries, and a shift of posing scenes. As the cars leave the pits, lap the circuit – once, twice or even three times, depending on the whim or requirement of the drivers – and take their places on the starting grid, those armed with full monty passes take the short cut to the piece of track that will be the focus of attention in the minutes leading up to the start of the Grand Prix.

This is a cameo performance surely unparalleled in sport. Mechanics make last moment checks and adjustments – more, you suspect, out of habit than necessity – while guests and journalists mingle, gawp and generally clutter up an already confined space. It is a bit like allowing selected mobs on to the pitch at Wembley as the Cup final teams go through their last warm-up routines, or on the Centre Court as the players knock-up for a Wimbledon final. Eventually, and reluctantly, they stream away, doubtless hoping the television cameras caught them.

The drivers are waved away on their formation lap before lining up for the start proper, and when the five red lights go out Hakkinen gets the grip and acceleration that wins him the race by the first corner. Coulthard's claim to second place is still more assured. All weekend for this. McLaren can hardly be held responsible, of course. The rest are simply not good enough and the onus is on them to make a Championship of it.

As McLaren go about their lonely business there is at least some activity, and controversy, in their slipstream. Schumacher has a sluggish start, loses two places, and regains them with a characteristically quick pit stop only to be told it was too quick. He pays with a stop-and-go penalty, drops down to fourth but regains third with another characteristically quick pit stop and this time it is deemed legal.

Eddie Irvine might have finished well up in the points after a blistering start, but ends up in the gravel trap with Giancarlo Fisichella, who gives the Irishman a piece of his mind. The Italian's boss, David Richards, accuses Ferrari of ordering Irvine to hold up Fisichella and so protect Schumacher. Irvine says: 'The Ferrari might be a useful car but it's not a helicopter and that's what I would have needed to avoid him.' The stewards fine Fisichella 7,500 dollars for 'causing an avoidable accident'.

Hill, who has also visited the gravel, manages to extricate himself but has to park his Jordan three laps later with a broken engine and returns to base fuming about the earlier incident, accusing Frentzen – the man who replaced him at Williams – of pushing him off the road. 'It's mindless, just stupid,' Hill tells the man from Radio Five Live. 'He's a brick short of a full load if you ask me.'

Alas for the 65,000 crowd, they have no inkling of these behind-the-scenes gems. Coulthard's self-analysis will tally with their perspective of proceedings: 'I was given a bit of a driving lesson today. At the beginning of the race I had such a fight with the car. I drove my maximum and wasn't quick enough, so it's back to the drawing board.'

Alexander Wurz gives Benetton the consolation of fourth place, immediately ahead of Barrichello and the much-maligned Stewart. It is a measure of their success, and Williams' failure, that the Brazilian has held off Villeneuve to claim those two points. The Williams, however, is good enough to frustrate Herbert. Frentzen, who tangled with Alesi on the first lap, finishes eighth. Magnussen comes in 12th, albeit two laps down.

The reaction at McLaren Mercedes is more restrained than it was at Imola. This is, after all, becoming a bit of a routine. There is no gloating, no flaunting. The one–two has been clinically accomplished; time to pack up and head for the next race. Spilling emotions are to be found along at Stewart Ford: jubilation, relief, a sense of vindication. This is the unscripted triumph of the Spanish Grand Prix.

'The last few weeks have been murder,' Jackie Stewart now feels able to say. 'We needed a good result here and we've got it. The really pleasing thing is that Rubens managed to keep Villeneuve behind him for the whole race. During the last third of the race I was incredibly tense. I just wanted it to be over. It was great that Jan finished. We just have to get his head in shape. We don't want to change him if he can get his act together, and maybe this is the start for him.'

Tented motorhome extensions are being folded away, teams of mechanics are now racing to load their transporters, and upstairs in the media centre journalists are writing and filing their reports. The Grand Prix has been dire and they are grateful for the material provided by Hill and Benetton. Unless it rains – or the cavalry turns up – the chances are they will have more tedium to grapple with in a fortnight. At least there should be plenty of distractions to help them through the weekend. They'll be in Monaco.

3

Monaco

IT'S SHOWTIME

Of course it makes no sense to run a Grand Prix on a circuit with the dimensions and limitations of the principality, but this tiny nub on the Mediterranean is the incomparable gem in the Formula One display cabinet. For the rich, the famous and, interestingly, the race fan, it has hypnotic appeal like no other. It is the place to see and be seen, a happening to be part of. For those actually keen on the cars, Monaco offers the closest and optimum vantage points.

Prospective sponsors are brought here by teams knowing the show will prove irresistible, even if the race itself is processional because overtaking is more difficult on this circuit than any other. A former McLaren commercial director had a favourite spot where he always took his guests. 'They got so close to the cars it blew their minds – and I knew they were mine,' he would say, the figures rolling in his eyes.

Some drivers hate Monaco. Nelson Piquet was one. Jacques Villeneuve has been distinctly uncomfortable here. Most, however, acknowledge the tight, twisting, climbing, tumbling streets as the greatest challenge on the calendar. The barriers leap out and grab those who lose concentration for a millisecond. Gerhard Berger, recovering from his fireball accident at the 1989 San Marino Grand Prix, was a spectator here that season and could scarcely believe what he saw as the cars speared through the tunnel to the harbour. 'They're all mad,' he gasped.

Monaco is a madhouse. An unreal though serene tax haven for most of the year, it loses its marbles on the sixth weekend after Easter. First practice day is conveniently fixed for Ascension

Thursday, a feast day and public holiday, thereby leaving Friday free and extending the possibilities for revelry. As a social summit it is a bizarre amalgam of royal pageant and warehouse rave; and somewhere down there, by the waterfront, teams are working on their cars and preparing for a Grand Prix.

Not that all of them are so lucky. So confined is the space by the harbour that the bottom four teams are condemned to car-park cells up on the rock, not so affectionately known as Alcatraz. Status is all in Formula One. The first reward for a reasonable season, in the minds of mechanics, is an escape from that wretched place. The engine suppliers have been locked in a tug-of-war for a final spot in the paddock. Mecachrome (née Renault) eventually win the right on the grounds they are the defending champions. The fact they are French, the others are assured, has nothing to do with it.

By mid-morning on Wednesday the Monaco scene is in place. Inside the caged paddock and at the adjacent Paddock Club staff are laying tables and positioning plants, while amateur poseurs strut the narrow strip of harbour on the other side of the fence. Security guards with dogs station themselves near the paddock turnstiles. Others keep watch on the vehicles on the top road. Monaco boasts zero crime but during Grand Prix week 'souvenirs' are targeted by the visiting hordes.

The pits here are hopelessly inadequate and garages non-existent, so the teams erect awnings by their trucks to create areas where they can work on their cars before and after practice sessions, and before and after pushing their cars up to the pits, several hundred yards away. An alcove has been made in the perimeter fencing to accommodate Portaloos, or VIP restrooms as they are labelled. Now here we are talking status. The troops are hugely amused to hear from the Stewart camp that Jackie and Paul alone are permitted use of the toilet in their team motorhome.

Curious holidaymakers mingle with dedicated racegoers in Casino Square and around the harbour. The sun glistens on the water, boats lilt gently, and it can be difficult to take in the fact Formula One cars actually race here. Many of the Italian contingent certainly have their minds on other things. Down in the Ferrari compound the sound of rock music competes with chatter about this evening's European Cup final in Amsterdam, where the Italian champions, Juventus, meet Real Madrid.

Ferrari's main man, Schumacher, is on parade at the official press conference, along with Hakkinen, Fisichella and Barrichello. Schumacher, rather than Hakkinen, the Championship leader and winner of the last race, is invited to speak first. Status is everything. The German expects to be more competitive here than in Barcelona and fends off inquiries about alleged dodgy brakes. Fisichella, having pointed out to his interviewer his name is Giancarlo and not Gianfranco, is gratified to hear from the other three drivers they feel the Spanish Grand Prix stewards were harsh in blaming him for the incident with Irvine.

Hakkinen is challenged on the issue of the sport's entertainment value and says: 'I wouldn't like to change anything. I have to say I like it as it is now.' That's honest enough. Perhaps, though, he is stretching things when he goes on: 'I am still fighting when I am leading, with myself and the car. I am not just cruising.' Schumacher contends this is not a key race, then admits he cannot afford to let McLaren get too far away.

Out in the warm sunshine, Herbert, with a young daughter on each hand, is attempting to negotiate a barrier and a way into the paddock, while posing for pictures and signing autographs. He seems to be accomplishing the multi-mission with familiar cheerfulness. The star-spotters have another sportsman in their sights, Alberto Tomba, the charismatic Italian skier. And this is only Wednesday. Wait till they start rolling up from the Cannes Film Festival.

A clear morning greets those descending on the circuit from the spectacular high corniche. The views are stunning. At harbour level a buzz of excitement along the paddock fence signals the appearance of a driver or a well-known team official. Schumacher is in no hurry to leave his compound, engaged as he is in discussion with an earnest-looking lady. The mood in the Ferrari camp is subdued. No one can quite understand how Juventus lost another European Cup final. Spaniards suddenly seem to be everywhere.

Clouds cling to the highest peaks above the principality as the bulk of the drivers head for the pits. Most walk; one or two, including Hill, ride on scooters. Schumacher checks his stride to take caps, programmes and scraps of paper from hands reaching through the fencing and return them with his signature. Irvine, unruffled as usual, brings up the rear but still has time for autographs and a chat.

The local television director is obsessed with activity around the pit-lane Portaloos. He captures Mika Salo stepping into one, Ralf Schumacher stepping from another. Jackie Stewart and Alain Prost, holders of seven drivers' Championships between them and now team bosses, are trying to talk above the noise of revving engines – or at least Jackie is. Alain is doing most of the listening. Flavio Briatore, dressed in a light-coloured suit which gives maximum effect to his tan, strolls towards the pits with the air of a man announcing his return. He has been brought in to pep up the Mecachrome operation and give the engine situation a little more stability. Berger, who worked with Briatore at Benetton, has been lured from his boat to cruise the pit lane.

Out on the circuit Michael Schumacher is bullying the Ferrari, to the appreciation of the German and Italian fans on the hillside beneath the Royal Palace. Even he has a limit and he finds it when he over-shoots the chicane. Hakkinen does not have to try so hard and still finishes the opening hour's session on top. Sly Stallone, working on a movie based on Formula One, gives Schuey the benefit of his advice but it doesn't work. Schuey crashes heavily exiting Casino Square, one of many who come to grief. 'It's like threading a needle with a jet fighter,' is Irvine's brilliantly graphic description of driving here.

Hakkinen spins but stays top. Villeneuve has no such luck. He attempts to take Rosset on the inside only for the Brazilian to crunch him into the barrier. The Canadian climbs from the stricken Williams, admonishes Rosset, still glued to his seat, and turns away in dismay. The collision comes at the end of the session and is seized on by the press pack desperate for something with a bit of edge. This is manna from heaven.

Back in the paddock Williams' press officer, pursued by a posse of journalists, is trying to find Villeneuve. Rosset is easier to locate. He is hovering sheepishly in the Tyrrell hospitality area. Pollock grins into his food. Has he seen Villeneuve? 'I think if he sees me he'll punch me on the nose.'

Rosset is coaxed into giving his version of events. 'I didn't see him. I was trying the car. I was concentrating on my lap and that is not an overtaking point. Two cars cannot go through there together. He jumped into me. He shouted at me a bit but I don't know what he said.'

Villeneuve has been tracked down and informed that Rosset is unrepentant. The champion shakes his head disdainfully and says: 'From the first race he's not been looking in his mirrors. He has no right to be in Formula One. What's the point in talking to him? It's not the first time he's done this sort of thing. He's always being overtaken so he should look in his mirrors. Every time I get close to him I'm thinking what's he going to do now? I think I'd better watch out. He's a liability. I've heard from other drivers they've had problems with him. When I got out of the car I just pointed for him to look at his mirrors.'

By the way, Jacques, what's with the new hair colouring? (The plain blond has given way to white with blue tinges). 'No reason. Just to get Frank angry.'

Jacques Laffite, a former Williams driver, is caught by the TV director in typically enthusiastic conversation with Prince Albert, fresh from his trip to the European Cup final, but probably only because they happen to be standing in front of those Portaloos. Briatore positions himself in the middle of the paddock to tell anyone interested about his plans to place Mecachrome with the top teams. 'I am interested only in winning,' he says.

Winning is a thing of the past for Hill, who acknowledges in the media interview room he cannot expect to score points 'except by luck'. He has joined a team struggling to make an impact but maintains: 'Regret is completely useless. I knew it was going to be hard. McLaren wasn't a possibility.' Talking about his old adversary is almost a relief. 'You only have to watch Michael Schumacher to see why he's so good. It's just fantastic the things he does. He's always on top of the case.'

Hill supports Prost's assertion that the racing would be more interesting if refuelling was banned, thereby creating changing car conditions which the brighter drivers would be able to exploit – à la Prost. 'At the moment there is no surprise,' Hill adds. 'You get an established race order after five or six laps.'

Formula One's commission of technical experts, drawn from the teams, is charged with the task of finding ways to improve the racing, in particular to make overtaking easier. Alesi, sitting alongside McLaren's Adrian Newey, reckons technical directors have too many vested interests to be 'completely honest'.

'There's an element of truth in that,' Newey concedes. 'Everybody's in it for themselves and looking at it from their own angle.'

Hill suggests: 'There's an easy solution. Give everyone a Minardi.' He gets the laugh he wanted but appears to be wishing he hadn't said that and tries to put an apologetic gag on himself. Too late. Word soon reaches the Italian team. Their boss, Gabriele Rumi, retorts: 'Pick another team to joke about. If by the end of next year we are still doing a bad job then people can joke.'

At the McLaren motorhome there are no diplomatic ripples to concern Hakkinen. One of his aides places his helmet on a table. The colours – cool to ice blue – never seemed more apt. Hakkinen is sitting at an adjacent table. He is wearing dark glasses and a demeanour of self-assurance as he gives an interview to three Belgian reporters. That done, he turns to face a Brazilian TV crew.

'I started the weekend confident,' he says. 'I just felt good. I knew what I was doing. I tried to continue from Spain. I had a plan to go with here also and it is going well.'

'You were talking to Ron Dennis before you went out,' the interviewer says. 'What was he telling you?'

Hakkinen throws him a disbelieving glance and smiles. 'You don't expect me to tell you that, do you?'

The interviewer, whose command of English is limited, giggles nervously and resorts to asking Hakkinen if he finds an advantage living in Monaco. Nine other current Grand Prix drivers are officially resident here.

Not really. Not as far as the circuit is concerned. It is another racing circuit, nothing like Monaco at normal times. The fact that you may be passing your favourite restaurant doesn't matter. But I do feel comfortable here. I am relaxed. I go to my own place and I sleep fantastically. I believe it is how I feel that is important to me. If I am in control of my plan I do not fear anyone.

Do not misunderstand me, I'm not saying I'm going to beat David and Michael in the race. I respect them and they are very strong, very dangerous. But I now know what I can do. I am working all the time to get the car I want, and that plan is working for me. If I stay focused like this, I have what I need.

The body language is equally positive. Hakkinen's best result in a Grand Prix here is sixth, in 1996, and even then he failed to finish the race, but times have changed. This is not arrogance, just the unmistakable conviction of a driver who has traced his intended course. With that he is dragged away to another appointment.

Late into the afternoon mechanics are poring over their cars in the row of canvas garages, entertaining thoughts of a serious night on the town – no practice tomorrow, chance for a bit of a sleep-in. The bar on the other side of the paddock fence is already shifting up through the decibels. The younger Formula One generation know little or nothing of the fabled Rosie's Bar, going up the hill. Even the Tip Top, just down from Casino Square, now seems to belong to another age. The trick is to make your money go as far as you can. Veteran members of the fraternity still come here on their annual pilgrimage, clinging to their own perception of Monaco. Its accommodation of young and old is testimony to Monaco's unique and enduring fascination.

A cloud cover has freshened the air and brought one or two concerns. Now is that outfit going to be suitable . . .?

The promised sleep-in is shattered by the early morning bleating of racing cars. This may be a day off for the Formula One drivers but those on the undercard are out there practising. The Grand

Prix workers blink into a bright day and are thankful for the stiff breeze to help clear their heads. The Ferrari camp is still quiet at ten o'clock. Other teams have turned in, although some of the boys are evidently relying on instinct for guidance.

The drivers will look in at some stage of the day, as much, perhaps, by way of courtesy as necessity; always good to show willing and an appreciation of the workers on the shopfloor. Coulthard pops round to the McLaren compound from his home in Fontvieille mid-morning and then returns to the other side of the rock that seats the palace and the old town above the rest of the principality to host a lunch for the British media. He was long ago indoctrinated in the ways of good PR. He is in big demand from the papers, magazines, television and radio, and this arrangement suits everyone, especially as the food at the Italian restaurant beneath his apartment is excellent and substantial.

'He's hungry,' Coulthard says, unwittingly finding a neat link with Hakkinen's appetite for success. 'He's fired up, no question. But I think I can do it. This is not like Spain. We were changing positions right through practice yesterday. Consistency is important in Championships. I'm the only driver who's finished all five races. We all want to win Monaco. It's one of the big three, along with Silverstone and Monza. It's the ultimate challenge, a journey into the unknown. You have to run within millimetres of the barriers.'

Every few minutes someone appears at his shoulder, waiting for the moment to interrupt and ask for an autograph. Mostly they are middle-aged businessmen, wearing suits and ties. An Englishman asks him to dedicate a message to his wife, Monica. 'Saves me buying her a present.' A glamorous lady is rather more demure and glides back to her table to share the treasure with her partner. 'It's a great privilege being well known, that's why I don't mind scribbling my autograph,' Coulthard says.

He was not always so readily recognised, as he recalls in a story against himself. A couple of years ago he was at a sponsor's event, right here in Fontvieille, where the MC presented him with a CD by the Irish band, the Corrs. 'He made a big thing about this band from my own country. He obviously thought I was Eddie Irvine!'

He will have taken that in his stride, as he takes most things in his stride. He is a polite, personable, even-tempered, well-turned-out, clearly well-brought-up man. The chaps find him good company and his girlfriends have tended to be tall, blonde models. But listen, David, isn't it about time you cut out some of this gentlemanly stuff and had a real go at some of your opponents, the way Our Nige used to? The hacks are only half joking. Mansell was always good value for the nationals.

'I'm not like that,' he protests. 'I can't bottle up anger for an hour and a half of a race and then let it go at the end. I don't think that's healthy. There's no point in losing your temper. It achieves nothing. I am what I am.'

Recognising his argument has fallen on fallow ground, he turns in mock panic to his management guru, Martin Brundle.

'Martin, help me. They're saying I'm boring.' Before Brundle, now extending his television repertoire with the 'Great Escapes' series, can think of a way out of this one, the hacks pounce again.

'Martin would have a go, he would mix it.' Brundle nods.

'Yeah, they even got me to pose in a T-shirt with "Bully Boy Brundle" on it,' he confesses.

Coulthard is grateful to change the subject. How about the World Cup? He's hoping to get to Paris for the opening match, Scotland's meeting with Brazil. A life dedicated to motor racing has, he points out, stifled his knowledge and experience of many activities in the world beyond, and such is the precarious nature of his profession his philosophy is to savour what he can where he can.

'I intend to enjoy life as much as I am able to. I could put it in the barrier tomorrow and it could be all over. I'd hate to think I could have wasted my twenty-seven years. You have to live for now. But it's not material things that I desire. Money is not the motivation. Success is.'

Coulthard is having to strive for success to the constant accompaniment of rumours that McLaren and Mercedes are intent on prising Schumacher from Ferrari. The stories have been fanned this week by a quote from Ron Dennis: 'When you have a very good car you want the best and Michael is the best.' Coulthard sees off yet more questions on the subject with his tiramisu.

'Ron has told me not to concern myself with the rumours and that is a nice commitment from the man. People may say I'm naïve but why worry about it? It's an ongoing thing. At the moment I'm comfortable. The crunch time will come in the future. I'll be talking about my contract in the middle of the year and worry about it in the unlikely event that will be necessary.'

Hakkinen is generally perceived to be the favoured son at McLaren, a privileged position that has as much to do with his near-fatal accident at the end of 1995 as his ability or personality.

'I've said in the past I've felt uncomfortable with Mika's relationship with the team, but I understand it because of all he's been through with them. If I have equal machinery and emotional support – because even if we are thought of as these tough heroes, we do need that – then I'll be happy. Success will help strengthen my relationship with the team and I've no reason to doubt I'll be with them beyond this year.'

Later on this 'day-off', Coulthard is on show for Mercedes and before that, at three o'clock, he's off up into the hills for a training stint on his bike.

'What time is it now?' Three. 'Oops!'

Johnny Herbert has been having a family lunch, but scarcely a private one, at the bar-restaurant on the other side of the paddock fence, fork in one hand, pen in the other, signing autographs for an endless queue. Schumacher has plenty on his plate with Stallone and entourage posing for pictures in the Ferrari garage. Stallone throws everyone by slipping out of a side exit but is spotted by a member of another team: 'He was picking his nose.' That piece of business attended to, he rejoins his men and they troop away in arrow formation. Stallone's hair is jet black, his jaw almost as perfectly sculptured as Coulthard's, his arms held wide and rigid, his chest bulging a modest-looking – but no doubt designer modest-looking – polo shirt.

Schumacher's paddock day over, he rides away on a motor-
bike, his identity hidden inside an unfamiliar helmet. Frank
Williams has to make a slower, more public exit. He is lifted from
his wheelchair into the passenger seat of a people carrier in view
of dozens pressed against the fencing, the indignity of it all
showing in his sad face. Even the sky is dark and sorrowful this
early Friday evening.

Saturday morning practice comes as a relief to everyone, especially the drivers. Even Stallone has to keep his distance now.
Schumacher's session is short-lived, however. He parks his sick
car halfway around his first lap and watches the rest of the
morning's proceedings because mechanics cannot repair it in time
and he is not allowed to use the spare. Villeneuve also pulls up,
while Coulthard, Hakkinen and Wurz fail to thread that needle at
some point or other. Irvine brings Ferrari's president, Luca di
Montezemolo, up to speed on events as they stand in the pits.

Max Mosley, the president of FIFA, is here on one of his
infrequent visits to a Grand Prix and makes himself available for
questions from the press. A lawyer and son of Sir Oswald Mosley,
the British fascist leader, he handles the conference with familiar
eloquence and charm, while brandishing a little barb when he
feels it appropriate to do so. 'You obviously weren't listening to
what I said earlier . . .'

He is asked why Sauber have not signed the Concorde
Agreement – the Formula One constitution – and refers the
questioner to Sauber. He is asked to comment on the lack of
entertainment in the racing and in particular the difficulties of
overtaking but he reiterates his conviction that not a lot is wrong
because TV figures have gone up 'by leaps and bounds'. He
dismisses Prost's proposal for a ban on refuelling as blatant
self-interest because the little Frenchman would be able to pass on
his strategic skills to his own drivers. Mosley signs off with a
commendation for Schumacher on his road-safety work, the
German's 'punishment' for driving into Villeneuve at the end of
last season. An hour on, the tall, smiling figure walks away
unscathed.

'He should be a cabinet minister,' a veteran cynic mutters with a resigned shake of the head.

Time for some therapeutic star-spotting. Footballer Ryan Giggs and athlete Merlene Ottey are here. So is singer Lisa Stansfield, the Rochdale lass and now neighbour of Hill and Irvine in Ireland. She was determined to make this race after Irvine introduced her to the delights of the Grand Prix stage last year at Monza.

'It were great,' she said. 'I wasn't keen on the helicopter flight in, though. I nearly wet myself.'

They say Eric Clapton is due, and Phil Collins, or George, as he is known to one of his new friends in the paddock. On his last visit to a Grand Prix he found himself at the dining table next to the elder statesman of the press corps, Jabby Crombac, who is Swiss or French – no one is quite sure – and has been covering motor racing since Fangio was a lad. Crombac, of course, had no idea who Phil Collins was but got it into his head his name was George and duly called him George all night. Collins, relishing the anonymity, cheerfully never let on.

Forecasts of afternoon drizzle prove unfounded and the McLarens again lead the way in qualifying. It is, however, an eventful session. Irvine has the biggest shunt but walks away from his twisted car unhurt. Hakkinen and Coulthard trade the number one spot before the former is confirmed on pole. Rosset's plight goes from bad to worse. He spins in forlorn quest of a qualifying place and compounds his embarrassment as he attempts the kind of power spin back on course that any half-decent Formula One driver routinely performs like the rest of us park in our garages. The Tyrrell rifles into a gap in the barrier and is terminally jammed.

Hakkinen talks of his satisfaction at overcoming the nerves and stresses of Monte Carlo and Fisichella, having beaten Schumacher to third place on the grid, gleefully says: 'Michael said there was no way for Benetton to be on the second row, but I am.' Coulthard reveals he will spend the evening at his apartment, studying in-car footage of his previous starts here to work out how he can take Hakkinen at the first corner. Since overtaking is near impossible here, the outcome of the Grand Prix could hinge on those opening few seconds. And, to the appreciation of the British press, he is talking aggressive, if not quite dirty.

'There will be a team thing in that we'll be told to make sure we don't crash at the first corner, but once we're off the line it's all to play for and if I get a wheel in front I will try to muscle ahead of him. I'm a lot more confident about trying that sort of thing this year than last year because the cars are quite robust now. You learn from experience, such as with Schumacher in Argentina. I'm not saying I'm prepared to push anyone off the track but if I create a gap I will hold my position. As normal.'

Prince Albert and his henchmen are patently resolved to hold their position as they cut a swath through the paddock throng. 'We were literally just pushed out of the way,' report two female paddock VIPs. A well-endowed lady with some advertising message on her chest has no difficulty finding enough space to pose for a batch of eager photographers. A cooling shower is perfectly timed.

Nine o'clock Sunday, race day, and already the teams are dismantling their canvas garages and packing their equipment. The cars have been pushed up to the pits and after the race they will be loaded into the trucks. The morning is again fine and warm but the harbourmaster is adamant rain will arrive at midday. The clouds over the mountains are supposedly the foolproof sign. 'Besides,' one of the motorhomers says, 'It's fixed for Schuey to win. To keep the Championship going.' If it rains, Schuey is well-nigh unbeatable, but this conspiracy theory is another matter. The Formula One bush radio is always giving out these bulletins and the people here believe them.

Presumably the rain will also help Barrichello, who was second to Schuey here last year, so he ought to look a mite happier than he does.

'Mmm,' someone in the Stewart Ford camp begins to explain. 'It was his birthday yesterday and he ended up having dinner at McDonald's because nothing was organised. We should have done something, really.'

Elsewhere parties have been in regulation swing and paddock folk are comparing notes. Seems a posh bash given by Jordan's sponsors was especially lively once the initial starch had cracked. It is related one old dear was particularly taken by a younger, male guest and made concerted attempts to whisk him away. The paddock women – motorhome staff, PR and press officers and sponsors' representatives – had their own do at the bar over the fence, which must be making enough this weekend to sponsor a team.

One of those surviving to tell the tale is Ann Bradshaw, as prominent a figure here as almost any driver. If Stallone decided to go for a 'Carry On' approach to his movie, Ms Bradshaw would be ideally cast in the Joan Sims role, the more mature, responsible sort but still with a twinkle in the eye. She is actually head of Tom Walkinshaw Racing's media affairs, and in Formula One that means Arrows. This is her 14th full season on the Grand Prix tour and she has been involved in motor sport for 27 years. The list of her associates in Formula One reads like a *Who's Who* of motor racing.

There were over seventy of us on the girls' night out. We went to perhaps the liveliest place on the circuit so it was inevitable one or two of the guys would have a look. It was a great hoot. EJ [Eddie Jordan, that is. They are big on initials in F1; there's DC and also JYS – John Young Stewart] sent us champagne and I did a little speech to embarrass him and he ran away because his wife was there.

I think there is as much fun as there used to be, but it's tougher in certain ways because you've got all the sponsors to look after. When I started in motor racing you'd get a couple of guys come along, they'd sit in the motorhome and they'd have the odd sandwich. Now you've got the Paddock Club, hundreds of people, and there are so many more things to do.

Also, you'd have half a dozen English journalists, half a dozen French, half a dozen Italian. Now if Nigel

Mansell or Damon Hill is doing well you can have fifty English journalists. It depends who's driving for you as to how busy you are. Because of TV, so many people know about Formula One, so many people want to know about it. It's a lot busier in every way.

I had a season with Lotus, eleven with Williams and this is my second with Arrows. So I've met and worked with a few people. I've worked with Mansell, Rosberg, Piquet, Senna, Dumfries, Hill, Coulthard, Villeneuve, Prost, Patrese and others. Riccardo Patrese I just adored. He had been with Brabham a long time but Williams became his spiritual home. People told us a lot of things about Alain Prost before he arrived, how political he was and so on. I found him a total gent.

I saw Damon go from a test driver to world champion. I sometimes felt I spent more time with him than Georgie, his wife, did. He's very private, a family person. Keeps himself to himself, not the sort of guy who's going to tell everybody his innermost feelings. He's a good guy. Damon found it more difficult to cope with the adulation than Nigel did. I think he was a worthy champion and I'm sorry he couldn't have shown more in the car. He took on the mantle of world champion and the responsibility that went with it. Being ambassador for your sport is very important and he played a magic role in that. He helped a lot of people, guided the drivers. He became the elder statesman.

Nigel was one of the most inspirational guys in a car, but I never knew how he was going to react from one day to the next. Nigel was . . . mercurial. I could have slapped him sometimes. Other times he was just wonderful. Then something would upset him again and he'd change completely. They are in this pressure cooker, but Nigel was his own worst enemy. And yet the people loved him and I don't think I've ever enjoyed watching anyone I've worked with driving a car so much as I did watching Nigel. He wrung the thing's neck. [You sense she would have paid a lot for such an opportunity.]

It's very difficult to talk about somebody like Senna. Everybody says he's the greatest driver who ever lived and who knows? He'd still be racing now, I'm sure. It's still an emotional thing. I worked with him twice, when he'd just started winning races and then when he'd got nothing to prove, and he was two very different people. Most people say they change when they become famous. I found Ayrton changed for the better, not for the worse.

At Lotus he was intense and so focused on what he wanted to do. He'd always been a bit of a practical joker, but he became a lot more relaxed. Happier. Cheerier. I remember at Aida, the race before he died, a lot of Japanese people stood outside the hotel on the first morning, waiting for him, but he had to go straight to the circuit. Next morning he came out half an hour earlier so he had time to sign autographs for all of them. In 1986 he wouldn't have done that. He'd achieved his goals and was happier with himself. In some ways he became less of a superstar and more human.

The big practical joker, of course, was Mr Nelson Piquet. Sometimes he was a little naughty, like hiding the loo paper when Nigel had the runs in Mexico. You never knew what he was going to do next. He would sometimes physically abuse people, grabbing parts of their anatomy. A lot of the time it was fun but he was also mischievous, like he'd say Nigel's wife was ugly. He could be malicious and seemed not to know when to stop sometimes.

Among the current crop I'd say DC is the girls' favourite. He's a sweetie. Everybody loves him. He's a bit of a softie. He'll never change. It's true to say he's politically correct because Jackie Stewart sent him through the IMG school [International Management Group, the agency owned by Mark McCormack] and at an early age he was told this is how you look, this is how you dress, this is how you act. But inside there is a really lovely guy. His mum and dad are nice. Like Pedro [Diniz] here. Brought up properly and they are nice to their mums.

Among those Ann has not worked with are Schumacher, Irvine, Alesi and Berger, but she naturally has her views on them.

I may not have worked with Michael but I've danced with him! People say he's arrogant, he may well look arrogant, but I've never found him to be so in a one-to-one situation. He's polite and a gentleman. As for Irvine . . . he's a lunatic. He's a yob. He's . . . [She breaks off lest anyone should get the impression she doesn't like him.] You couldn't be indifferent about him. He used to live quite near me in Oxford and one day he told me he'd chased a woman down the Banbury Road because he thought it was me. He got up alongside and discovered it wasn't. Poor woman was probably petrified. Sometimes he says things for effect but you can't accuse him of being bland. He's like Jacques, who's very much his own man. I think it might be no coincidence they spent time in Japan, as did Mika Salo. It probably helped them develop a sense of humour.

I know a lot of girls say Irv looks the sexiest of the drivers but I've got to say I prefer those with the Latin looks. They always seem to look right in their race-suit. But then as a racing driver you're always going to do well with the birds and Irv uses it to full effect.

Alesi seems a bit of a Jekyll and Hyde character. When I've met him he's been great, but you don't get the impression he's a person you'd like to work with. He's another you'd probably describe as mercurial. It's funny that Berger, this good guy that all the journalists like, suddenly comes under a scathing attack from one of his own mechanics. Most drivers have most of us in tears some time because we want them to do something and they don't want to do it. They are always going through bad patches because of problems on the track, so there's frustration.

That's the drivers. What about some of the bosses?

Frank Williams today is a very different character from the one I first knew because then he wasn't in a wheelchair. He was very focused on his team. After a race when everyone was waiting at the airport for a flight home, he'd be heading somewhere else, doing a deal. After his accident the only way he could find out things was by relying on people coming to him and he became much more of a people person. You hear stories of when he lived with his mates in Harrow, getting up to outrageous things. For a bet Frank ran round the block with no clothes on and they locked him out, things like that.

The TV cameras like to catch him in the garage looking very serious. They can't get in front of the others because they are on the pit wall but if they could, you wouldn't find them smiling during a race. You'd find them concentrating just as hard as he does. Frank loves his sport. He loves talking to people, and if a pretty woman arrives Frank will talk to her for hours about things other than motor racing.

There are people here you can love or hate, and you have to say there are people, perhaps through jealousy, who don't like Ron Dennis. But in a way he has got character. Although he tries to put on this stern exterior you every so often hear of his having outrageous parties when his guys do well. And then there are the stories of the practical jokes when he was with Senna and Berger – throwing briefcases out of helicopters and those sort of things. I think he threw Stefan Johansson's briefcase into the boating lake in Montreal. If you're a television viewer, you would never imagine Ron Dennis doing anything like that.

On another occasion in Australia, Senna made the mistake of revealing to Dennis and Berger he did not like frogs. Subsequently he returned to his hotel room to find frogs in his bed, wardrobe, bathroom and any other crevice. He dragged the furniture into the corridor in his frantic search for every last croaking creature and was near demented when told one was not accounted for. And oh, did you find the snake?

What does Ann think of the bosses of bosses?

Bernie's frightening! He has this great knack of unsettling you when you're having a conversation. He does it on purpose. He'll bark at you, 'What do you want?' and you instantly know you've got ten seconds and you'd better not screw up. He's put you on the back foot and he unnerves you. I don't feel comfortable having to say something to him because I know he's so difficult and you have so short a timespan to talk to him.

Now Max ... At Suzuka we'd all been to the Log Cabin [a watering hole near the circuit] and were all a bit happy. Another girl and I jumped on our moped. She was driving, I was riding pillion and Max stood on the back. We were riding through the hotel complex, came round the corner, found the police doing their drill and scattered them. We end up in the foyer of the hotel, abandon the bike and run to our rooms and lock the doors with the police looking for us.

I know this is a sport led by technology and money, so in that sense it's not a sport, it's a business, but it's still the people who make it fascinating for me. These things don't work by themselves. We all say how great the McLarens are doing, and whether you like them or not they're doing a fabulous job. But as far as I can tell, it's people like Mario Illien [of Ilmor, who build the engines for Mercedes] and Adrian Newey who make that work, and while they are absolutely brilliant at what they do, they are two of the nicest, most ordinary people you could come across. After work they'll have a silly evening and not mention a racing car.

It was interesting listening to those scriptwriters who came down to Barcelona. They said they'd got their material from the paddock, they'd not seen a car. So many people come and never see a live car on the track. I can't remember the last time I went out to the track and watched the cars. But the number of people I've come across over the years who have said they went to Monaco in 1969 and met so and so, and still talk about it. It stays with them.

Give Bernie his due, he's created a bit of plastic that's worth, to some people, millions, because that's what they are having to pay to get them, these paddock passes. At the end of the day the sponsors are paying for these as well as their name on the car. There are not many things in the world you can't buy but this, in the ordinary sense, is one of them. If you make something exclusive then everybody wants it. It's brilliant marketing. Whatever anybody says about Bernie, and I hate being fenced in, doesn't it make people want to be here, because you make it almost impossible to get in? You can't just walk up and get a pass. Bernie's made it like that.

But then there are twenty-two guys in here to race these cars, and there are not many things which you can say only twenty-two people in the world do. So here they are in a confined area with twenty-two fairly rarefied people. Can't wait to get home, though.

Showbiz and sporting celebrities are the most conspicuous of these sponsors', team or Formula One hierarchy guests, drawn by the arena's cleverly manipulated magnetism, the prospect of personal projection or simply the genuine thrill. Sponsors receive an allocation of passes as part of their deal. Today there is talk that Bruce Willis and Lennox Lewis are coming, although there have been no reported sightings. Better informed intelligence confirms Hugh Grant and Liz Hurley are on their way.

A source in the Mercedes camp has provided an intriguing

twist on the will-they-won't-they go for Schumacher saga.

'If Schumacher came here he would get all the credit and if for some reason we were not so good next year, we would get all the blame. Now everyone can see how good we are because we are winning without Schumacher. It is better for us to be beating him.'

Warm-up beckons and Schumacher marches through the paddock gates on to the track at La Rascasse corner to an explosion of roars and klaxon horns. He waves to the fans, who sustain the din as he makes his way up the short rise and around the corner to the pits. Enterprising fans in the stand overlooking the entrance to the pit lane pass down caps on pieces of string for the great man to sign. He returns to the paddock with second fastest time, having split Hakkinen and Coulthard.

Still way off the pace are the Jordans, yet down at the team compound there are no outward signs of catastrophe. The hospitality area is tastefully appointed, the dark-grey tables, chairs and cupboards, the polished floorboards and tall plants neutralising the sponsors' yellow paint job on the bus. Catering staff walk by with platters of food and the view to the harbour, where gently bobbing boats are decorated with sunbathing females, is as good as most will reckon it can get.

Even Bette Hill, mother of Damon, and wife of the late Graham, is reasonably calm as she relates the ordeal she and a friend experienced near Antibes the previous evening, when four young thieves on two motor scooters snatched their handbags, containing cash, passports and race tickets, from the back seat of their hire car.

'It was frightening,' Bette says. 'I've been coming here for years and nothing like that has ever happened to me before.'

Inside the air-conditioned bus Eddie Jordan is confronting the latest stage of his miserable season with a characteristic mix of frankness, defiance, optimism and blarney.

'We seem to have gone backwards. This isn't good enough. I'm not looking for mercy. It will be very painful and I'm not ashamed of that. You can bet I'm kicking bums here. I fight best when my back is to the wall. But there is no quick fix to this. I have had serious talks with the drivers but they have done a particularly good job in difficult circumstances. Damon had a difficult start with us but I've been really impressed with his motivation, being world champion. I'm sure it will be turned round here and I think Damon will want to see it out.'

Hill now apparently off the hook, the finger appears to point at Mugen, the new engine suppliers, and the team's technical director, Gary Anderson. Jordan observes that Prost too are having problems with their Peugeot engines after the two teams changed partners. Anderson's role is a more delicate issue. Jordan, nestled into a bench seat which arcs around a table at a raised end of the bus, considers his response for several seconds.

'The things we have done to the car have not made a difference, so now we have to take a more radical approach. Gary and I have faith in each other and have to solve it together.'

But are not the sponsors putting him under pressure, especially when they are seen to be under-achieving at the most prestigious race of all?

'I put myself under pressure because if I was paying the money they are I'd want to know. But they put no pressure on me and good sponsors tend not to jump from one team to another. It is the most important race for sponsors but there are so many other things for them to do, to see and enjoy here, and they are really not always looking at qualifying times.' The man-eater at the party springs to mind.

Paddock banter suggests Jordan enjoys the hedonistic perks too much to be a winner in Formula One. The latest joke in circulation poses the question: what would Frank Williams, Ron Dennis and Eddie Jordan do with their last £100? Answer: Frank and Ron would spend it on their racing cars, Eddie would spend it having the barnacles cleaned from the bottom of his boat.

Jordan, who has cultivated the fun side of his team's image, may not be amused by the serious implication in that joke, but there has been speculation he might sell out and the name of Honda – due to return to Formula One in two years and the parent company of Mugen – has inevitably been mentioned. Honda are said to prefer an autonomous operation and Jordan contends he is not ready, 'even at fifty', to put his feet up. However, he is leaving the door open to parties interested in joining forces with him.

'I could sell out but I'm still ambitious and have a lot to achieve. I've done nothing yet, I know that. But if there was the opportunity of a technical partner having a piece of Jordan, that would not be selling out. That would make business sense to help the team become stronger.'

Outside the bus, in the hospitality area, Chris de Burgh has joined Jordan for lunch. Along the waterfront one way, Merlene Ottey is eating chez Sauber, the other way Fergie – the Duchess of York, that is, not the Manchester United manager – has opted for McLaren. Stallone is still cruising, smiling for cameras; but he refuses a request to pose holding a baby. 'No, I can't. Insurance,' he explains in those well-honed gravel tones.

The Williams motorhome area, at the near end of the paddock, is relatively quiet. No sign of celebs here, just a few regulars asking if Mr and Mrs Head and newly arrived baby Luke are well. Apparently so. Villeneuve is wandering with a plate in his hand, evidently seeking sustenance. A group of British national newspaper journalists, sitting at one of the tables, are assailed, albeit playfully, by Ginny Williams, a bright, chatting, engaging woman of middle years, for always being rotten to her Frank. Her Frank, of course, has a propensity for parting company with champions, the journalists counter – albeit playfully.

Drivers set off to the pits for the last time on this, the longest weekend. Some mechanics, who work in the pits and therefore have to wear similar protective suits, are mistaken for drivers by fans straining for autographs or merely shouting their best wishes for the race. A young, dishevelled man in Tyrrell gear, walking alongside their driver Toranosuke Takagi, is drawing on a cigarette. 'Must be Rosset,' someone cruelly speculates. Coulthard and his girlfriend stroll hand in hand in the sun – so much for the harbourmaster's expertise – as young lovers would on a Sunday afternoon. Two of his compatriots in kilts, tammies and ginger wigs, jig on the other side of the fence – as you would, dressed like that in Monaco.

The Grimaldis, of more sober attire and deportment, arrive in the royal box and apartment owners fill their balconies as the cast of thousands smother the grid. Liz Hurley is asked who she fancies. The Irishman, she says. Presumably she does mean Irvine and not Coulthard. Still time for another picture of Stallone and photographers almost come to blows in the scrummage.

The Grand Prix gets away first time, Coulthard backing off at the first corner and Hakkinen speeding clear. Fisichella holds off Schumacher. The McLaren pair trade fastest laps before, on the 18th lap, Coulthard's engine blows as he descends the hill from the tunnel, and he rolls his crippled machine up the escape road. Hakkinen maintains his concentration to win the race and extend his Championship advantage to 17 points.

Schumacher performs his usual pit-stop trick to get ahead of Fisichella only to find Wurz in front of him. The German tries his muscle-man routine and although he eventually forces his way past the Benetton, the contact has damaged his car. He loses three laps in the pits and registers an academic tenth place. Wurz crashes heavily but is unhurt. Fisichella finishes second, Irvine third, Salo fourth, Villeneuve fifth and Diniz sixth. Herbert and Hill are next, outside the points.

Hakkinen takes his slowing-down lap as slowly as possible, savouring the moment. Back on the grid he is deliriously happy. This is what they mean when they say winning at Monaco is special. The Finn may not yet rank among the greats who have dominated this event in recent seasons – Senna six times, Prost four times and Schumacher three times – but he has taken a huge stride towards the world title. Asked to share his feelings, he says: 'I'm sure other drivers have found it difficult to explain the feeling of winning here, and it is the same for me. Maybe tonight, tomorrow or the next day I will know what it means to me. I wanted to enjoy the slowing-down lap, look at the people and experience the feeling. I don't want ever to forget it. And I had some fun. The team were shouting things at me on the radio, Finnish words I have been teaching them.'

He thanks the team for supporting him through the 'incred-ible' pressure of the Monaco Grand Prix. He says he thought his race was over after hitting a barrier and that, although relieved of the battle with Coulthard, the torment was unending.

'The grip level changes and to keep your concentration throughout the race without a mistake is incredibly difficult. You remember Ayrton Senna going off some years ago here. Don't misunderstand me, I'm not comparing myself with him, but it's so easy to make a mistake. You think you can slow down but these cars are not designed to drive slowly, so it becomes a nightmare.'

Fisichella puts on his little boy smile and asks Hakkinen to let him have a win. Hakkinen responds with an unequivocal 'No.'

'Why not?' the Italian persists. 'Just one.'

Coulthard reveals he was thrown a chocolate and given a drink of beer by a fan after abandoning his car, and contends all is not lost.

'I know 17 points difference might look too much but I can recover. It's a question of keeping your chin up.'

Irvine has his family in attendance and goes through his Kevin routine again. He is trying to use his mobile phone and eat an ice cream, a task which further tests his dexterity when he bites off the bottom of his cone and has to cope with its dribbling contents. At the same time he is tapping Sonia, wanting to know where they are going on to, while his mum – holding his trophy and presentation flowers – and dad are telling him to keep his voice down.

Stewart Ford have nothing to celebrate this year, two retirements cutting short their day. The Cosworth engineers, having worked until two o'clock this morning and got up again at 6.30, are thankful their engines were not the cause. The motorhome staff, similarly exhausted – at least one of them nodded off during the race – console themselves with the thought they won't be serving champagne until ten tonight. Ann Bradshaw is not the only one who can't wait to get home.

4

Magny-Cours

YOU'RE NOT SINGING
ANY MORE

The rain is hitting the pavement like spears as a woman makes a dash from the boulangerie to her car, cradling baguettes. It is unseasonably cool as well as wet in Burgundy, and out in the fields big, white Charolais cattle stand in pathetic resignation of their plight. It is a morning made for solemn moods. Perhaps that suits the woman at the filling station, just down the road from the Magny-Cours circuit. Her modest little business place is a shrine to Ayrton Senna. Every square inch of wall and shelf bears dedication to his memory: photographs, signatures, helmets.

Up in the paddock, a man is sifting through framed photographs to be hung in the hospitality area of the Ford motorhome. He discreetly discards a picture of a smiling Jan Magnussen. 'We won't be needing this,' he says. Stewart have finally given up on the Dane and replaced him with Jos Verstappen.

Much has happened en circuitous route from Monaco to the French Grand Prix. Ricardo Rosset has survived a threat to his job at Tyrrell, who, in the guise of British-American Racing, have also announced a deal with Briatore for a supply of his Renault engines next season; Mika Hakkinen has gained a wife, Erja, six years his senior, but lost ten points of his advantage over Michael Schumacher in the World Championship, while the German has managed to stir up more controversy. He won a chaotic race in Canada, despite incurring a stop-and-go penalty for forcing Heinz-Harald Frentzen off the track. Williams' protests were echoed by their other driver, Jacques Villeneuve, after Schumacher insisted he had not seen his compatriot and attempted to shift the attention to what he considered dangerous driving by

Damon Hill. Villeneuve concluded Schumacher lived in his own world, or 'Planet Michael' as he sardonically termed it.

The European season, and with it normal paddock life, resumes at this generally unloved venue. The facilities are excellent, space generous, but the circuit is a typically uninspiring product of the age and the atmosphere little better than at Barcelona. There are, however, ingrained prejudices, since France's previous venue was down in Provence, at Paul Ricard, within reach of the Côte d'Azur and its accompanying delights. Almost any place would suffer by comparison but this corner of the country has its hidden gems, such as the tiny, medieval village of Apremont-sur-Allier. The Allier river feeds into the Loire just west of Nevers; further downstream is Sancerre, which offers its own refreshing reward for the traveller; and over all this reigns a hot, regal sun. Usually.

The open expanses of the square paddock, laid out on a slightly lower level than the pits, accentuate the inclement nature of the elements this last Thursday in June. Potted plants, strategically positioned on the tarmac, still out-number people early in the afternoon. As the rain relents, and the temperature creeps upwards, awnings are unzipped. Team personnel arrive in batches, drivers one by one. Just about the first is Verstappen, who is pounced upon by a Dutch TV crew for his thoughts on returning to active Formula One duty.

Rather more attention is focused on a new Ferrari rig, parked alongside two regulation trucks which carry the cars and equipment. This latest model has on its roof a satellite dish the size of something you might expect to see at Jodrell Bank, and giant antennae reaching to the sky. Along the side of the vehicle is a narrow strip of tinted window. Ross Brawn, Ferrari's technical director, climbs the steps which lead to an outer balcony and a sliding door, activated by the inevitable swipecard. Inside is the team's mobile office, divided into three sections. But will it help them win races?

'It should do,' Brawn says, beaming proudly. 'We can exchange information between here and Maranello.'

David Coulthard appears to have enlisted Rubens Barrichello

as his personal porter. The Brazilian drops off a bag for the Scotsman at the McLaren motorhome and heads for his own camp.

'I've got to be good to him if I want to be his team-mate,' Barrichello says in passing.

Coulthard is wearing a white T-shirt bearing the legend: 'David Coulthard, powered by Mercedes-Benz'. He needs all the force he can muster to resuscitate his Championship aspirations after another setback at Montreal, where he led until a throttle linkage problem derailed him.

'There's no point thinking it's all or nothing for me this year,' he says. 'If I do well in the next two races things can change to my advantage. I don't want people thinking I don't care, because I do want to win the Championship, but I'm not going to get screwed up about it because that would be counter-productive. I'm third in the Championship, so there's no reason to be downhearted.' It sounded suspiciously like resignation again.

'Not at all,' insists Martin Brundle. 'He's not given up and he doesn't think he's out of it. He's been genuinely unlucky. He's gone out in races he should have won. Don't write him off.' Brundle might well say that, of course. It is in his interests for Coulthard to be successful. The reality is probably that Coulthard is deliberately trying to fend off the pressure, which is entirely sensible.

Schumacher has been patently caught out by the weather and turns up in shorts. He looks still less comfortable when it is put to him at the press conference that he does not command the level of respect attained by some of the sport's former champions.

'I believe when you go back to Alain [Prost, who is seated behind him], other drivers didn't always like some of the things he did. It is normal for drivers at the front to be criticised. I'm not saying I did everything right, but if you take the middle ground that is probably right. There is no way the things I did were as extreme as they put it.'

So how about speaking to Hill and clearing up the debris from your latest skirmish?

'I've not had a chance to speak to Damon. If he runs over me

I will. It's not so easy to find him.' He is evidently relieved to smile at the expense of his old adversary.

Another old adversary, Frentzen, is in no mood for light-hearted reconciliation. He is adamant Schumacher should quit his position as joint spokesman – along with Coulthard and Hill – for the Grand Prix Drivers' Association.

'A driver like Michael, the way he drives, he can't be our spokesman. He is always going on about safety, and then drives the way he does. At our next meeting I'll call for him to step down.'

At paddock level, Hill groans at the first mention of Schumacher.

'I don't want to talk any more about him,' he pleads. 'Let's talk about the World Cup.' So he does, in particular his forlorn efforts to get his seven year old to concentrate on England's cause.

Michael Breen, Hill's lawyer and the man who negotiates his contracts, has turned up for this race. Time for talks again? Breen came in for strong criticism after Hill lost his place at Williams and missed out on a move to McLaren. Against that, he has helped make Hill a very wealthy man. Rumour has it Jordan and their sponsors are reluctant to shell out another fortune to retain the former champion.

Back up the steps, on the open plateau behind the trucks, Coulthard and Villeneuve are locked in conversation. A little way on, the brothers Schumacher have their heads together. Photographers and caption writers lap up the opportunity. Stewart's press officer senses the chance to involve their new driver, Jos Verstappen, in a golf day.

'You like golf, don't you?'

'Not really.'

'Then how come you list it as number two in your likes?'

'I like hitting the ball but I don't like walking two hundred yards to find it.' The press officer, nonplussed, turns away.

A windswept and ruddy-faced Irvine looks as if he has just been at sea. Apparently he has. He chats with his engineers and retreats to the Ferrari motorhome. He settles on a beige, soft-leather seat, in front of an Italian television programme and asks for a 'nice cup of tea'. Irvine has a reputation for saying what he thinks, or at least saying what he thinks might ruffle a few feathers. He expresses some characteristically forthright opinions between sips of tea this late Thursday afternoon. Most senior drivers maintain they could compete with Schumacher on a level playing field but Irvine derides such claims, and he believes the last two champions were fortunate to find themselves in a Williams.

> If Michael puts pressure on Hakkinen and Coulthard they're gone, they're history. Simple as that. I don't think either of them is consistently fast enough at all the circuits. You look at Michael, he's just on it everywhere. It's soul-destroying but that's the way it is. The great drivers, like Senna and Schumacher, are always up there. They modify their driving style for every corner. They just know how to get the maximum all the time. That's the killer.
>
> I challenge DC and Hakkinen to put every penny they've got on a head to head, in the same car, with Schumacher. I wouldn't do that because I'd lose my money. And neither of them would do it. They'll talk a big fight, but when it comes down to it they'd get destroyed. I'm not saying you couldn't beat him in another team because he has got weaknesses, but in the same team his ability is unreal.
>
> Hill and Villeneuve have just not got the natural driving ability that Michael has. Coulthard is definitely better than Hill. You saw it in the second half of the year they were together. DC really blew him away. I'm surprised no one could see through the car's superiority. Formula One is about the car. Same with Villeneuve last year. Frentzen has been on top of Villeneuve every race this year.

Much of what Irvine says is greeted with derision elsewhere in the paddock. He is considered by many to be mercenary, prepared to forfeit his pride and suck up to 'St Michael' for the sake of his contract. He maintains, however, he does not always agree with his partner and when asked whether he likes him, pauses for careful thought first.

Michael sometimes values his opinion a little bit higher than I think it deserves, but because he's two-times world champion everyone will listen to him before they listen to me, for instance. It doesn't necessarily mean his opinion is right, but no one will pay attention to mine, even though it may be better than his. It's the same with all the other drivers. No one's going to pay attention to them because Michael's the better driver.

I don't think they're knocking him because they know he's a better driver. They're just knocking him because they see it's slightly unjust, which to a certain extent it is. He's not particularly liked. Senna was liked. Michael, for whatever reason, isn't liked.

I understand he's got bad qualities I don't like and he's got very good qualities I do like. In some ways he is arrogant. But he's very honest, which I like a lot. He's very straightforward to deal with, which is more than you can say of some. And if he's your friend, he's a proper friend, which is a lot more than you can say about a lot of drivers around the circuit.

He's a friend to me. He's been very supportive of me in the team and to be honest there's been times when I've needed it, and he's stood by me a hundred per cent; and not because it suits him, but because that's what he genuinely feels. It is good to know where you stand with someone. We work well together. The tyres I choose he likes, set-ups I choose he likes. There are so many similarities it's unreal, but he just seems to be able to get that little bit extra out of it, which is disappointing for me.

But then there are the consolations, as Irvine willingly acknowledges. He may not be making the £78 million a year Schumacher is said to earn from various sources, but his £3 million-plus goes a long way. As usual, there is a price to be paid, although Irvine does not include foibles of the paddock environment among them.

The last week I've had has been just mind-blowing, you know? I'm sitting on my own yacht, down at those islands off Toulon. It was like the Caribbean. Blissful blue water, with a bunch of good friends, and just heaven, absolute heaven. I've got a jet waiting at the airport to pick me up, I've got the helicopter, and I'm thinking 'Wow [his laughter emphasises his difficulty taking this in]. This is madness.' One guy, and I've all these people working for me. It's a company. It just can't be right, you know? And you feel guilty. You have to say it's an unfair world. It's totally unfair. But the good thing is I'm going to enjoy it, because as someone once said to me, 'I've never regretted anything I've done, but I've regretted a lot of things I didn't do.' It's so true, because you're a long time dead.

I quite like paddock life, because there are a lot of good people in Formula One, a lot of very interesting people. The dangers are obviously a downside. I might not get the chance to spend all this money. [He laughs again.] But apart from that, the travel gets to you, and not being at home a lot. But people who are at home a lot want to go away. Humans are never happy with what they've got. You always want something different.

I'll never be a hundred per cent happy because I am an ambitious person. At the end of the day I've got to beat Michael Schumacher, and that's difficult. I don't go out there every weekend thinking I'm going to let Michael beat me again. I know I can't beat him. I know he's better than me but that doesn't mean to say I'm going to let him beat me. It's like the defender who goes up against Ronaldo. He knows Ronaldo is better than him, but that doesn't mean he's just going to lie down and say, 'Hey, that's the net, go ahead my son.' You've got to work out how you can beat him. You might not beat him on talent, but you can beat him another way. So I've got to look at how I can beat the guy because he is the guy to beat.

The Hakkinens, the Coulthards, the Hills, the Ville-neuves, I don't give them a second thought. I know I can beat them. But Michael, that's going to be hard. For sure I'll not beat him in the same team. But for sure I won't beat him in a Jordan, either, or a Minardi or whatever. Coulthard and Hakkinen have beaten him because they are in a McLaren. You've got to be in a different team, but I don't want to go out and be a number one and be finishing eighth, beating my team-mate. It's a good job for Formula One Michael is there. It's a shame to have to say that, but that's the reality.

The early evening is still grey, a relief from the oppressive heat of past years, and there is always the World Cup to watch ...

Back in Germany, Schumacher has managed to join the hooligans on the front pages. Asked how he would handle the thugs wreaking havoc and injury at the football fest here in France, he replied: 'They should be treated like animals, and if an animal bites a person it would be put to sleep.' Unsurprisingly, his remarks caused a stir in the Fatherland. Unsurprisingly too, his subsequent discomfort is being enjoyed in corners of the Magny-Cours paddock this Friday morning. As Irvine observed, his team-mate is not the most popular figure in the fraternity.

Johnny Herbert is a likelier candidate for that status. He has positioned his two Weetabix in front of a television under the Sauber awning to watch Sky News. 'I'm not a three Weetabix man,' he confirms. Neither is he a mercenary or a willing number two.

Eddie is in a situation where he's accepted he's number two and longer term it's helped him out. He's done a good job, but I would never be a number two, even for the rewards. He's being paid well and he's getting good results now, but that's not what I'm trying to achieve. If

you're not being allowed to try and win I don't understand why you would want to stay, but Eddie's happy
with that. It depends what goals you set yourself, and
obviously his goals haven't been too high. My goals are
higher than that.

Herbert's team-mate, Jean Alesi, is among a pack of drivers
mooted as candidates for a job at Williams next season. Herbert
is not.

It doesn't get me down when I'm not mentioned, but I
don't see any reason why anyone should dismiss me,
especially after this year with Jean. There's no point
sulking and thinking it's not fair. It makes me fight all the
more. Doing well against Jean should put me in a better
position because my team-mates last year, three of them,
didn't push me. This year I'm with a 'name' and probably
haven't had a fair comparison since I was with Mika at
Lotus. We were equal there but I never got in the right
position.

Williams would be a nice challenge. At the moment
they are not the best team in Formula One but they have
the know-how to get back to the top and that is something
I would like to be involved with. I have to say I am happy
here and don't want to go anywhere unless it's better.
Things are okay with Jean. He has his mood swings but
our relationship is fine. I just don't want to stay around to
make up the numbers. If that was the situation I would
have stopped ages ago. I would have been fed up and not
bothered. I feel I am still driving well and I want to drive
further up the ladder. If you're doing something you're
not enjoying it's pointless to go on. I still have a desire to
make it.

Out in the paddock the plants are at last out-numbered by
humans but the sun remains reluctant to grant its blessing.
Diagonally across the tarmac from Sauber is McLaren's camp and

Herbert's former team-mate, the newly wed Hakkinen, is showing no ill effects from the nuptials. His boss, Ron Dennis, appears similarly recovered, doubtless to the relief of the driver. Hakkinen went to great lengths to warn Dennis that Finnish weddings tended to be 'different'. Through a brief northern night and out the other side into a bright early morning, Dennis discovered how different. The Finns do like a drink and have the stamina to indulge their fancy. Dennis was impressed.

McLaren in general, and Dennis in particular, are not perceived (to borrow a much-used word from what is mockingly termed Ron-speak) as a fun bunch. The livery of their motorhome, and those of their partners, shades of grey, fits the image. Order, appearance and discipline are paramount. Dennis applies his swipecard to enter the bus and sits in an unfussy, functional upstairs section to work his way through a sheaf of papers. The fun, he explains, has its place, too.

While we are here we are working. If you go into most serious people's offices – doctors, solicitors, people in business – do you think you'll walk into some sort of flippant, showmanship-like environment? You'll walk into an environment conducive to the people in it doing their job. All I expect our team to be, at a Grand Prix, is focused and professional. We are here to do a job.

Yes, it's a show, but I think there are too many people who think the show is as important in the paddock as it is on the circuit. For me, image is important. We can't win all the races but we can look the best and that's important to this team. But we're under no illusion. The show is the race, not in the paddock, motorhome, garages. I don't see that at all. I see the paddock, motorhomes, garages as the team's office. I expect everybody when they're in their office to be doing their job above all else – and I don't care about the criticism that's directed at myself or the team.

There are, as there are in an office, the coffee-breaks, the lunch-breaks, and they tend to be consolidated into the post-circuit evenings, and our post-circuit evenings are as lighthearted as anybody else's. We tend to work hard, play hard, and try, and sometimes fail, to bear in mind we've got to go into the office the next day. Sometimes you find yourself having too free a spirit on an evening before practice, but that's where discipline comes in. You get very focused and stressed during the course of a day so you try to balance it off by being relatively relaxed at the end of the day.

Ayrton didn't know the concept of a practical joke till he joined the team, and Gerhard and I tend to come from the same mould when it comes to practical jokes. The most important thing about a practical joke is its complexity, and the recipient can't begin to comprehend that what appears to have just unfolded has been planned. I have a bit of a perverse sense of humour. Some people would call it almost child-like sometimes. The reality is there is an important place for humour and lightheartedness at McLaren, but at the right time and in the right place, and that's not at the circuit.

Our current drivers are in a quite different situation from Ayrton and Gerhard in that I've grown older. The age gap between me and the drivers is greater and I'm probably a bit more intimidating to them because of that than I was to Ayrton and Gerhard. So they are a little bit more cautious about me, but not away from the circuit. Away from the circuit and certainly between Grands Prix there's nothing held back and anything goes.

Dennis, at the age of 51, has worked and played his way back to the top for the first time since 1991, when McLaren won the last of their six Constructors' Championships under his command. A former mechanic, he does not now take for granted a reclaimed position of pre-eminence.

We didn't have expectations coming into this season and it wasn't until Brazil we could start to get a feeling for where we were. Inevitably the gap gets closed, as hard as you try to maintain it. We're entering the second half of the season with a measurable advantage, which can quickly disappear if you have any unreliability. That is probably the most vulnerable aspect of our performance package.

I'm more concerned about that than the threat of Schumacher because it's something we have control over. We're pretty comfortable the problems we had in Canada won't repeat themselves. Michael's optimism is part of his psychological approach and his competitive spirit. It doesn't work at all, either with our drivers or the team. Data available to us indicates we still have an advantage over a Grand Prix distance. Over the thirty-odd years I've spent in motor sport I've often become embroiled in the psychological approach drivers bring to their own efforts, but it's wasted on us. We know where we're going.

But since Schumacher is now in second place, surely it might become prudent to implement team orders so that the drivers' title should not be yielded to the German.

We don't have a strategy here based on how we are going to win the Championship. The strategy here is based on how we are going to win the race. We're a long way from needing a strategic approach. It's always nice for a driver to win the World Championship, but the team's primary goal is the Constructors' Championship. That is the mission. I would prefer as many race wins as possible, even if it was detrimental to one of our driver's chances of winning the World Championship, because that's our objective.

Having said that, that's the best environment for the drivers as well, because we are offering each driver equality, the opportunity to demonstrate he's better than his team-mate, and if in the process of that the driver from another team achieves his personal goal to the detriment of his team-mate, fine, I understand that. It's their prerogative to run their team that way, but it's not the way we ever run McLaren, and I think McLaren's results speak for themselves when it comes to justifying that strategy.

Of course there's a special relationship with Mika. That comes from the fact that he's been with the team longer, and he's sustained injuries in an accident in one of our cars, even if it was caused by debris puncturing the tyre, allowing us the consolation that it wasn't our fault. After an accident, if that driver recovers and returns to form, and if you are human, you can't possibly not have it in your mind when you are part of the team. But it absolutely does not have any relevance to whether each driver receives equality of equipment and support. If you are in Formula One as a driver you should have the strength of character to understand and cope with these sorts of issues, and I know David has that strength of character. To ignore it is foolish. You've got to recognise it and handle it. If Mika chose to retire at the end of this season and another driver came, David would find himself in that position as well. It's just a normal human relationship.

That said, Coulthard's contention that Dennis gave him assurances about his future at McLaren brings a puzzled expression to the boss's face.

I can't remember saying it, but that doesn't mean it's not true. The simple fact is that historically this team has demonstrated fierce loyalty to its drivers, which is something we expect back from the driver. That's not new. It's why Senna and Prost won three Championships. We are about loyalty and that's not going to change. David and Mika should feel more comfortable than any other drivers in any other team, because of the approach we take as a team.

That has to be qualified by recognising we exist to

win, and at a certain point in every year we evaluate the performance of the other drivers in Grand Prix racing, compared with the performance of our drivers, and if we believe we can enhance our chances of winning Grands Prix, then we will take difficult decisions. But we are not in that position now. As such, both of our drivers have every reason to believe that the philosophy within McLaren is conducive to their staying.

If Michael is available on the market, and assuming we are in a contractual position to consider it, we will consider it, because it's our job, it's my job. But that situation doesn't exist at the moment, so it's academic. As you would expect, I have a great deal of knowledge that I cannot share, but the result of the thought process is that our driver pairing is more likely to remain as it is than change. The situation could change. David or Mika could fall over in the bath and break a leg and I would have to make a decision. Teams can have three bad results, drivers become demotivated. It can happen. To pre-empt a decision at this stage is just not possible and is counter-productive to our primary goal.

We've got a stable environment, we enjoy the environment we've got and we don't really want to change it. I would be disappointed if we were not able to demonstrate to any driver who joined our team that we have the ability to provide both drivers with the same equipment. I don't believe any driver, if he is really convinced the team is capable of doing that, would look for an unfair advantage.

Steering McLaren through relatively lean years, back to the head of the pack, is cause for satisfaction by any standard. Dennis, however, does not permit himself any sense of achievement at this stage of the season.

It's inevitable your mind strays to all kinds of thought processes, and that's where we try to bring our corporate discipline to bear. It's a luxury to think that way, a luxury we can't afford. If there's any time we can afford it, it's got to be after the last Grand Prix. I block it completely out of my thoughts and all my colleagues follow the same route. So many teams or individual athletes find themselves back in form and fail because they think they've made it. They lose sight of the goal and fall, sometimes not even at the last fence but well before.

Talking of matters 'corporate', how about Hill's suggestion that Coulthard and Hakkinen are shackled by corporate considerations, and restrained from enjoying their success and speaking their minds? Dennis' response is stern and withering.

I hope he enjoys not winning races. I don't think he's a particularly happy person at the moment. I have a healthy respect for many aspects of Damon, but if this is his observation I think he should focus on what your primary goals are if you are a Grand Prix driver, and that is to win races. If, for example, I thought our drivers could enhance their ability to win a Grand Prix by standing on one leg for half an hour a day and I could give them a valid reason to do so, I would expect them to do it, because that's what we're about. I say to our drivers, after you've done the job go and enjoy the satisfaction, but don't come to a Grand Prix with anything on your mind other than what is required to win that Grand Prix.

There are many instances of drivers getting themselves into a form of media tennis: one driver says this in one paper, another driver says that in another paper. What a complete and utter counter-productive waste of time. Great for the media and maybe it's of interest to the consumer, but does it do anything to enhance the image of the driver? It might make him a little more colourful but will it help him to win races?

What our drivers receive is guidance – this is the advantage of adopting this or that approach, this is the

disadvantage of adopting it. They're not automated individuals with our corporate media people behind them
with their hands up their backs pulling strings. We are not
trying to de-colour the drivers. We give them advice, not
instructions, on the upside of taking a path which doesn't
put them into the sort of controversies that you see
occasionally coming into Formula One and other sports.

Hill claims also that he had no genuine opportunity of joining
McLaren, the inference being he was made an offer he had to
refuse. So could Hill have joined Dennis' team? 'Absolutely,' he
replies, then explains the procedure he follows when determining
his drivers for the following season. McLaren put their current
drivers 'into a box' and evaluate all other available drivers,
eliminating those who are of 'no interest' and those who have
contracts. That process leaves them with a maximum of five
candidates, who are considered for 'evaluation' against the two
men in the box.

> When the discussions stopped between the team and
> Damon, we had not reached the need to evaluate Damon
> as an option against our two existing drivers. We were
> still at the stage when we were saying, 'If this is the
> proposal, what is your response?' His response to that
> suggested path was, 'I'm not interested.' Therefore it
> never went beyond that point. If he had said, 'I'm inter-
> ested,' we would have evaluated him as an option versus
> our two drivers, and there was a possibility – unquantifi-
> able because those circumstances never developed – that
> he could have been a driver for this team. Why spend
> hours and hours of discussions, going backwards and
> forwards to Germany [and Mercedes] if there was a
> decision already taken not to change?
>
> I think the offer, taking everything into consideration,
> was an offer that should have been accepted. If people
> don't convince the management of McLaren and
> Mercedes Benz that their primary goal, above all else, is

to win races, there is no place for them in this team. Simple as that.

Dennis' team is about to take to the track for practice. The morning is cloudy but dry and the McLaren still looks the best car out there. All the more reason for Bernie Ecclestone to be thankful he has Schumacher to take them on, and he grasps the opportunity to speak in the German's defence.

Ecclestone, never a man to shun box-office controversy, says: 'I get a bit fed up with all these complaints about Michael Schumacher's driving. He's a racer and it's a pity we've not got more like him. He's good for the sport, and like Senna and Mansell he's prepared to take a few risks. We don't want drivers pussy-footing, we want them racing and competing. Michael's a big boy. He'll cope with the criticism on and off the track. Whingers are losers.

'Schumacher shouldn't have been penalised in Canada. I saw nothing wrong and there was no accident. The stewards should never have done what they did. He didn't have the chance to give his side of things. He's happy at Ferrari and there's no reason for him to leave. He's the man taking it to McLaren and making them fight for it.'

With that he scuttles away, knowing full well the ripples will have reached every corner of the pits and paddock by the end of the day. 'Whingers are losers' – he will be especially pleased with that.

Hakkinen is fastest today, by 0.082 seconds from Irvine. Coulthard is third, Frentzen fourth, Schumacher fifth. Irvine, in demand from the media, says: 'I hope I can make it tough for McLaren on Sunday. I put my money on Michael for the Championship at the start of the year and see no reason to change my mind now.'

The sun at last burns through the clouds during the afternoon and brings life to the village square. Two women from a travel company responsible for the movement and accommodation of most British personnel in Formula One are camped at Jordan, struggling to cater for the whims and petty jealousies of teams as they allocate flights and hotel rooms for forthcoming races. Theirs is a nightmare beyond all others in this paddock.

Behind the pits, mechanics are tending their tyres like caring shepherds. A man in an official bib checks the tyre allocations against his sheet of paper. Long-serving members of the press corps, engaged in convivial banter around a sample of the local grape, are restructuring Formula One.

'Might as well erect the Paddock Club next to the M25. It would be more interesting. At least something happens.' The chortles are prolonged by a challenge emanating from Ecclestone's appearance nearby. 'I'll give twenty pounds to anyone who goes up to Bernie and says, "What's a man of sixty-seven doing still sporting a Beatles haircut in 1998?"'

Hairstyles are in discussion again later in the evening, as television sets around the paddock are tuned into England's World Cup match against Colombia. A British press dinner at Tyrrell is a particularly enthusiastic scene. A close-up of Carlos Valderrama, he of the amazing blond mop brings the cry: 'He's got Eddie's wig on.' Martin Brundle offers the thought that if Bernie ran a football team he would field 12 players and get away with it. Murray Walker is invited to dub over the German cable TV commentary. Since he declines, someone mimics him: 'It's minute forty-two, so after this it will be minute forty-three, minute forty-four, minute forty-five and then half-time.' Murray just laughs, as he has laughed at the mickey-taking down the years. He laughs all the way to the bank.

McLaren, just across the way, have outflanked the rest again. They have picked up BBC Radio Five Live's commentary and the unmistakable tones of Alan Green are booming into the night. The Tyrrell gathering out-shouts all-comers when first Anderton, then Beckham score splendid goals for England. One bemused diner in their midst is the team's Japanese driver, Takagi, who hid himself away inside the motorhome until his interpreter showed up. He probably wishes he hadn't ventured out.

The final whistle on England's 2–0 win and passage to the second round is greeted with another eruption. The tearful Colombian goalkeeper finds no sympathy in this company.

'Always look on the bright side of life,' is the gloating refrain. The singing goes on until England's barmy army finally run out of steam and wend their way back to their hotels. A man is left to water the lonely paddock plants in peace.

Early Saturday morning cloud lifts, encouraging a Ferrari fan, wearing a red cap and joyfully waving a rolled-up red umbrella at passing cars, to cycle more than 20kms to the circuit. The noble old cathedral of Nevers dominates the skyline. Traffic leaving the town for Magny-Cours moves less freely than the cyclist as it encounters squads of superfluous gendarmes along the road.

Bernie's bus, positioned behind the team trucks and away from the paddock, is receiving its morning brush-up from a man on a stepladder. A chorus of good-mornings exchanged by team personnel competes for the airwaves with the throaty growl of engines. When the beasts are uncaged, the McLarens are still kings of the jungle. Hakkinen rules in morning practice and, more importantly, in qualifying, securing his fifth pole of the year. He will be joined on the front row tomorrow by Schumacher. Coulthard is relegated to third on the grid for the first time this season. Irvine is fourth.

Hakkinen expresses confidence in his prospects for the race, as does Schumacher, who predicts he and Irvine could give McLaren a hard time. Coulthard acknowledges he has more to gain by taking risks and talks an aggressive strategy. He aims to play Schumacher at his own game but is mindful of Irvine's proximity.

'I'll be hot to trot, so stand well back,' the Scot says, to the puzzlement of some listeners. 'The opportunity to make up the two places might come only on the first lap, so I've got to be ready to take it. Eddie's the wildest card in the pack. He'll be fired up so expect him at his wildest. I'm not going to have a mountain of pressure building up on me, but anyone who questions if I'm pushing myself is not looking at the situation closely.'

Under close scrutiny late in the afternoon are the Italian football team, taking on Norway for a place in the last eight of the World Cup, and it's standing room only in the Ferrari hospitality motorhome. Alesi has a seat on the front row. Schumacher opts for the quieter 'team only' motorhome but watches no less intently. Fisichella joins Minardi for the match. A profusion of Italian flags flutter in the breeze. Early oohs and aahs give way to a thunderclap of a roar as Vieri gives Italy the lead.

Herbert has wandered over to Ford, where there is less empathy with the Italian cause. Villeneuve, despite having spent much of his life in Europe and having raced in Italy, has scant interest in football and occupies himself responding to Ecclestone's contribution to the Schumacher debate.

'Taking risks for yourself is one thing, putting other people at risk is something else. It goes beyond what I consider acceptable. I believe you don't do to someone else what you wouldn't want doing to you. There again, if you believe you are a higher being than anybody else, that nothing can happen to you, I guess you're allowed to do anything you want.

'Everybody tells you that you can't overtake in Formula One but you can, as long as you are prepared to take risks. The problem is, if you go off that's not accepted in Formula One. Taking risks is much more acceptable in CART. Drivers crash more and they don't get as much blame for it.'

Villeneuve raises his eyebrows at a yell of anguish from the Ferrari camp. Must have been close. He could, of course, have his ten cents' worth by joining the Grand Prix Drivers' Association, but that option has no appeal to the Canadian.

'I wouldn't want to be part of a group where it's just a few people bitching at each other and accomplishing nothing. The drivers won't stick together on anything, so it's a waste of time.'

Italy, meanwhile, are still leading 1–0 and over at Minardi Fisichella and friends are anxiously counting down the minutes. Where's Murray when you need him? At last the referee blows and Italy are through. Roars of relief, clapping and laughter fill the paddock. Alesi, the Frenchman born to a Sicilian family, trots back to Sauber with a huge grin on his face. Next up on the football fields of France are Brazil and now it's Barrichello and Rosset indulging in a show of patriotism. Rosset has been wearing his No. 9 Ronaldo shirt under his race-suit all day. Barrichello now dons the golden shirt of his country, and although he is upstaged by Rosset – no number, no name – he goes to sleep a happy man. The favourites have booked their place in the quarter-finals.

The sun and dark, rolling clouds are playing cat and mouse on race morning. Equally uncertain is the attraction of this Grand Prix on an afternoon when France are playing their second-round match in the World Cup. On the face of it, it's a ludicrous clash, one that must have been anticipated. Precisely, say those convinced Machiavellian forces are at work here, intent on undermining Magny-Cours' position and taking the race back to Paul Ricard. The organisers, it is said, have endeavoured to cover their backs by giving thousands of tickets to schoolchildren. The political jousting, actual or imagined, is one of the main topics of conversation over breakfast.

It's the turn of the only French team, Prost, to gorge on the footie fest and a girl, decked in blue shirt and white shorts, and carrying a football, is escorted to the pits for a photocall with the team. Opportunism is endemic in this game, and not all of it is acceptable to everyone.

'You've got people here just waiting for the chance to tread all over somebody and rubbish them, that's what I don't like about Formula One,' a driver's manager protests. 'Teams chasing each other's sponsors is something you have to live with. Business is business. But wanting others to fall on their faces, that's something else. There ought to be a greater element of fair play and more friendship in the paddock. There's some, but not a lot that I can see. It's all pretty ruthless.'

It's all pretty predictable in warm-up, the two McLarens leading the way from Schumacher. Coulthard takes the top spot, and is now in animated discussion with his engineers in the garage, using the flat of his hand to indicate the movement of the car and clenched fists on an imaginary steering wheel to emphasise his point. Hakkinen is more subdued, confining his communication with an equally earnest-looking Dennis and Adrian Newey to verbal observations.

Paddock guests congregate in small groups to chat and bask in the occasional shafts of sunshine. A larger group gathers at the foot of the steps from the pits to catch returning drivers. Alesi is at ease with his admirers, Coulthard is content to talk, Hill strolls casually to lunch. All are evidently relaxed. Jackie Stewart is accompanying Edsel B. Ford II, great-grandson of Henry Ford, who is making his first visit to a Grand Prix for a decade. He 'can't believe the way this scene has changed in that time. That Paddock Club is something, isn't it? For fifteen hundred bucks or something all in, that's pretty good value.' It would be next to the M25, you can hear someone mutter.

On the grid, little more than 20 minutes before the start of the race, Irvine is content to declare his intent: 'If DC wants to win the Championship he'd better keep out of my way.' Hakkinen parks his car at the front, climbs out and wanders off for his pre-race pit stop. Most drivers go through the same ritual, whether or not they really need to go. Irvine is standing under an umbrella held by his sister, Sonia. An umbrella is shading the cockpit of Schumacher's Ferrari but the driver has disappeared to the little boys' room. Coulthard is wandering on the grid, chatting, smiling, looking incredibly relaxed. 'Right,' he says, 'let's get on with it,' zips up his suit and reaches for his helmet. Just time for a final picture of the girl in the French football kit, now standing in front of the Prost crew with a placard pledging the racing team's support for the nation's World Cup campaigners.

The grid is cleared and the cars line up, engines revving to a crescendo, only for Verstappen to stall and the start to be aborted. Hakkinen is especially frustrated after getting away in front, followed by Coulthard. The crews are not exactly ecstatic having to lug their equipment back on to the grid and fuss about for another two or three minutes before the starter tries again.

This time there are no problems, except for McLaren. Schumacher launches into the lead, followed by Irvine who, good as his word, forces Coulthard to take evasive action and zips past a stuttering Hakkinen. Irvine plays the dutiful number two, holding up the McLarens as Schumacher opens a healthy advantage. It goes from bad to worse for the Championship leaders, Hakkinen spinning in a desperate attempt to take Irvine and dropping to fourth, Coulthard losing time at his first pit stop because of a faulty fuel-hose mechanism.

Coulthard's second stop is even more catastrophic. The fuel rig refuses to cooperate and the Scot sits there shaking his head as the points slip away. He is sent off without taking fuel on board and is called back a lap later after Dennis has satisfied himself they can fill him up. They manage, eventually, to refuel the McLaren but now Coulthard is down to seventh and only a last lap manoeuvre takes him past Alesi to claim a point.

Schumacher has long been out of reach, leaving Irvine to resist a renewed attack by Hakkinen. The Finn makes a lunge at the last corner, both cars twitch and cross the line rally style, but Irvine takes the flag by 0.172 seconds to complete Ferrari's first one–two success in eight years. Hakkinen's advantage over Schumacher is down to just six points, with Coulthard a further 14 points behind. Schumacher's embrace for Irvine tells all.

McLaren feel the restart was unnecessary but Coulthard is concerned that more problems have been self-inflicted.

'The team have apologised and it's just one of those things, but we know it's not good enough. If you're going for the Championship you can't afford things like today. In pure racing terms I guess I've got to win the British Grand Prix to stay in it.'

Irvine returns to the Ferrari motorhome to chants of 'Eddie, Eddie,' from the mechanics, who are seated and ready to feast, bottles of champagne placed on the tables. Irvine, too, is fizzing.

'McLaren have missed the boat and now the Championship is ours,' he raves. 'Michael will destroy the McLarens at Silverstone. It will be more of a race but he'll put them in the shade.'

Schumacher has been inching his way back to base, signing autographs and shaking hands before breaking free and sprinting the last stretch, then sneaking into the side entrance, through the kitchen area, where staff are preparing the pasta, while Irvine holds the media at bay. Even now, the Irishman is covering for his number one and earning that lucre.

5

Silverstone

OVER THE EDGE

The British Grand Prix is the same as every other Grand Prix – two days of practice and race day – and yet it is very different, or at least so it seems. It seems bigger, longer, busier than all the others, even Monaco and Monza. The event at Silverstone has somehow grown into a monster that spreads itself over a fortnight. During the week before practice begins, the teams are here for testing, which is the normal pattern. Not so normal is the packed paddock as teams ship in hordes of guests whom they cannot accommodate on the race weekend. This is zoo time.

It is also a barometer of the whole Silverstone show, a production which has become something beyond the wildest fantasies of its pioneers. The four-day festival – cars in support races go round on the Thursday – attracts a crowd of 225,000, the Grand Prix is watched by a live television audience of 350 million people in 130 countries and it generates £30 million annually for the local economy. And this weekend Silverstone's Grand Prix celebrates its golden jubilee.

Across the landscape of that half century, this exposed, wind-swept plain on the Northamptonshire–Buckinghamshire border has played host to some of the most spectacular encounters in motor racing. It all started when a bunch of motoring enthusiasts ventured on to the former bomber training base, near Silverstone village, to satisfy their thirst for recreation in the aftermath of the Second World War. The RAC, seeking a site for its planned Grand Prix in 1948, were alerted to the possibilities and acquired a lease.

For that event the organisers laid out a track which utilised not only the perimeter road but also the runways. Since the cars would be hurtling towards the intersection from opposite directions before turning sharp left, canvas screens were erected lest any wimpish fears should enter the drivers' heads. Unsurprisingly, this section of the circuit was changed the following year, when the race formally took on the title of the British Grand Prix. On 13 May 1950, Silverstone staged the first round of the inaugural World Championship.

It was never the most loved circuit in the world. It lacked the atmosphere and mystique of Monza, the awe-inspiring splendour of Spa and the natural amphitheatre of Brands Hatch, for instance. But it was fast – blindingly fast. Keke Rosberg qualified his Williams Honda for the 1985 race at a record 160.725 mph. Radical alterations had to be made for safety reasons in 1992, and they have since been fine-tuned to the wider approval of drivers and spectators alike.

Improvements off track have kept pace since the days of straw bales, oil drums and roped-off public enclosures. For this year's Grand Prix, 53,000 grandstand seats are in place. Hospitality and catering facilities expand by the year. On Sunday, Silverstone becomes the world's busiest airport, with nearly 4,000 helicopter movements.

Testing, the drivers will tell you, is when the really hard work is done. Most teams have designated test crews and test drivers, who pound out lap after dreary lap to try this part against that part, this set-up against that set-up, this tyre against that tyre; three or four days of nine to five toil and tedium to gain the odd tenth of a second. Significantly, senior race-team personnel as well as race drivers are on duty for the Silverstone test. This is, after all, the home race for seven of the 11 teams. Jordan are based just across the road.

This is still a barren season for Eddie Jordan's camp and, as last year, Hill arrives at Silverstone seeking his first point of the season. His tone is positive.

Formula One is always a test of your staying power, because it's hard work. I'm not complaining. It's something I want to do. But it tests you in every area. The one thing I've learned is that if you work hard at it you invariably get a reward. As much as it's hell doing three days of testing, round and round doing 250 laps or something, it teaches you things you need to know. Also, I feel a responsibility towards the team, the mechanics, who work incredibly hard, and the people back at the factory.

Running second in Canada was fantastic. You don't want to get out of the car when you're actually at the sharp end. It's reward for everything. So you've got to travel in hope. You have always to think you'll get there. My hope is that we've bottomed out. We had this terrible Monaco race and we were kind of shaking. But we seem to have pulled ourselves up a bit. Eddie has taken a closer look at his team and what needs to be done. He's taken on new personnel but he's also managing the personnel he has and optimising his resources. He doesn't have the resources of Williams.

We want to win races, but you have to be realistic about what you can achieve with what you have. I want to win. I don't have many more years left when you consider Ralf is just twenty-three, so I'm impatient to progress with Jordan. I don't think there are signs yet that I'm less competitive than someone who's very young, a very fast driver and reputedly as talented as his brother. So I'm proving myself against the toughest challenges I can find and still feel I can hold my own and be competitive.

My relationship with Ralf is very good. We don't speak much, I have to say. He's a very quiet boy and doesn't really involve himself with me that much. I think he feels a bit awkward about some of the things Michael says about me. He's not like Michael in that regard. He has to position himself carefully within the team. I find him just fine, no problem at all.

Unfortunately I have a slightly reactive streak in me and so I have to check myself and I have spent many seasons holding my tongue about Michael, and the innuendoes and comments still keep coming. If he continues like that then I'll lob some back his way, but I would regret it if it should get to that. I want people to know I have a sense of humour. Honestly. It doesn't bother me a lot. It doesn't really concern me. I think it's laughable, most of it. Utterly laughable. Since when has he been interested in regulations? It is a joke coming from him. I don't know what it's about with him and me. As for this business that I ignore him, what am I supposed to do? Ask for his autograph? If he can crack a smile about it then we're going to be fine, and I'll be happy with that.

Hill made his Grand Prix debut at Silverstone in 1992, and won the race in 1994. Another landmark would be appreciated this time and he welcomes all the help he can get from the gallery.

When I got my point here last year I could hear the cheers in the car, so I know I've got some support. This year there will be a lot of support for David also because he's actually got Championship hopes. It's great being a British driver at the British Grand Prix. There's a Herbert faction, a Coulthard faction, an Irvine faction, and when you see all those flags it has to be worth something. I just hope it helps me get in the points again.

I'd love to be in Mika's position, leading the Championship, but I would not feel so comfortable with Michael second in the middle of the season. Dozens of things can happen. It's certainly far from over for David. If you are in a top team it can swing so quickly. I think Mika is on it. He looks as if he's enjoying himself and he's not someone who'll crack under pressure. I think he's got some good people around him. He feels supported and strong.

That sense of security is apparent in Hakkinen's demeanour within the McLaren compound. He is comfortable, relaxed, at home. Put him on display at an official press conference and he is visibly awkward, slow in his responses. He can come across as dour, even dim. He is acutely conscious of this clumsy public image.

'When you see me answering questions I look serious because I am concentrating and thinking what I am saying,' he explains. 'And this is in a foreign language. In private life I am relaxed. That is a different situation and I can be different.'

He is aware, too, that many in Formula One considered him too cocky by half during his early days at McLaren. A life-threatening accident at Adelaide in the last race of the 1995 season gave him a new perspective on himself and the world he still belonged to.

There is a danger of becoming big-headed in my situation now. You just have to listen to the people you work with and keep your feet on the ground – very heavily. [The delivery of those final two words brings a slightly twisted grin to his face. Like Hill, he has a sense of humour. Honestly. Just mention Eddie Irvine.] Eddie's comments are always funny. It makes him happy but he's fourth in the Championship and should keep his mouth shut. You don't worry about words. They give you a good laugh but what people say can't hurt you. It worked on Damon a couple of times. [Another grin.] I have been around in racing for many years and have a huge experience. I don't think I will crack. The pressure is always going to be there, but when I am on the race track I really don't feel Schumacher's psychology or all these mind games will affect me. That shows a weakness. On a race track you can lose your temper in certain situations, but it happens rarely to me. I try to stay calm. Racing is about control-ling your emotions. If you get excited and negative you start making mistakes.

I have been expecting to be in this situation since I came back into Formula One in 1991. It has taken a long time and it does not feel strange. All the time I have been racing I have been preparing for this, to be in a leading position. It is what I have been waiting for, I just wish I had more points in the lead, but I can't expect everything. I'm going to work even harder. Of course David has still got a chance. He is a very quick driver but he has to beat me first. I'm not fighting against my team-mate, though. I try to make him an ally, a friend rather than a driver who is competing with me. It is not necessary to talk of David helping me. He deserves his chance. If he's saving my bum it's not right.

Coulthard concurs:

I believe too much is made of this master plan at Ferrari. Eddie has moved over for Michael in only one race, at Suzuka last year. I have actually given up track position twice for Mika. A lot of credit has been given to Eddie, but the fact is that Eddie is just not as quick as Michael. Not even Eddie believes he is as quick as Michael!

I have shown my loyalty to the team and now it's for the team to just keep doing what they're doing, which is allowing us to go out there and race. The Championship should be won because you have beaten everyone. It's a recent thing, this putting all your eggs in one basket. Why? The team is capable of supplying equal machinery so I don't see team orders as an issue. I'm not going to adopt the attitude it's an uphill struggle and go all negative. I am going to try to win the British Grand Prix and take it from there.

A distinctive feature of the British Grand Prix is the traffic. Nowhere on the Formula One tour is it worse. Even on this Thursday lunchtime, a queue is building up along the main road through Silverstone village. Dozens of fans are camped at the gate to spot the drivers and the more famous team officials. Some are optimistically attired in shorts and T-shirts, others have judiciously opted for sweaters and anoraks. As yet the day is benign, but the inevitable threat of dark clouds looms on the distant English summer horizon.

Another battalion of fans, with tickets for the infield, home in on the paddock gate. They and their like will be there all weekend. For now they must content themselves with the spectacle of a man carrying a colossal flower arrangement which totally engulfs him and obliterates his vision yet, as if by remote control, he manoeuvres past all moving and stationary obstacles on course for some motorhome. Compared with the bedlam of the test, the paddock is now a scene of tranquillity. It will get busier, of course, but passes for the real thing are still at a premium.

Even rarer is a Michael Schumacher victory in the British Grand Prix. In fact there is, as yet, no such thing. Silverstone is one of only three venues on the current calendar that have eluded his skills. Another is Australia and the third, Austria, which has staged only one race during his Formula One career.

'I've tried many times to win here and I'll try again,' says Schumacher, embarking on his seventh attempt. 'I need the car to finish and me to do well.'

He is genuinely puzzled when asked whether he might consider giving his team-mate a race in return for his generosity in France.

'I'm going for the Championship and can't give any presents. I need presents for myself.' The very idea, his expression adds. As Irvine has said, you know where you stand with this guy – no prevarication, no phoney diplomacy, no chance.

More presents are on offer from Ferrari and the word in the paddock is that Schumacher is about to accept a new two-year contract, which would stuff another £50 million or so into his back pocket. 'There is a good reason that will happen,' he concedes. Fifty million would seem a good enough reason.

This being the British Grand Prix, Johnny Herbert gets a higher profile than normal. Yes, he's looking forward to racing in front of his home fans; yes, it gives him an extra push to do well; yes, he's happy at Sauber but he has to see what his options are and Williams would be good.

Hill is in still greater demand. He acknowledges that although expectations are always high, he would be feeling greater pressure as leader of the Championship.

Homely sentiments come with the territory and most drivers are conditioned to self-censor their comments for public consumption. Villeneuve and Irvine tend to exempt themselves from such restrictions, which makes their contributions all the more welcome. Schumacher is witheringly blunt when it suits him to be so. However, even these usually uncompromising characters can demur when offered open confrontation. Villeneuve and Schumacher meet and shake hands in the cold of Thursday afternoon and Villeneuve denies he has hurled any grenades Schumacher's way of late, suggesting the media must have recycled the stuff from Canada. Schumacher takes the same course, reasoning he answered the accusations of Canada. And yet there is a discernible edge, as there is about almost everything here. Perhaps it is the time of the year, contract time; perhaps it is a particularly tense period of the Championship for winners and losers alike; perhaps the added responsibility of a home Grand Prix, which this is for most teams, gnaws at the nerve-ends.

When it is put to Hill that Coulthard may be considering resigning from the Grand Prix Drivers' Association unless they agree a code of conduct, the Englishman says: 'It is for FIA to apply the rules and I would urge David not to leave the GPDA, and Jacques to join because he could contribute something.'

Villeneuve manages the thinnest of thin smirks. If he's not careful he'll be getting the reputation of a shrinking violet. But what colour is the hair now, Jacques? He takes off his cap to reveal the answer: purple. Schumacher, who is more likely to sign for Minardi than dye his hair purple, has some intelligence on the Coulthard issue.

'I spoke with him in Magny-Cours but I did not get the impression he wants to leave. He wants stability. FIA have to give the guidelines. Some drivers don't know the rules.' Is that another smirk, Jacques?

The threat of rain by race day is no smirking matter for Villeneuve, as a member of his team ruefully acknowledges.

'He doesn't like the wet and admits it. When it's raining at tests he comes into the garage!'

Schumacher is better than an umbrella in the rain. He has

innate and unrivalled ability to control a car in the most demanding of circumstances because he has an innate and unrivalled
ability to control a car in the most benign of circumstances. He
simply has what it takes, as one of motor sport's most knowledgeable observers, John Blunsden, a former correspondent for *The
Times*, confirmed for himself at last week's test. For half an hour
he watched and listened from the inside of the track at the exit of
Copse as Schumacher went about his work. He noted the power
of the Ferrari was on longer than other cars and the sounds from
his engine and exhaust were different. Those who watched and
listened to Senna said much the same. Anyone can be quick in a
straight line. The test comes at corners, wet or dry.

Early Friday morning the clouds are still a peripheral threat.
Arriving hordes, most of them experienced race-goers, are prepared for any eventuality. The drivers profess themselves
similarly primed as they roll in for practice, and yet that edge is
apparent again. Silly season is here. Drivers are on the move, on
the look-out for a move or fearing a move. There is harder
conjecture that Williams have lined up the reigning CART champion, Italy's Alex Zanardi, and that Heinz-Harald Frentzen is
seeking employment in America. Knowing nods greet the 'news'
as ancient history. No one likes to admit to being caught
unawares.

Schumacher, now said by Italian sources in the know to be
staying with Ferrari until the end of 2002, is exchanging light-
hearted banter with Ross Brawn outside the motorhome.

'That's it,' the technical director says with that huge schoolboy
grin as his driver walks away. 'The script is worked out.' The
knowing nods are now coming from those of a cynical disposition.

Brawn takes up the issue of suspicions about the legality of
his car.

'Did you see that in the paper this morning? Ron Dennis says
he's not paranoid, then goes on to talk about traction control at
Ferrari. Totally paranoid.' The grin remains huge and defiant.

Schumacher has made little progress and is trapped in conversation again, but since the language is German he is comfortable

and makes no effort to extricate himself. He is wearing a Ferrari sweatshirt, blue jeans and trainers. His arms are folded, his legs splayed. Irvine, in Ferrari T-shirt, blue jeans and trainers, stands talking a few yards away. No edge here, although Irvine is being linked with Williams and Craig Pollock's team. Seems he is being advised by his aides to play down the 'dutiful number two' bit. Ferrari are said to have been rejected by Zanardi but don't want to pay the Irishman more money. Negotiations, conducted for Irvine by his Bolognese manager, Enrico Zanarini, are approaching a delicate phase.

The faces at the fence are rewarded when Coulthard, wearing a brown suede bomber jacket and carrying a briefcase, does a U-turn inside the turnstile and answers the clamour for autographs. He inches his way along the fence, signing dozens of programmes and sheets of paper thrust through to him. He doubles back to satisfy the next wave. Chants of 'David, David' ring out from the schoolgirl choir. Herbert shares the burden. So does Hakkinen, winning a few new friends in the process. The ever-friendly Coulthard peels away and is asked to be pictured in front of a buckin' bronco contraption. He politely declines – friendly, but not gullible.

Villeneuve's screaming new hairdo catches the attention of the faces at the fence as he hurries from motorhome to transporter. He smiles, waves and disappears. Patrick Head covers the ground at a more leisurely pace, secure in the knowledge he will not be hounded, not by fans at any rate. But what's the score with Zanardi?

'Oh, God,' he sighs wearily, then maintains no contract has been signed, that Zanardi is on a list of drivers being considered. As for Villeneuve, Williams are waiting to hear from him what his plans are.

With less than an hour to practice, there are plenty of faces to spot for offspring being dragged around the paddock by off-duty team members. Hill is posing with pouting models, Frentzen is stuck with Mickey Mouse. There's Ron Dennis being interviewed by a television reporter. There's Eddie Jordan being interviewed by a radio reporter. There's Mika Hakkinen . . . There's Jackie

Stewart, being interviewed by no one.

'Where's Chris Evans?'

'Who?'

'Chris Evans. I heard somebody say Chris Evans was coming.'

Practice is a merciful relief, the sight and sound of Grand Prix cars.

'Yes, but where's Chris Evans?'

'Where's your mum?'

Morning practice is predictable; Hakkinen, Coulthard, Schumacher. Afternoon practice less so. Coulthard first, Hakkinen second, Schumacher seventh. The media, the British media especially, home in on the McLaren pit to find out what Coulthard, the British title hope, has to say. A smartly dressed doorman stands at the back of the McLaren garage, presumably to ensure no unauthorised person steps on the £40,000 grey marble flooring. Someone explains it is actually polished granite, laid by a sponsor, and is probably worth £25,000.

Either way, 'Bernie heard about it and sent Ron a message saying he'd got him a better garage and would he like to move?'

Coulthard steps from the said flooring into the daylight and steers towards 'my friends', the familiar faces of the regular British press corps. He talks of his emotions, of a 'twinge in the stomach' driving in front of his own fans on the circuit where he stood as a wee lad, watching the cars in wonderment. It would be a dream come true to win this race. It would also be a fillip for his Championship aspirations, he recognises with a little encouragement.

Suddenly he is not so easy, as if reality is blotting out the dream. And now there is a definite edge, as well as discomfort, when he is asked if he has a psychological problem racing Schumacher in the wet.

'We haven't beaten him yet in the wet, so to that extent we have a problem,' he says. 'He's had some amazing races in the wet.' His response veers off course and he puts on the brakes. 'I'm not really answering your question, am I? I don't have a psychological problem with him, but I prefer it to be dry. I think about my own race. I've got respect for him but he's human. I've beaten him before and I intend to beat him again.'

The McLaren–Ferrari friction is bristling nicely backstage. Irvine provokes Dennis by suggesting McLaren should have the advantage here because they are playing at home, but over the season he still backs Michael. He passes on the opportunity to repeat in Dennis' hearing his contention McLaren have blown it.

'Put it this way, they should be further ahead of us than they are.'

Dennis retorts with a steely cold put-down: 'He's wrong. Most opinions drivers express are wrong. Inevitably, when you are pushing everything to the limit you make mistakes. If anything, what he says motivates us more. I think this is a mischievous attempt to destabilise our situation. I don't see it as malicious. It doesn't worry me at all.'

Schumacher looks totally unworried, sauntering through the paddock after visiting brother Ralf at Jordan. He has preserved his tyre supply today, so that seventh place is not representative of his potential. He's relaxed and would prefer to talk about his daughter, Gina Maria, now 17 months old.

'She's great,' he drools. 'I think there is something special in the relationship between a father and daughter. We would like to have more children.'

He goes on to charm children of all ages at a Ferrari stand, out there in the real world, beyond the paddock, belying his unpopular stereotyping. Could it be he's just a big softie, really, and simply misunderstood? 'Yes,' affirms a resident critic with heavy sarcasm.

The spectre of hostile weather has hung over proceedings all weekend and although Saturday rouses with a bright countenance, the air is cool and the menace is ever closer, lurking, brooding, seeking the moment. Perhaps qualifying will escape the rain; perhaps it will not. Anoraks are zipped to the chin, wet gear is at the ready. The enemy is out there somewhere.

In the Jordan compound the mood is dark, the atmosphere tense. This is the team that has cultivated an image of levity amid the gravity of modern Formula One. They like to be known as the team with a smile on its face. There are no smiles this morning. Ian Phillips, the normally affable commercial man, a former journalist and wise to the sparring between drivers and reporters, growls: 'I hope you're not here about that garbage in the tabloids.' He shakes his head in exaggerated disgust and draws long and hard on his sponsor's soothing product.

That 'garbage' is a story that Hill will consider quitting if Jordan cannot give him a car to his liking, garnered from an interview conducted at the test here, some ten days ago.

'It's certainly not the message we've been getting from him the last few days,' Phillips pursues. 'In fact, nothing could be further from the truth.'

Michael Breen, Hill's solicitor, is keeping his head down, intently eating his breakfast. Hill emerges from the motorhome, changed for work and determined to laugh off the matter.

'I've not spoken to anybody this weekend,' he says, quite truthfully, and barely checking his stride. Challenged again, he replies: 'It's not something I'm considering.' He dives for the sanctuary of the garage.

Eddie Jordan arrives and is briefed by Phillips. The expression confirms this is an irritation he could do without. Jordan ponders over his breakfast as Phillips goes about his commercial work with a caller, who is enthusiastically displaying glossy illustrations and applying the requisite spiel. The breakfast dishes and glossy illustrations are removed, and Jordan and Phillips retreat to a distant corner to put their heads together again. They can stall no longer. Phillips smiles defensively, Jordan talks.

'I think these stories are preposterous. This is wholly inconsistent with the conversations we've been having with Damon over the last couple of days, over the last couple of weeks. I'd be an incredibly bad judge of the mood of the situation if that was true. He's well fired up. We want him to stay. We look in far better shape for the second half of the season.'

Jordan and Phillips are aware of course that Hill, who has the option to stay, has taken the opportunity to apply a little pressure. All part of the posturing. This is contract time. Since Hill is reported to be buying a £5 million Learjet it is reasonable to assume retirement is not high on his agenda. Hill has also used the media to demand more concerted effort from Honda, which has evidently embarrassed Jordan. This is a time-honoured ritual in Formula One. Senna frequently leaned on his team and their partners. Schumacher does the same with Goodyear. But Hill is no Senna or Schumacher, and Jordan's ire cannot be disguised.

He is doubtless relieved to see, filling the mouth of the awning, the figure of Willi Weber, manager of Michael and Ralf Schumacher, even if he is attired in the red of the older brother's team. 'Get out of here,' Jordan calls in mock disgust. Weber beams and, undeterred, ambles towards Jordan. They shake hands and seat themselves out of earshot.

'There's a performance option on both sides with Ralf, which neither side can achieve. It can't kick in, so that's why they're talking,' Phillips explains. 'We want Ralf to stay as well. He's quick and, OK, he's made mistakes, but he's young and we'd hate him to mature somewhere else.'

Michael astonished everyone with his maturity the moment he arrived in Grand Prix racing with Jordan as a 22-year-old in 1991. One of his team-mates at Benetton, Riccardo Patrese, the most experienced driver in the history of Formula One, marvelled that the young German 'never did or said anything stupid'. Ralf is no Michael, but then Michael, as we have heard, does not command universal approval. He now delivers a riposte:

People are just jealous. I'm always at the top and if there is someone at the bottom I can understand they don't like to see me always at the top. But I know what I do myself and I have no reason to be upset about what I am doing. It is a particular group. They are not very successful at the moment. For sure it's frustration. Imagine you are the world champion last year and this year you struggle to get into the points, and suddenly you make mistakes like Jacques did.

I want to be liked rather than disliked but if I can't change it what can I do? My first motivation is to win the

Championship with Ferrari. I don't care about the record of fifty-one victories. If they come it will be nice. But the nice thing is to get the goal and win the Championship for Ferrari. That's what I want to achieve and I'll never give up till I achieve it.

Security is a prime consideration at all major sporting events in Britain and a police squad with sniffer dog check out the pits and media complex. All seems in order off the track and on. Hakkinen, Coulthard and Schumacher again set the pace in practice. Interestingly, they are followed by Ralf Schumacher, Hill and Villeneuve. The breeze has picked up but the clouds are high and there is no imminent prospect of rain, to the relief of the faces at the fence. German voices cry out to Frentzen as he climbs the steps to the Williams truck. He smiles but keeps moving.

Williams' main sponsor, Winfield, is consolidating its reputation for attracting the biggest names to its hospitality motorhome this Saturday lunchtime. As George Harrison departs, Sylvester Stallone and entourage arrive. Ecclestone makes his regular visit and mischievously moans he has 'had it up to here' with the precious divo, who has pulled out of his planned ride with Martin Brundle in the specially built two-seater McLaren tomorrow. 'Macho-man Rocky-Rambo's bottled it,' reports the bush radio with unrestrained glee.

'No, it wasn't right. He wasn't comfortable,' insists a diplomatic Brundle. Max Mosley is still on for his ride today.

Gerhard Berger, the new one million dollars a year ambassador for BMW, Williams' next engine partners, has popped in for a jacket. It is getting colder out there. Helicopter companies are particularly anxious following a gale warning for tomorrow. Stallholders have been told to batten down their businesses. Nothing, however, disturbs lunch chez Karl-Heinz. Barry Briggs, the former speedway champion, is enjoying the fare and the crack. Alan Jones, Williams' first world champion, hovers at the doorway. Leo Sayer, a popular singer when Jones was a driver in his pomp, chats outside.

Schumacher sets the first competitive time in qualifying but

Hakkinen betters that, betters it again and cannot be unseated. Schumacher improves to secure second place but Coulthard is relegated to fourth by Villeneuve. Hakkinen's jubilation in the pits compounds the Scotsman's misery. Coulthard is more than a second down on his team-mate. It is Hakkinen's sixth pole of the season and talk of rain cannot dampen his satisfaction.

'There's no reason to worry,' he is adamant. 'If it rains it rains.'

A modest-sounding Schumacher contends there is no reason for him to relish a wet race. Any driver should be able to handle a racing car regardless of the conditions, he argues. Maybe he is not being so modest after all. Villeneuve is savouring the chance to compete at the sharp end again after 'we were looking like idiots'. They are interrupted by the roar of the two-seater McLaren. Schumacher reckons Brundle is enjoying himself driving Mosley.

'I'd like to take Bernie,' Hakkinen says. 'At least he would fit in.'

This frivolity contrasts starkly with the heavy heart Coulthard now bears. Twenty-four hours ago he talked of his dream; today he is thrust headlong into a living nightmare. Even he does not feel up to – or trust himself to be exposed to – public scrutiny right now. He needs time to shower, to think, to compose himself and compose his pronouncement. At last he reappears outside the McLaren motorhome, spruce yet sullen.

He describes this afternoon's ordeal as the biggest disappoint-ment of his career. He felt he was running up against a brick wall. He cannot understand why he is so much slower than Hakkinen and has to find out. But he has no reason to doubt he is receiving equal treatment. He was so submerged in his own despair he had no interest in what was happening elsewhere, around Mika or Michael or any other driver.

Hakkinen and Schumacher are sympathetic and supportive. They, too, are puzzled by the gap. It is too big to be normal, Schumacher says. But it will come for David, Hakkinen main-tains. Coulthard is not easily consoled or reassured. His stunned expression could almost have been cast in stone. The rain might be a blessing, or at least a lottery. That is beginning to look his best chance of a winning ticket.

Hill is less depressed with his seventh place on the grid and gratified by the backing of his home crowd, although he still feels the need to agitate for a better engine.

'I'm not lacking support, just a little horsepower,' he declares.

The rain arrives at 3.30, virtually clearing the paddock but for a few sheltering in wet-weather gear or under umbrellas. Yet still the faces are up at the fence, undeterred, unyielding. They, too, have their brollies. More importantly, they also have their heroes and fantasies, so what of the rain? And the police visitors are insulated against the elements by Karl-Heinz's hospitality. His is one bomb they are positively thrilled to see and hear go off.

It is still raining on Sunday morning. It is also cold and windy enough to be November rather than mid-July. This day of the British Grand Prix and the World Cup final has been billed as 'The Glorious Twelfth'. That now seems a highly presumptuous fanfare. Campers are resigned to their soggy plight, thousands stuck in traffic to their torpid progress. Those paddock personnel taking a designated route along a cart track park cars caked in mud.

A helicopter service is even more appealing for those who can afford it. The winds are not as ferocious as forecast and the world's busiest airport today is fully operational. Helicopters fill the sky like hornets, up to ten of them in range of the eye at any moment.

Race fans with their feet on the ground stand patiently in long queues at the gate, shoulder to shoulder beneath multi-coloured umbrellas, arms full of provisions. An opportunist hawker calls out: 'Get your Ferrari mac, get your Ferrari mac'. At least the queues are moving and the punters are generally good-humoured. This is all part of the deal. At the paddock turnstiles the power is down and the swipecard points are inoperable. Alan Jones and another of Williams' former champions, Nigel Mansell, are among those held up until the staff are told to open the turnstiles and check passes with the human eye. Somehow there's a perverse sense of triumph for those who prefer the personal touch. It just feels better.

Mansell, accompanied by his wife, Rosanne, is here as a guest-cum-ambassador of Ford, for whom he is competing in three meetings of this season's British Touring Car Championship. His milky tea is at the ready, his breakfast is about to be served.

'Things have definitely changed since I was last here, in 1992. These things, for a start,' Mansell says, disdainfully fingering his out-of-action paddock pass.

He would not be alone in fondly reflecting on the years when the Silverstone paddock was situated in a grassy enclosure, separate from the pits area. On sunny days it was like an idyllic village green and most drivers did not mind running the gauntlet of fans between paddock and pits. Today, alas, it would have been a quagmire up there.

'Ferrari must be rubbing their hands,' says Mansell, who had two seasons with the Italians, looking to the heavens.

Mansell won three times here and had two victories at Brands Hatch. He caused an outbreak of Mansellmania and at the height of the fever fans invaded the track. The last time he appeared, and won, at this circuit, he was a month away from securing his World Championship. Now he saunters through the paddock, hunched inside his coat, the once familiar moustache gone, apparently unrecognised by the faces at the fence. The three years since his final Grand Prix is a long time, the six since his last race here an eternity. A new generation of fans now look on, wearing the London Rowing Club cap in allegiance to Hill, sporting the red of Schumacher or chanting for Coulthard.

Spectators picking their way through the puddles to the stands or the banks see little or nothing of the cars in the early part of warm-up, lost as they are behind a screen of spray. The times come down as the rain eases and the track begins to dry. Coulthard draws encouragement from his time, the fastest of the session. Hakkinen is next quickest, followed by Fisichella, Irvine and Schumacher.

After the drivers' briefing, Charlie Whiting, FIA's race director, and Herbie Blash, a long-time cohort and now a FIA observer, are locked in earnest conversation, anxiety etched on their normally serene faces.

'We've had all sorts of problems this morning with the power going down,' Blash explains. 'I've got to sort out some generators, in case it happens again.'

The show must go on, and the celebrities are duly rolling in. *Ballykissangel* star Stephen Tomkinson and Robson Green of *Soldier, Soldier* fame, catch the attention of the faces at the fence. 'If you go over there, you'll never get away,' Green cautions. Instead they wave and take pictures of the fans taking pictures of them. Trevor McDonald, *News at Ten* front man, joins them. All are suitably fascinated by a glimpse of Villeneuve's hair. Someone dressed as the France '98 World Cup mascot is managing to attract the attention of photographers outside the Jordan motorhome. He just happens to be waving a flag of the team's major sponsor. Models reporting for duty at the team sign autographs until another heavy shower forces them to take cover beneath the awning. Hill is already inside, which accounts for the scrummage of TV crews and photographers.

Beyond the Jordan compound, into the 'second division' of the paddock, TV and Page Three stars are thinner on the ground but the puddles aren't. For those more interested in racing legends than racy legs, there is ample consolation. Phil Hill, the 1961 world champion – an American and no relation to Damon – has engrossed company at Ford. Not everyone would relish a ride in that two-seater McLaren with Brundle, but he would – 'Why not? Do you think he wants to kill himself for *you*?' Put that way . . .

The inevitable air display – another acquired taste – is laid on to entertain the public. Mercifully, it passes without incident.

Down on the grid, Coulthard and his crew are contemplating their tyre choice. The rain has stopped but the circuit is still wet in parts and dark clouds loom.

'It's half and half,' the Scotsman says of the track conditions. That suggests 'intermediate' tyres to start with. Coulthard's car is pulled well back in its grid position, allowing air to the tarmac it will occupy when it lines up for the start proper. Smart thinking.

Schumacher, whose thinking is generally one step ahead of the rest, is musing over the settings of his Ferrari: wet, dry or a compromise?

Tomkinson, Green and McDonald are more interested in taking pictures of themselves in front of the cars than logging such finer details. Eventually they are ushered away with the rest of the gawping throng, clicking and giggling to the end. Team officials are stern-faced as the cars pull away on the parade lap and spots of rain fall on the grid. Too late to change anything now.

Hakkinen makes a clean getaway, followed by Schumacher, then Coulthard. Irvine makes a sluggish start and is sucked back to tenth. Schumacher hounds Hakkinen for a couple of laps but cannot sustain the attack, and on the fifth lap, loses second place to Coulthard. Irvine, meanwhile, is taking on the pack. On lap eight he passes Hill and Villeneuve to go sixth. On lap 12 he takes Frentzen.

An intensifying drizzle is making driving more hazardous and three laps later Hill is caught out. He loses control at Brooklands and careers across the gravel. He climbs solemnly from the silent Jordan and makes his way back to the pits. He mutters a brief and critical self-analysis to the advance guard of press and media, which amounts to 'pretty pathetic'. He takes cover, leaving the growing media pack out in the increasingly heavy rain. Hill is patently embarrassed, the more so because this is Silverstone, perhaps still more so in light of his much-publicised demands. Jordan, it can be safely assumed, are not impressed. Hill, aware his team-mate is having a stirring drive from the back row of the grid, prudently joins the crew at the pit wall and watches with mixed feelings.

Frentzen comes to grief and Irvine moves ahead of Alesi in the pits. Alesi endures more frustration behind his team-mate, Herbert, before the Englishman joins the list of casualties to the weather. Then, on lap 38 of 60, Coulthard, negotiating back-markers, spins and is beached. As his car is winched away, his title hopes are surely gone also. Coulthard, like Herbert, cuts a disconsolate figure as he wends his way back to base.

Herbert walks into a furious row at Sauber. He was ordered

to give way to Alesi and claims he tried to do so, but not everyone in the camp is convinced he tried as hard as he might have done, least of all Alesi, who is forced to retire and issues an ultimatum to the team: 'Next year it's him or me.' Herbert seeks refuge at the Ford motorhome and murmurs: 'All sorts of things are going on there.' The normally smiling, lighthearted Herbert is melancholy and teetering on the edge.

Alongside him, and in danger of falling over the edge, is Coulthard. He, too, is sad and confused, torn and seemingly near desperation. In his turmoil he ignores the comforting embrace of the fans, and for that he will later chastise himself. But now he is inconsolable. He complains of conflicting weather forecasts within the McLaren camp and of being given the wrong tyres at his first and what proved his final pit stop.

'I am very angry, very disappointed,' Coulthard says, his usually cool, clear eyes ablaze. 'I find it remarkable there can be one set of tyres for one driver and different ones for the other. Maybe the forecast wasn't clear and they were trying to cover the team for either eventuality. But it didn't work out for me. I was put at a disadvantage. I'm not sure if there was any favouritism. I am just trying to understand why there was a difference. Things seem to be a struggle just now.'

The drama back here, played out to a tiny audience, is as compelling as that running parallel out on the circuit, witnessed by millions. Human emotions are unleashed, the cover of machinery and technology discarded. And for David Coulthard, this could prove the defining act in his Championship.

Hakkinen, meanwhile, is stretching further away, not only from Coulthard but also from Schumacher. For once the acknowledged master of the wet appears to have found his match. Even when Hakkinen goes off, spinning wildly and with potentially catastrophic consequences, the McLaren traverses grass and gravel and returns to the road. In the process, the Finn actually increases his advantage over Schumacher to 42 seconds. His only danger now appears to be the umbrellas blowing across the track.

However, two laps later the safety car is sent out into the monsoon and Hakkinen fears the worst. When normal racing is resumed, with 11 laps remaining, the lead is a mere, fragile two seconds. Schumacher hounds for two laps before Hakkinen goes straight on at Becketts. Again the McLaren's momentum carries him back on to the circuit, but this time he has lost the lead and he knows he cannot catch Schumacher. What is more, the other Ferrari is on his tail. He fends off Irvine and settles for second place; or does he?

A flurry of activity in the Ferrari pit indicates one of their cars is in trouble. Then comes the information Schumacher has been penalised ten seconds (for overtaking under the yellow warning flag, which is not permitted). At the end of the 60th and final lap, Schumacher enters the pits and follows the routine of a stop-and-go penalty. He drives back out on to the circuit, but in the meantime Hakkinen has taken the chequered flag and is celebrating. Seconds later, Schumacher is declared the winner. Confusion reigns.

Schumacher brings his car to a halt still not sure who has won. His brother, having presented Jordan with their first point of the season, greets him with the news he is the winner. Hakkinen, hearing the same verdict, sits in his car, distraught. He gathers himself and salvages honour for his dignity as he follows Schumacher on to the scales and offers a handshake, albeit limp. But he cannot bring himself to join in the podium frolics, and quietly leaves the stage to the cavorting Ferrari pair.

It is explained that since notification of the penalty was given to Ferrari within three laps of the end of the race, the stewards were empowered to add the ten seconds to Schumacher's time. Therefore, as Schumacher completed the 60th lap, in the pit lane, 22.4 seconds ahead of Hakkinen, he is deemed the winner by 12.4 seconds.

And now the weather is fine.

Schumacher reveals he had opted for dry settings in the minutes before the race and had been disadvantaged accordingly until the intervention of the safety car. Hakkinen said his car was 'pretty knackered' after his first excursion and knew he would not be able to resist the German. He did not wish to claim the stewards' verdict was unfair or make any other comment he might later regret. The team would handle that and, unsurprisingly, they protest.

Irvine's sixth podium finish of the season is his 13th in all, a record for a driver without a win. It may be a dubious distinction but it reinforces his position and, for good measure, provides him with the opportunity to have another dig at Hill for weaving in front of him. He brands the former champion a 'sad old man' and a 'menace' on the track. 'Still, he got his punishment when he went off.' This is perhaps the most cruel cutting edge of all this traumatic weekend.

Some three and a half hours later, McLaren's protest is thrown out. Furthermore, Schumacher's time penalty is rescinded on the grounds notice to Ferrari was not given within the stipulated period. Schumacher has won by 22.4 seconds and now stands just two points behind Hakkinen with seven races remaining. McLaren's lead over Ferrari in the Constructors' Championship is three points. Unsurprisingly again, McLaren appeal, which means the case will go before FIA, at a date to be fixed. Those who subscribe to the conspiracy theory that Ferrari must be top this year, or BMP (Bernie's Master Plan), laugh it off as a fight they cannot win.

The hornets are disappearing into a grey sky and still the faces are pressed against the fence. Most of the teams are packing and leaving but the Prost motorhome is intact for the World Cup final, France v Brazil. Whistles and horns greet the host nation's 3–0 triumph. Jean Todt, the French sporting director of Ferrari, who is said to have flown over for the match with Ecclestone, is probably the happiest man in the world tonight.

6

Zeltweg

THE GRAVY TRAIN

Those who knew this place last time round, before Austria's ten-year exile from Formula One, lament the passing of another of the real circuits. The old Österreichring was up there with Spa in its beauty, its majesty, its challenge, its terror. The home of the Austrian Grand Prix since last year is no longer the Österreichring, in name or character. They call it the A1-Ring, in deference to its sponsor, the mobile phone company. If that's a sign of the times, so is the track, its scale, pace and personality sacrificed in accordance with modern safety requirements. In that sense the change of name is right and proper. This is almost an insult to the legend of the Österreichring.

Not content with renaming the circuit, they have tried to rename the location. It was always Zeltweg, a small town barely a couple of miles across the valley. Now they want you to know it as Spielberg, an even smaller town but barely one mile away. The A1-Ring and Spielberg are welcome to their unreal alliance. Zeltweg and the Österreichring may represent an era of more traditional movies, but the thrills and drama were incomparable and purists will stubbornly respect their identities. So, it seems, will the locals. A woman cyclist, waiting at a level crossing in Zeltweg, is nonplussed by a request for directions to the A1-Ring. Asked for the way to the Österreichring and all is explained. The Österreichring it remains.

And so, mercifully, gloriously, inspiringly, does everything else about this corner of the continent, tucked under the foothills of the Niedere Tauern range of mountains, a two and a half hour drive south-west from Vienna. The scenery, the people, the very

atmosphere here are divine. Austria has the natural splendour of
Switzerland and more besides. Its embrace is somehow warmer,
more personal.

The approach roads meander through emerald green mead-
ows, bordered by forests of conifers, climbing towards elusive
peaks; they wind alongside cool, rushing streams, past woodyards
and impeccably maintained chalets, decorated with window-
boxes of effusive, tumbling geraniums, red, orange and pink, by
cycle paths that reflect the gentle nature and pace of civilisation
here. This Thursday morning in July the sun bestows a final
blessing.

Beyond Zeltweg and the level crossing, grazing horses are
disturbed by a truck delivering Portaloos. Thanks to an enterprising farmer, the horses will have to share their field with campers
this weekend. Many have already established their base and
staked flags declaring their allegiance. This may be Alexander
Wurz's home race, but it is more obviously part of the Schumi
central European tour, and the red of Ferrari proliferates.

Schumacher's long-term commitment to Ferrari has been
confirmed since Silverstone. McLaren's appeal over the British
Grand Prix is to be heard on Monday, while the stewards have
been summoned to appear before the FIA on Wednesday.
McLaren stress they are forcing the issue as a matter of principle
and are not challenging Ferrari's conduct. The stewards are being
universally condemned for the shambles. A man is hammering
down a step outside the McLaren motorhome. They have had too
many mishaps of late.

The fortunes of Schumacher are boundless: three successive
wins and now a £20 million a year contract until the end of 2002,
plus, plus, plus. But then he is not alone, travelling in luxuriant
style aboard the Formula One gravy train. Craig Pollock's British
American Racing organisation have announced Jacques Villeneuve is to join their great adventure. His salary for next year is
estimated at anything from £6.5 million to £10 million. It is said he
will also have shares in the business headed by his former teacher
and manager.

Williams, on the face of it, are in a mess. Fourth in the

Championship, neither driver in the top six, one driver going, the other apparently unwanted. Heinz-Harald Frentzen is on the wrong end of some typically caustic comments from Patrick Head in a magazine article. The German is castigated for falling asleep during races and changing his settings at inopportune moments. Someone relates an incident in the Williams pit, when the engines were cut, suddenly giving full range to Head's bellow: 'The problem is, Heinz-Harald, you're too slow!'

Frentzen effectively retaliated first by stating whoever drives for Williams cannot expect to win over the next two years. He is now being linked with Prost, as well as Sauber and CART, but rule out none of the rest. The scramble for the gravy train is the day's talking point. Zanardi is still said to be bound for Williams, but could join Villeneuve. So could another CART man, Jimmy Vasser. Hill, too, is a possibility for BAR. The permutations are being chewed and digested up and down the paddock.

The latest gossip will always find a place on Di Spires' bench, out the back of the Ford motorhome. Di, 50, and her husband Stuart, 52, have been motorhomers since 1978, when they worked with an 11-strong Surtees team. 'Twelve counting John,' Di expands. They have provided food, water and a shoulder to lean on for so many drivers and team members since then that they are known as Mum and Dad to the paddock family. They have no children of their own, having taken the decision to adopt Formula One. They have homes in the Midlands of England and the South of France, but see precious little of either. Usually they are on the road.

The Spires have brought on board another couple, Graham and Tracey Ogden, who produce some of the finest fare in the paddock. Over a race weekend they will serve some 300 breakfasts, 150 lunches and 60 evening meals to Ford and Cosworth personnel, VIPs and journalists. Today's racing teams number more like 50. As well as the motorhome, or bus, which Stuart drives, towing a Ford Galaxy, they have a 17½ ton truck, which Graham drives, to carry the equipment.

Di has a particular affection for this place, going back to a time when space was less confined, her view of the mountains was not obscured by a canvas barrier separating the Formula One and Formula 3000 paddocks and the gravy train did not exist.

We won our first point here with Surtees in '78. Things have changed a lot since then, not much of it for the better. I don't like the politics. That's got worse because the money's too great now. I don't think that will change till the cigarette people go. When everybody has to fight for the same sponsors it might be a bit different. Same with the drivers. They sign contracts which never seem to mean anything.

The job is still interesting but the social side isn't what it was. We were all couples and used to mix with couples from different teams. Now it seems to be the drivers and their chefs, and hostess girls, who can change race by race. There's not the same community there used to be. I don't even know some of the girls. We also have contracts to do Ford's Formula Three and rallying, which gives us a bit of a change. With the rallying you get to meet different people, go to different places, and it's far more relaxed.

We used to have trestle tables, no electrics, and lived in the motorhome. Now we have proper tables, posh cupboards and blinds, wide-screen TVs . . .it just goes on and on. It is nice to get away at nights and sleep in a hotel. Nobody sleeps in the motorhomes now. People say to us what do we do between the races, but we have to be here on the Monday, setting up. There's hardly any in between. And we have the rallying on top. This race is back to back with Hockenheim, then we'll go home for about four days before going to Hungary. From there we go straight to Finland for the rally, then straight back to Spa, and for the first time we'll be late for setting up there.

I don't think you get the personal touch in a lot of hospitality areas because they're just girls from a catering agency, chefs from an agency. We try to keep our place cosy. A lot of teams have gone in for the clinical look. I think a lot of them are competing with each other. I

The bigger the name... (*Above*) The 1997 world champion Jacques Villeneuve obliges autograph-hunters, while (*Below*) Michael Schumacher meets the Dekraheads.

The Formula One paddock is an irresistible attraction. (*Above*) The Jordan team's Damon Hill and Ralf Schumacher enjoy the company of two of England's most famous models, Jordan and Melinda Messenger. (*Below*) Jackie Stewart escorts Princess Anne at the Austrian Grand Prix.

Di Spires (*centre*) and husband Stuart (*top*) have become known as Mum and Dad to the paddock. They recruited Graham and Tracey Ogden to work with them in the Ford motorhome.

Minardi may not have much success on the track, but their pasta is renowned in the paddock.

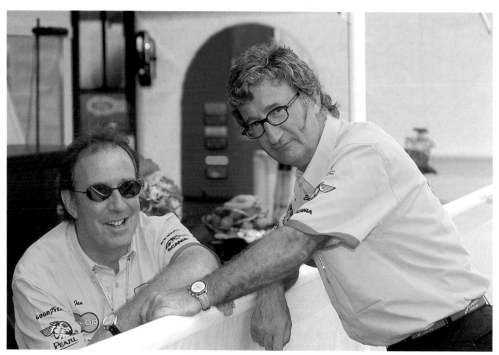

Ian Phillips and Eddie Jordan, a double act that has worked together since 1991, polish up their routine.

Craig Pollock and Harvey Postlethwaite in suitably reflective mood.

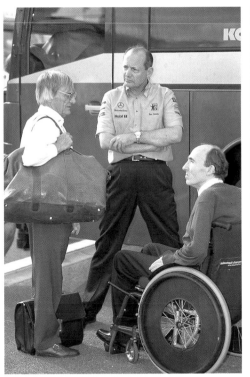

(*Above*) Bernie Ecclestone, Ron Dennis and Frank Williams in high-powered discussion. (*Above right*) Ann Bradshaw, the Arrows media relations officer, has worked in Formula One for 14 years and is as prominent as many of the drivers.

(*Right*) Herbie Blash and Charlie Whiting, FIA race officials, are a classic case of poacher turned gamekeeper.

The Drivers' Story

(*Left*) Mika Hakkinen at the French Grand Prix, where he was pipped by Eddie Irvine for second place. (*Below*) David Coulthard, his team-mate, talks shop with Norbert Haug.

(*Right*) Johnny Herbert contemplates a tricky manoeuvre through those fiendish turnstiles with his two daughters Chloe and Aimelia at Monaco.

(*Below*) Eddie Irvine with his manager, Enrico Zanarini, minding their own business.

(*Above*) Martin Pople tends his tyres with care. (*Right*) 'Slyvester' Stallone, a member of the 1998 supporting cast, gives his views to ITV's Martin Brundle at the Hungarian Grand Prix. (*Below*) The imposing Ferrari base at the Austrian Grand Prix.

certainly don't want anything to do with that. That's not what it should be like. A lot of the girlies have done these cordon bleu cookery courses. We had one. Didn't know how to make an omelette. Graham's very good. We'll do pasta, because everybody loves pasta, and another dish for lunch.

The drivers have definitely changed. There aren't the characters there used to be. They are all a bit too programmed. They should start to loosen up and have a bit more fun. I listened to Wurz the other day. He's in bed by ten o'clock every night. I suppose his doctor man has told him he's got to be in bed at that time. He's twenty-three or four, a young chap, he'll be all right anyway. You've just got to relate back to your Nelsons and Nanninis, and those sorts of people, who enjoyed themselves.

The Spires worked with Nelson Piquet and Alessandro Nannini at Benetton. Piquet, as we have heard, was a sometimes cruel joker. Nannini, an Italian, smoked, drank far more espresso coffee than was deemed sensible and had a penchant for English breakfasts, which he preferred in the middle of the day. His Formula One career ended after a helicopter crash in 1990. Surgeons saved his severed right arm and he subsequently returned to racing in touring cars.

Di's warm, homely face breaks into a smile as she recalls these two and a few others.

Nelson and Sandro was the best pairing we ever had. They were so much fun. I always remember Nelson being late for testing at Monza. We were really worried. We thought he'd gone down in his helicopter. Suddenly he arrived and put it down – in the middle of the paddock, instead of the heli-pad. He got out, slammed the door and said he'd got so-and-so lost. He'd had to put it down in a field, next to the motorway, to check his maps. When Sandro had his accident, Nelson was straight over there, to the hospital. He wasn't even in the country. Just to sit by his bed. That's Nelson. I believe Nelson became a dad again, and a grandad, last week. That's Nelson, as well!

Years ago, at Toleman, we were so short of space we had to store stuff like crash helmets in the shower. If you didn't release water from the waste tanks, the water would come up into the shower. On the morning of the Monaco Grand Prix, we came in to find the helmets of Bruno Giacomelli and Derek Warwick floating. Luckily, we got in at six o'clock, so I had time to use a hair dryer on them, trying to get the foam dry for when they came in so they wouldn't know any different. And they didn't. I told them afterwards.

Derek and Bruno were characters. Gianni Morbidelli was another. I think Michael [Schumacher] would be a character, if he was allowed to be. He's always having a bit of fun, pinching somebody's cap, that sort of thing. But they're all so serious now and they've all got their doctors. They're not doctor-doctors, they're sports doctors, and there are millions of them, giving their massages and all making a lot of money.

We had Michael at Benetton. He's quite a private person, but he talked to us and trusted us, I think possibly because we were his first team, after his one race at Jordan. He still speaks to us. He'll always stop if he sees us. If Corinna's at a race she'll try to come up. I even have a cup of coffee in the Ferrari bus with her, something that wouldn't happen otherwise. But they can't even walk in the paddock in peace, which is quite sad. Drivers just can't stroll around and mingle and have fun the way they used to. The media have their jobs to do, though.

Di saw a Schumacher very different from the common perception after Ayrton Senna's death.

The race was stopped when Ayrton crashed and nobody knew exactly what had happened. Not officially, anyway. Michael came back to go to the loo and asked if there was any news. We said no, but we'd never have told him anyway at the time. It was obvious they were going to restart the race. It was afterwards that he found out what had happened and I think at that moment he would have given up Formula One because it suddenly hit him that even Mr Invincible, something could happen to him. I don't think it had ever occurred to him.

A lot of drivers had never seen it before. I've never known an accident have such an awesome effect. It's always tragic, but the drivers suddenly got a jolt, realising Ayrton Senna could be killed, through the simplest thing. Michael was semi-blaming himself because he was pushing Ayrton. He said, 'It's my fault.' I said, 'Michael, of course it's not your fault. You're a driver, it's your job to push, you weren't pushing him out of control. He'd been around a long time.' But Michael was so distraught. Everybody was. He cried. We all did.

People don't know Michael, they don't understand him. They see him so intense about things, and he is intense about his racing, but he's beginning to relax a lot more. He loves people, he loves animals. He's doing a lot of charity work. I wouldn't think he'll carry on till thirty-five or something. He's got so much to enjoy in life. I just hope he keeps safe and can do it. He's very sincere. It would be nice to see him socially still, occasionally, but that's impossible. One day, maybe.

We see Johnny [Herbert] socially. He's just about the only remaining character. But then I don't really know all these new ones. I've never spoken to Villeneuve. You stand outside and Villeneuve doesn't even raise his eyes if he passes. In the old days everybody would say, 'Hello, how are you?' and that sort of thing. He'll probably go off and never have spoken to me.

We get on well with Eddie Irvine's mum and dad, and Sonia. His mum and dad are always here for tea. What Mum tells me about Eddie – it's a different Eddie from the one we all see. I think he's probably a lovely family person. I think he's a shy, nice person.

A lot of our old mechanics come round for a bacon sandwich. They come to the bench at the back for a natter. We're on our fifth bench now, all autographed. When we left Benetton after so long – fourteen years when you count the time they were Toleman – and then missed a couple of races before starting with Ford, we had to apologise to Ford because at one time we had five of our former drivers under the canopy and they'd all come to see us. They were all in their different sponsors' shirts but Ford didn't mind. Some other teams are funny about that.

We've known so many people over the years. The girls who have just started next door at Arrows are gobsmacked when they hear people say to me, 'Hello, Mum.' They think it's so funny. A lot of people really do think Johnny's related to me because of an article where Becky said she watched Johnny winning with Mum and Dad. They think Becky's our daughter and Johnny's our son-in-law.

Di sees differences out on the track, as well as in the paddock, and wasn't surprised to read about the conspiracy theory in a recent article.

It appeared somewhere I was reading, that it is all master-minded. I don't know how it can be, but so many strange things seem to happen. They don't seem to go out and just race any more. You see moves in IndyCars that if they tried here they'd probably get ten second penalties for, or be. banned for a race. But that's racing. They're not allowed to race here any more. It's all move over, let me by, wave me through sort of thing.

Ferrari are definitely going to win this year because of the fear of Formula One without them. My money's on them anyway. If they don't win this year, somebody somewhere is going to say, 'Well, why are we in Formula

One? We've put every penny we've got into it, best driver in the world, best design team, best engines, but we still can't win so we might as well stop.' I would imagine Bernie's terrified Ferrari are going to pull out. That would be fifty per cent of the world's interest gone, and then everybody would watch IndyCars, or motorbikes.

I keep saying we'll do one more year. I shall go on as long as I enjoy it. When you dread the first race, it's time to stop.

It's time for Mum to join Graham and Tracey in the 'kitchen', a small compartment at the back of the canvas hospitality area which can be unpleasantly warm at the best of times. This sweltering lunchtime, it is like a sauna. Stuart is working in a compartment at the side of the bus with what appears to be a water pipe.

Along the paddock, Hill is sitting at a table in the Jordan hospitality area, perusing *Autosport*. He is wondering aloud whether Coulthard should be careful about 'fouling his nest somewhat'. He suggests it can have costly repercussions, 'as I know from personal experience', and acknowledges 'whingers' win little sympathy.

If Coulthard is concerned about his job it doesn't show as he saunters in, wearing shorts, tanned, hair newly trimmed. It is the familiar Coulthard rather than the Silverstone version. He reveals that the day after the British Grand Prix, he had a meeting with Ron Dennis, who explained that circumstances, rather than the team, had conspired against him in that race and he should not react so hastily. Coulthard is suitably contrite but convinced his place is safe, not least, perhaps, because Schumacher has signed a new contract with Ferrari.

'Ron didn't think I was being constructive. He told me it wasn't the thing to do. My frustration got the better of me. I was wrong. But if you look at the last two and a half years, and what I've given the team, I think I can feel comfortable. I'm a team player. I don't believe one weekend of frustration after three races of problems through no fault of mine is unreasonable. I don't believe he would base his decision about his drivers on something like this. He will base his decision on who are the quickest drivers.'

Schumacher explains he has unfinished business at Ferrari, that money is not his prime motivation, otherwise he would have accepted a higher offer, presumably from McLaren Mercedes. He had one other offer, presumably from BAR. He values the mutual 'loyalty, understanding, trust and respect' he has at Ferrari; 'We now have a stable team.'

Domestic attention is focused on Wurz, who makes a valiant attempt to satisfy most interview requests before his bedtime.

'There has been a lot of stress but now the driving starts and I'm looking forward to it. I feel the emotions, like the spectators. We have blue skies and sunshine.'

Wurz should know better than any driver here that the weather in these parts is as fragile as a Formula One contract. After the young man has retired for the night the skies turn violent and prevent some from reaching their beds.

The workers return on a cloudy, fresher but calm Friday morning with horror stories of the long night before. Thunder, lightning, hail the size of golf balls – 'honestly, they were, literally' – have left a trail of devastation; houses and walls destroyed by water and mudslides, trees toppled, power lines brought down.

The most dramatic personal account hereabouts is related by Chris Leese and his weary motorhome staff at Arrows. Steeling themselves through the terrifying electric storm, climbing a mountain to their hotel, they found themselves marooned on a bridge between two raging torrents. The fire brigade, alert to these local difficulties, arrived to lead them back down the mountain to the sanctuary of a bar. Alternative rooms were located for the Arrows seven but the road to that Gasthof was also under water and impassable. At five o'clock they returned to their motorhome and crashed out there, to be discovered later by the team's puzzled mechanics. Breakfast was a mite behind schedule. '*Everything* has been late this morning,' Leese says.

Most people around the paddock look sufficiently rested and

relaxed. Karl-Heinz welcomes everyone within earshot 'to my country'. The Schumachers are engaged in easy conversation with a confidant outside the Jordan camp and, as Di observes, there is no respite for Michael. Photographers are pointing their lenses up his nostrils yet he never remonstrates, never flinches, never changes his benign, brotherly expression. When at last they split and go their separate ways, the confidant reveals Michael has advised Ralf not to rush into re-signing for Jordan because an opportunity at Williams may present itself and that, despite their current plight, has to be the better long-term option.

Practice is less than an hour away and the Benetton crew are working on pit stops. There is a discernible new sense of purpose in the team, doubtless focused here by Wurz. Towards the end of the morning session, however, he parks his car and his team-mate, Fisichella, takes the first of the weekend's honours. Come the afternoon stint the sun and those blue skies, dappled with just a few docile, white clouds, reappear. Fizzy just misses out this time, by a thousandth of a second, to Coulthard.

Déjà vu for Coulthard? Conscious of events following his promising start to proceedings at Silverstone, the Scot declines to voice any extravagant expectations, preferring to acknowledge Nigel Mansell's pep talk at a post-British Grand Prix golf day. Of course it was a boost, he is content to confirm, because Nigel had more hard luck stories than anyone and got there in the end. He was a driver he always looked up to.

BAR's first driver signing is 13th in the Williams. Villeneuve concedes his move could be a gamble, that nobody knows what to expect. What he does not expect, he maintains, is a 'Michael situation', outright number one status.

'That's not right and you do that if you are afraid you can be beaten. I'm not afraid.' Mmm. He has also a little barb for Zanardi. 'He's a fighter, but in Formula One he'll have to calm down a bit. You can't bump people as he did last year.'

Another BAR signing has been less publicised. In fact, it has gone through totally unnoticed by the outside world and probably by most inside the paddock. Martin Pople, truckie, tyreman and designer of transporters, has been lured from Arrows for what we can safely assume is something less than £10 million or even £6.5 million. 'A few noughts off that, I think,' he feels at liberty to tell, taking a break, perched on a crate at the back of the garage. In fact, a raise of about £3,000 takes him up to an annual salary of £35,000. He will also pick up a bonus of £20 a point and expenses. He currently receives £30 a day when not fed by the team, around half that when he is. Pople has worked in Formula One since 1991, with Benetton and Arrows. Once at the track he is responsible for tyres, but unlike the mechanics he drives to all the European races. He and his mate share the wheel of one of the two race trucks, which he happened to design, £450,000 worth of gleaming grey and black rig. The 'clean' truck carries the cars and incorporates a spacious office section at the front. The high-floored 'dirty' truck, or support truck, carries the pit equipment and incorporates a workshop, complete with lathe, grinding wheel and welder. It also houses a large fridge for the drinks. The rigid truck alongside carries the engines.

The trucks left the factory in England on Sunday and arrived here on Tuesday, to be washed and polished and emptied. The garages were set up in readiness for the mechanics, who joined their colleagues on Wednesday or Thursday morning.

Pople, a lean 35-year-old from Kent with a weathered hue, leaves Arrows after the next race.

> I'll probably stick on tyres at BAR. I've got to design three artics because that's what we're having instead of two and a rigid. There's so much equipment we've got to step up, like the top teams. I've also got to help design two motorhomes, similar to the McLaren one, with a raised outside area. For me it's a good career move. It's not gone quite to plan here. A bit political, really. Too many people pulling in different directions. I don't get on with the chief mechanic and my job has been getting undermined. BAR came to me, I looked at it and thought, why not?
>
> McLaren are pretty good payers. I think they've got the highest paid truckie in the pit lane, close to £40,000. And they get points money, which is pretty good this year.

You work hard, and long hours, but you wouldn't get that sort of money outside Formula One being a truckie. It's also a way of life. You have to enjoy it and enjoy motor racing. The drivers are in a different world from us. It would be nice if they paid them a couple of million less and spread it around the team, but it doesn't work like that. At the end of the day what they say is if you don't want it somebody else will come and do it. There's been a lot of moving around over the last couple of years.

We mix with the other lads all the time, but you don't have as much of a laugh as you used to because it's so much higher profile now, and when you're bandying around figures like fifteen million dollars for drivers, well. There's so much more at stake. Sponsorship is so much more the essence, the bull side generally. You look at the trucks and things, and all the money coming to this end of the pit lane now. That's what Bernie wants, I think, to bring the whole game up.

But the whole work rate gets more and more and more. The fun goes out of it because you're doing later nights, at the factory as well as here. You don't have time to chill out on the road any more. It's go, go, go. It's the whole game for everybody. And we've got sixty to seventy people at a race with our own engine people. But you've got to make it enjoyable because you're doing it a lot of hours.

Michael is definitely the best driver I've worked with. I never worked with Senna. I suppose I'm lucky that I've worked with Damon Hill and Michael. As it comes over on television, everybody thinks Damon is the perfect gentleman and Michael's the ignorant pig, but it's definitely the other way round. Michael will take the time with you. He sees me and says, 'Hello, Martin.' Damon didn't even know my name.

The way Damon comes over is just not professional at all. Michael is so dedicated. He's a racing machine, he's in tune with everything. He wants to know every single detail, and he will stay there until he gets every single detail. But he's also a really nice bloke. He's down to earth. He hasn't gone up into the clouds, as a lot of them do. Johnny's another nice bloke. He's probably not going to be world champion but he's a good driver and a nice bloke. You do get them.

But Damon, he's a funny one really. I don't rate him at all. Unless the car was dead right, when he could be quick, he wouldn't produce it, whereas Michael would always drive around a problem, and that was often the trouble at Benetton. He would drive around problems and the second driver couldn't handle it. He's just streets ahead. I don't think Damon was really liked by any of the team. The feedback from Jordan is of the same problem. He slags the team off.

When it was the Schumacher–Hill scenario, Michael was always praising the team, upping the team. It seemed the opposite with Damon at Williams. He was the first one to slag the team, say the car was wrong, the tyres were wrong, the engine was crap, this and that. Frank eventually took him on one side, or this is what I heard, and said you've got to start upping the team and being part of the team, and he changed. Suddenly he started praising the team a lot more, but I think it was too late. He'd already sowed his seeds.

Pople was a member of the Benetton team that signed Berger and Alesi after losing Schumacher.

Now I know why Ferrari never won a Championship with that pair because they were so unprofessional. I couldn't believe it. What a total contrast. Even compared with the likes of Johnny and Verstappen. One race, Alesi came in, walked to the back of the garage and pushed a set of tyres over. It's not the sort of thing somebody paid five or six million pounds to drive the car should do.

But, then, he is Sicilian and you would be kind of

disappointed if he didn't show it. Berger, you would expect to be different, especially since he supposedly learned so much from Senna.

I thought Gerhard would be really good, but he'd whinge about this, he'd whinge about that. Again, if the car was good, he could put in a good performance, but those drives were few and far between. I think he was living on his past glory. I didn't rate either of them at all. I suppose it's a problem if you compare anyone with Michael, but take someone like Mika Salo, here. He's probably not the quickest, but he's good and putting a lot of effort into it. A lot of drivers are. We had Zanardi as test driver at Benetton years ago, and he really was good.

Just as Ann Bradshaw is intimidated by Bernie Ecclestone, so, it transpires, are the men on the shop floor.

Bernie's a very similar sort to Flavio. You see him walking towards you and you give him a wide berth. He just has this air about him. Everyone knows what he is, even though he's just a bloke. Flavio would either say hello to you or just look straight through you as if you weren't there. Same with Bernie. Nobody really talks to him.

Communications between Formula One workers and their partners back home have often broken down and marriages are inevitable casualties of the job. Pople long professed himself a committed bachelor. Two years ago he married.

'Yeah. It's getting difficult, though. I'd like kids, but it's difficult with the wife stuck at home and me away so much. She's known me long enough and the job and everything, but it doesn't get easier.' He munches a chocolate biscuit, handed out by one of the motorhome girls, and favours an optimistic outlook: 'Let's hope that with me and Villeneuve at BAR the sky's the limit!'

The workers are still busy when the sky is dark over the paddock. Sauber are entertaining the British media this evening, a ritual come-and-get-to-know-us soirée re-enacted on a rota basis with different nationalities and by a number of the teams throughout the season. The timing of this dinner seems a trifle unfortunate considering the Alesi–Herbert spat at Silverstone. The drivers are sitting at separate tables, but then that is the usual arrangement on these occasions and the atmosphere is pleasant, even if this is not going to be one of the great bashes in Formula One history. Sauber is a Swiss team, after all.

Peter Sauber makes it clear Alesi is under contract for next year and that there could still be a place for Herbert. Silverstone is consigned to history. He plays down the prospect of recruiting Frentzen, who left Sauber for Williams two years ago. Interesting this, because Frentzen was a member of the Sauber Mercedes 'junior' team in sportscars. One of his partners was Michael Schumacher, and they tell you here that Frentzen was the quicker of the two. However, Schumacher worked and learned and improved. Frentzen was less inclined to work and was subsequently overtaken by the younger man.

'Frentzen has around him this group of journalists who still tell him he is better than Schumacher,' a member of the Sauber staff says. 'Dah! They do not help him and he should see that. Michael worked at everything. In the evenings he would practise press interviews. He thought of everything. I don't usually believe in these things, but he is a true Capricorn. Now look at him. And look at Heinz-Harald.'

The Frentzen camp set their sights on a second Schumacher when Ralf arrived on the scene. They attempted to diminish him with their jokes. For example: what's the difference between Ralf and God? Answer: God isn't Ralf Schumacher. Perhaps that loses something in the translation, or is it just German humour? Try this: how would Ralf commit suicide? Answer: by falling off his ego.

Frentzen himself has, as he promised, taken on Michael personally here, calling on him to resign as an official of the Grand Prix Drivers' Association during a highly charged meeting. The two exchanged views – presumably uncomplimentary – in their own language as the rest looked on. Schumacher stood his ground and, as we now hear, no one else cared to challenge him.

Damon Hill, passing on his way out of the circuit, stops to fill in Herbert, who was otherwise engaged and could not make the meeting. Hill reveals that other, lighter side to his character as he relates in an exaggerated, self-mocking way, how he and the others kept their heads down, not daring to question *Der Meister*'s authority. 'No fisticuffs but peaked cap to peaked cap, you know. And we're all, "Yes Michael, no Michael, whatever you say Michael".' The laughter pierces the night air. Hill is the official who has actually stood down, to be replaced by Wurz – younger man, fresh ideas and happens to live in Monaco, where the organisation is based.

Hill and members of the Jordan team wend their way home. Eddie Jordan pauses, intent on some mischief, and has to settle for a few accurately aimed insults. Squads of mechanics are leaving well after ten o'clock. The Benetton boys grip comforting bottles of beer. Out on the road they have to negotiate fans who have patently been necking the amber stuff all evening and are now lurching uncontrollably in the headlights. At least there's no storm. Then again, that might actually make the journey safer.

Schumi's Army are on the march in ever greater numbers this cloudy, menacing Saturday morning. Hakkinen's fans are fewer but they have managed to bring along what just might be the world's longest hand-held flagpole. Others, unsurprisingly, are still stirring, watched by wide-eyed cattle, as they endeavour to find their bearings.

Hakkinen is second to Coulthard in morning practice and McLaren appear on top of the job. Then, on the stroke of midday, the skies throw another tantrum and the circuit is under a deluge. At one o'clock the rain eases and Schumacher sprints from motorhome to garage, but no one is in a rush to venture out on the circuit. Another shower further discourages them.

Takagi and Hill are the first to take the plunge, at 1.27. The Japanese spins twice and returns to his lair. Schumacher shows them how, but as the rain stops and the water drains, so the times tumble. Schumacher hesitates over his tyre choice and is overtaken in the frantic and spectacular final moments. Alesi goes top, then for the first time, Fisichella. Hakkinen pushes Schumacher to fourth. Coulthard is 14th, Hill 15th.

Coulthard owns up to a 'bad session' but Hill complains about a miscalculation. He has completed only 11 of his permitted 12 laps and could, he contends, have been out there at the end, claiming a place in the top four. 'Everyone is upset, but that's no good to anyone.' Behind him a team official rolls his eyes.

In the Benetton camp, all eyes are smiling. Mechanics hug Fisichella and hug one another. They have quietly gone about their work this season, almost unnoticed. But they have scored consistently enough to head Williams in third place in the constructors' standings. That near inconspicuous approach is apparently preferred by David Richards, midway through his first full season in charge following the departure of the ostentatious Flavio Briatore. The team steadfastly retains Italian features, such as two potted olive trees positioned outside the motorhome, and next season they will create an Italian-style piazza between their motorhomes. One of the motorhomes serves Japanese food, in deference to the team's main sponsors, and that flavour will be retained, but Richards' calm, measured strategy is unmistakably British.

However, anyone who might be thinking he is a soft touch should beware. He has an extremely impressive business and motor sport CV. This weekend he is keeping tabs also on events at Snetterton, where his British Touring Car Championship team are running, and in New Zealand, where Colin McRae and his Subaru crew are competing in the latest round of the World Rally Championship. Formula One is the last frontier but does not intimidate Richards.

When you come into something new it is far better to listen and learn rather than just say anything, until you've established yourself and got something to be proud of. I've got my credentials in other areas but there are a lot of people in Formula One who are far more experienced, far more qualified to talk on the subject than I am, and it would be rather rash and perhaps improper of me to take that position at the moment. Now, it doesn't mean to say that I haven't got my own opinions and doesn't mean to say I'm not building up a file of experience, and that when I do make some moves they won't be fairly bold and strong.

It's not so much expressing myself as the way we will go about things in the future. I wouldn't wish anybody to be lulled into a false sense of security, just because I'm fairly quiet and amiable at the moment. Clearly the paddock is full of very strong characters who like to get their own way and I perhaps have a different approach to getting my own way, and would rather persuade people than bully them. But don't misjudge me.

I don't think the money in Formula One is surprising. The budget is about double our rally budget, which sounds a lot but in real terms it's not. I guess our rally budget's bigger than many lower Formula One teams. The thing that frustrates me about Formula One is the inward-looking approach. This is unique, one of the strongest business groupings I've ever seen in any area you can think of, and yet they will not cooperate with each other. Everyone would rather poach each other's staff, nick each other's sponsors and spend all their time arguing with each other instead of looking at the big opportunities outside. I think Bernie's the only one who's got that vision.

We've got to look at the whole spectrum of the way we do our business, the broader picture and the diverse tool that we have in Formula One. It's got far more to offer than just stickers on cars and a few tickets to the Paddock Club. The commodity we have is unique and I think that because of the excesses of cigarette sponsorship people haven't been as creative as they might have been in developing all the other opportunities, and we are going to have to be in the future.

What I'm talking about is well away from pure sponsorship. For instance, I'm looking at setting up a management school at the factory with Oxford University. We've got a number of ideas, very diverse. I think the opportunities are enormous. There are some extraordinary talents in Formula One, and that's been one of the interesting things to see. Everyone's very keyed in and focused in the little area they're working in.

I don't see any danger of steering away from the racing. What you have to do is ring-fence the racing activity and draw from it all the time. That way you can keep reinvesting in it and keep it funded properly. You mustn't ever take your eye off the ball. You have to keep focused on the task, but that doesn't mean to say you can't use it more effectively.

Like Tom Walkinshaw at Arrows, he might be said to be asking too much of himself, controlling a Formula One team as well as his other activities. Walkinshaw responds by likening himself to the admiral of the fleet, with good and trusted captains at the helm of each ship. Richards, who somehow manages to remind you of Tony Blair and Richard Branson at the same time, answers this way:

I very much rely on other people. If there's one skill I believe I can bring to this operation it's the ability to build teams and work as a group. The rally team and touring car team work very efficiently. I'll go there when it's necessary. But my input is not needed when things are going well. You only need to be directly involved when you anticipate problems or you have problems. There's not a lot to put right here. The results the team are achieving this year speak for themselves.

It is the whole essence of the team to be young and dynamic, loyal and committed. that develops from within. I think we are one of the youngest teams, there's no dead wood around the place. It was a totally deliberate policy to go for two young drivers. We're well equipped in terms of the facility we've got, and well funded. A brand new wind tunnel comes on stream next week at the factory. It's an unbelievable thing. It's enormous and can take a full-scale car. The only thing we are missing is the manu-facturer link, and that is critical. I'm certain within the next two years we will have a long-term, established relationship with a suitable partner.

Any team would be acutely affected by the departure of Schumacher. Benetton, for a time, looked positively dazed and have still not returned to the fore. Richards maintains the spectre of the great man no longer hangs over the team.

That's gone now. It's back in history. I think we're left with a very different management style from the one that Flavio had while he was here. Flavio was very outward looking. Flavio only focused on generating income, and the outward profile of the team. Now that's all very well and it's obviously generated the money. It was right for the time and I'm not detracting from his success. My style of doing things is, I feel, adding more substance for the long term. I want to have an infrastructure in place that will be self-perpetuating. I want a team that actually doesn't need me there. It's got to be a team that is not reliant on one individual, not me or any driver, engineer or team manager. It's got to be a team that will work seamlessly, everyone feeling comfortable with each other. And that's my role, putting that into place, and that's only in its infancy.

Our two drivers are confirmed for next year and we have an option on the year afterwards. I think continuity is important. If you have talented people working together, then you'll only get better. You'll have hiccups and down-turns, but you've got to ride through those to learn from those experiences to go to the next level. The worst thing possible when you have these problems is to throw it all out the window and start again. Yeah, occasionally you'll have personality clashes and issues where people aren't willing to accept change, and when people aren't willing to accept change they have to go. It's not happened yet, but change has to happen, it's a natural process and an on-going process. You question the decisions you made yesterday, you revisit them all the time. You have to keep refreshing and you have to keep challenging.

Of the current crop of new drivers, ours look to be the best. Now, I think they're in a very good car and a very good team, and that obviously helps them. It's always hard to pinpoint how good the likes of Trulli might be in one of our cars. But we have had no thoughts of changing, and they need to know that. They need to be reassured this team is working round them. We need to focus our effort on the one who is under-performing at any time and be sure he is aware of our support.

I feel I haven't yet made my mark on Formula One. I'm still watching. It is much as I expected, an extension of everything else I've done for the last twenty years. I don't think I've suddenly changed my style of doing things because I'm here. I do enjoy dealing with other people. I would prefer to do business more openly and in a more businesslike manner so there are times when I find it frustrating. I find some of the ways things are done to be slightly unprofessional.

People tend to look for Machiavellian things but I often think the simplest answer is the truth. People give the most long-winded scenario about why somebody's done something and it's normally the most obvious thing. Looking back at Silverstone and the stories and suggestions around that, frankly I just put it down to incompetence on the day by a few people. To think there was anything more sinister and events could have been manipulated is just not on. I give no credibility at all to the conspiracy theory. Sure, there might be favours done here and there, but not in the true sense. If you call a favour giving an extra car-park pass and an extra couple of places in the paddock, OK, but nothing more.

I'd like to think we could get closer to challenging Ferrari and McLaren but the reality is that a strong third place in the Championship would be no disgrace. I think we could see ourselves more regularly on the podium in the second half of the season and who knows? The second half of last season saw a victory for Gerhard and we're coming to the tracks that probably suit us.

The drivers are getting more comfortable and confident, and I think they've taken the opportunities that have been afforded them. People may think we lost a win in Canada but the reality is we survived to finish second. Fizzy was missing third gear. He was not at all out-psyched by Schumacher. These guys don't take prisoners. Alex showed that in Monaco against Schumacher, and Giancarlo against Villeneuve in Canada. They hold their ground now.

And yet they are very much part of the team here. They get on very well together. The joy of it is they are very different characters, from different countries, and regard themselves as the new generation. I think it will be a number of years before we can make the judgement about who is the better.

Giancarlo is typically Latin, fairly laid-back, obviously great natural talent, probably a little susceptible to the emotional side. The early part of the year clearly unsettled him a bit and we were very happy to see him back on form again, and to show that we could help him do that. Alex has a far more clinical approach, he is far more strategic in his thinking. He knows what he's going to do this year. He's probably got his life mapped out for the next five years. All these drivers are very self-assured. They don't have a lot of self-doubt.

Does Richards have any self-doubt? 'All the time, but I have a good strong team of people around me who reassure me.'

The day makes an apologetic retreat into a grey veil of drizzle and by evening another downpour sends visitors and locals alike scurrying for shelter. Those who seek refuge and sustenance at a humble Gasthof in a tiny, unheard-of village barely 20 minutes up the valley from the circuit are intrigued by the presence of police and discreet yet obvious security personnel. Natural curiosity is satisfied when it is confirmed a party of guests dining with Jackie Stewart includes Princess Anne. Buck House this is not.

Sunday morning means another drying-out operation for the many who did not have the roof of even a humble Gasthof over their heads last night. Soft white clouds are sitting on the mountains like whipped cream on apfel strudel, but the campsites and car parks are like treacle pudding underfoot. Anyone who camped here in the early eighties will be consoled to know that the field alongside the approach road to the circuit is not flooded, as it was on one infamous occasion. The poor, blighted souls packed their stuff in the middle of the night and fled; all apart from the occupants of one small ridge tent, who defiantly stayed put in the middle of the lake. Nobody ever found out what became of them.

Richards checks into the paddock with a particularly jaunty step. Jordan's stride seems more laboured. He is none too pleased with Hill's comments the previous afternoon. 'Yes, we got it wrong, but we didn't say anything when he went off at Silverstone.'

Come warm-up the sun is suitably soothing. Hakkinen first, Coulthard second, Schumacher third, Irvine fourth. Business in the paddock is also returning to normal. Here's Jordan talking to Bernie, there's Jordan talking to Pollock. On the bench at the back of the Ford bus one of the catering staff is laboriously peeling spuds. Fit for a Princess, perhaps? FIA officials are anxiously mobilising police and stewards. Fans have broken down fencing at the top end of the circuit and there are concerns they might venture on to the racetrack.

Stewart escorts the Princess through the paddock towards Bernie's bus for an audience with Formula One's monarch. Several minutes later the party re-emerges with Bernie just as, on the other side of the fence, two black limousines sweep by followed by a police outrider and, slightly bizarrely, by a man wearing a dark suit and carrying a walkie-talkie, running. Bernie's party and the Austrian political dignitaries converge at the gate and are lost in the mêlée of photographers and film crews. An American female photographer makes an uninterested withdrawal. 'No one I recognise in the limos. Must be someone European.'

A team of fighter jets put on a lunchtime display and this, too, is tame compared with the troop that appeared in the eighties. Their daredevil antics would be allowed nowhere now. They were Italian and were affectionately, and sympathetically, known as the Arrowvedercis, because it was reckoned each year their number was reduced by one. Ah, but just take in the views today. The valley and the backdrop of mountains and forests are resplendent in the bright sunlight.

Richards is happy with the heat. It should suit their tyres. Fizzy? He'll be fine. The pressure at the front won't get to him. Pollock wanders on to the grid, exchanging banter and back slaps with one of Hill's chums. Patrick Head prowls the grid, eyeing the other cars for who knows what. Peter Sauber is on a similar mission. Jean Todt is in discussion with Schumacher, who still finds time for another TV interview. Hakkinen makes for Fisichella, shakes his hand and wishes him well. An old pro's ploy.

Hakkinen duly launches past Alesi and Fisichella to lead at the first corner. At the second, Schumacher is up behind him. They distance themselves from the chaos midfield and at the back of the grid. The Arrows drivers take each other out and brace themselves to confront a fearsome Walkinshaw. Coulthard loses his front wing. Fortunately for him, the safety car is sent out and although he takes his place at the rear, his car is repaired and he proceeds to scythe through the field.

Schumacher, carrying a lighter fuel load than the McLarens, tries desperately to pass Hakkinen but the Finn resists for 17 pulsating laps. Then the Ferrari goes wide and leaps wildly over the gravel, losing its front wing and other accessories. Schumacher ushers it to the pits and now he is last and embarking on a charge. His toughest task is negotiating his brother's Jordan. Ralf puts up a spirited fight and Michael almost loses control again before going by. Irvine slows and Schumacher takes third place, behind Hakkinen and Coulthard.

At the end the brothers shake hands and smile. Hakkinen is hugged by an unusually ebullient Dennis. This is an enormous win, and Coulthard's second place completes McLaren's comeback from a mini slump. Coulthard rates it the best race of his Formula One career, yet concedes it now looks like his teammate's Championship. Schumacher owns up to a 'stupid mistake' but, to scornful titters, claims brake problems forced Irvine to give way to him.

Nature's final contribution to the day, a gorgeous sunset over the mountains, is altogether more wholesome.

7
Hockenheim

DREAMS AND REALITY

There is no respite just now, just seamless toil, and four days after Zeltweg the workers more or less have things in place again. Grey, solemn skies beckon this morning, chillingly apposite here at this dark, forbidding circuit, where the past still casts a shadow over the present. The home of the German Grand Prix is a curious amalgam of long, superfast straights through the forest, interrupted by chicanes, and a meandering section contained in a huge stadium bowl.

Jim Clark, an all-time great in the realms of Senna and Schumacher, was killed in a Formula Two race here in 1968. The Frenchman Patrick Depailler died after an accident in testing here, in 1980. Another gruesome crash in heavy rain during practice for the Grand Prix in 1982 ended the Formula One career of his compatriot Didier Pironi. Racers are imperilled by rain on any circuit, but on no circuit more so than here, where spray hangs between the trees like deathly curtains. The grim prospect reaches out a cold hand of greeting across the vast western plain of Germany, fields of maize and cowering sunflowers.

But this is Schumi's home race and nothing must dampen the fervour of the Red Army. The young, middle-aged, even the elderly, are decked out in Schumi and Ferrari regalia. On Sunday there will be 130,000 of them, most massed in the stadium, creating an atmosphere to rival any in sport. They will be relieved to hear the ubiquitous Portaloos are being delivered to the forest this very hour.

The paddock is quiet this wet Thursday lunchtime, its travel- and labour-weary dwellers easing themselves into proceedings.

Ralf Schumacher is winkled from his shell to speak to German TV but can throw no light on his future. Besides, he feels he should concentrate on this weekend. Elsewhere, Irvine has been confirmed for another year with Ferrari, Barrichello has been linked with Williams, while McLaren, it has been revealed, attempted to intercept Villeneuve *en route* to BAR. Professions of their faith in Coulthard are beginning to look distinctly hollow. The team's appeal over the Silverstone fiasco has, as expected, failed, but the stewards, their cards doubtless marked, have done the decent thing and fallen on their swords.

FIA's World Motor Sport Council have given further consideration to the thorny subject of team orders, declaring they have no problem with the basic concept but do not find acceptable 'any arrangement which interferes with a race and cannot be justified by the relevant team's interest in the Championship, or any arrangement between teams'.

Confused? Jean Todt appears to be, fumbling his way through interrogation by the press. He is equally uncomfortable about his communications with Ron Dennis and persistent stories about the legality, or otherwise, of the Ferrari. 'This is a world of rumours,' he states profoundly.

One of those rumours suggests Irvine's relationship with Schumacher is not as cosy as it was, despite the Irishman's new contract. Asked what this race will mean to Michael, he replies curtly: 'I've no idea.' He says Michael runs the whole show and feels he 'owes me', but Irvine expects no pay-back unless the number one has the Championship in the bag. A theory going the rounds reckons Schumacher would rather have had on board Alesi – a neighbour in Switzerland, where their wives have apparently become friendly – as part of a deal taking Ralf to Sauber, with one of Ferrari's better engines. It is a weird and wonderfully convoluted theory, but then this is a world of weird and wonderfully convoluted theories – and rumours.

Not to be outdone by Benetton's olives, Ferrari now have topiary shrubs outside their motorhome: a peacock, another bird and an abstract design that defies description. Ford have taken to decorating the back of their bus with posters heralding the venue of the race and the route from the previous circuit. Stuart Spires is checking carefully for any embarrassing spelling errors. Last week's poster indicated they had reached Zeltweg via Salzsburg. The middle S has been a source of inevitable, lampooning comment.

Ricardo Rosset has been the target of ridicule, scorn and downright disdain all season. Even within the Tyrrell team, there are sniggers that any outside interest should be shown in 'the slowest driver in Formula One'. He has twice failed to achieve the qualifying time – 107 per cent of the pole position holder's time – this season, the only driver to suffer the indignity, and when he does qualify it is usually on the back row. He had a couple of wins in Formula 3000, but pays for his drive in the Tyrrell and Villeneuve is not alone in considering the Brazilian out of his depth here. Now, with pernicious irony, the BAR team which will supersede Tyrrell have signed Villeneuve at considerable expense and are not expected to retain Rosset, who celebrated his 30th birthday just three days ago. And yet, like all of them, he still dreams of becoming world champion and maintains he is an underestimated and misunderstood driver. Sitting with his wife by his side, he talks about his Formula One life and what is in store for Villeneuve next season.

Villeneuve was not really a friend but we were team-mates for one race, at Macau, in Formula Three. I used to get on with him fairly well, as I do with a lot of drivers. It was disappointing he reacted the way he did with me at Monaco. First, it wasn't my fault, and even if it was, why make so much of a thing about it? It was a crash, nobody got hurt. It's bad to go on like that. I try to forget it.

I don't think all the drivers are like that. But I think sometimes they forget they have been in a smaller team and what happens in overtaking. He was lucky. He went straight to Williams. I think maybe next year he will realise how hard it is at the back of the grid in Formula One. Because he came from IndyCars and it's more level there he doesn't realise the struggle it is in a Tyrrell. Even

Schumacher would have a struggle in a Tyrrell.

Some drivers do understand, some have short memories. I understand their side as well. Sometimes they are fighting for the Championship or to win a race and it's bad when you've got a backmarker in the way. But you have to understand the backmarkers in a race are having their own race, fighting for position, and sometimes the leaders catch us in the middle of a corner. You cannot just go off and let them pass. Sometimes only one car can go through a corner and they have to wait. Sorry.

Some don't show enough respect for the guys at the back, some do. Michael, for example, has a different way. He's very clever, very smart. He shows a lot of respect. I get respect from him on the track when I'm on a qualifying lap. If he's done his run and is slowing down, he will actually put his wheel on the dust to let me pass. So he's intelligent, because he knows in the middle of the race he will catch me and lap me, and by respecting me he knows he will get my respect. That's being smart.

But some of them don't do that. Some do a qualifying lap or come out of the pits quickly, stay on the line and screw my lap. So why should I respect him when he comes behind me? He has to overtake me and he can make it easier if he wants to. Or you can just play fair. With some drivers I just play fair. Some I make it easier for when I respect them.

Again, off the circuit, some show respect, some don't. If I name those who don't, it just goes on and on. We are in the same job and we see each other all the time. Schumacher is one of the good drivers, in and out of the car, and will say hello if you see him in the hotel. But some wouldn't know your name. They don't know that you exist, which is stupid. Everyone comes to me and says Schumacher is arrogant and so on. I say he is the best out there and shows respect. I played football with him yesterday. I don't understand why people say this. Some of them are just fortunate to be in a better team.

I don't know where I will be next year. It depends on so many things. Williams have to sort out both drivers, so where are they going to come from? That's what we have to find out. I think there is a chance for me at BAR. I want to stay in Formula One and would like to stay here. I think it will be good here and Jacques will be a different person next year. He will realise the life on this side is a lot different.

I hope the team will be at the front straightaway. It's a lot, lot easier to drive a good car than to drive a bad car. People don't realise that. It's a lot easier to drive a McLaren and be there fighting to win the race than be here, fighting to qualify at the back end of the grid, because the car is not good. When the car is good you can do what you want to do with it.

Ninety-nine per cent of people do not know how good I am. And especially the specialised press. Every day I read the papers and some guys you think know the sport just write so many stupid things. They don't realise. People don't understand what it takes and how it works. Once someone told me it's because I'm a paying driver. 'Ah, you're a pay driver so you're no good.' But I said what would Formula One be if nobody brought in money? Half of the grid here would be out, there would be no TV and these guys who are writing the bad things would be out of a job.

That's Formula One. What can I do? There are teams that don't have money, my sponsors want to be involved, what's the problem? What's wrong? Schumacher probably has his own sponsors involved, and he even came through with Mercedes. That's the way motor racing is. Unfortunately, some drivers can't find sponsors and will not make it. If they could make it I am sure there would be three or four Schumachers around. The men who manage to find sponsorship and keep the sport alive get bad press.

He breaks off to ask his wife for a coffee. He is dark-haired but paler than you expect a Brazilian to be. His face has the expression of the hounded. Then again, Senna often had that haunted, pallid look and Barrichello, though usually cheerier, could be north European. The search for the 'new Senna' put intolerable pressure on Barrichello and to varying degrees burdened all other aspiring Brazilian drivers. Rosset sips his coffee and goes on:

> When Senna died it was very difficult for Brazilian drivers because the people wanted someone to replace him straightaway. Rubens had a really hard time with that. Now the years pass and I think they realise it is not that easy to replace him. Now you're getting a new era and people are cheering for you to see if you can get better. In Brazil I don't get such a bad press as in England and in Italy. At least the national press in England have asked me what are the problems.
>
> But I've never felt like leaving Formula One. It makes you angry and want to prove yourself. And you get stronger. Every time they punch you down it can lift you up. It's very, very hard, but every time you manage to do that you become a stronger driver. Until you explode, I think.

A hint of Friday morning sunshine tempts the sunflowers to peep over the parapet. Stallholders are setting up on the road to the circuit. If you want anything but red, or the black, red and gold of the national flag, you should move on. The throng waiting at the main gate for a glimpse perhaps of any driver, but above all a glimpse of Schumacher, are disappointed. The main man has taken a secret track through the forest and breezes into the paddock with his manager Willi Weber in attendance. Weber, still in red, is in demand for pictures and interviews here almost as much as his driver.

Klaxon horns herald the start of practice and a booming firecracker announces Schumacher's entrance. He is a low-key sixth behind Coulthard and Hakkinen. Nothing unusual there. Glaringly unusual is Hill's fourth place. Rosset is 22nd and last.

Hill goes one better in the afternoon, behind Hakkinen and Coulthard. Schumacher is one better, also. Rosset is still 22nd and last.

This is a timely statement from Hill, whose future remains uncertain despite his assertion he is 99 per cent certain of staying with Jordan.

'It's very satisfying to see my name in the top three again,' he says, bounding out of the back of the Jordan garage. 'This is the most encouraging Friday of the season for me. And we're not kidding ourselves, either. We did this with fuel. The car seems inherently good here and we are knocking on the door of being a regular top-six runner again, which is the key. We have built up a momentum and I can see light at the end of the tunnel. Now I want to sustain this form and hopefully score points on Sunday.'

Around him the mood is less than euphoric. A team member screws up his face and says: 'It's only Friday.' It is and that's what they all say today. This, though, seems personal. Martin Pople's comments come to mind. So does the team's disquiet when Hill spoke his mind last weekend. Honda were not amused and informed Jordan as much. Now there are hints Jordan are not rushing into a new deal with the former world champion, not at £5 million, anyway. Further inquiry reveals Hill's option to stay with the team expired three days after the British Grand Prix. Now the option, and the ball, are said to be in Jordan's court.

Jordan have been advised they do not have to pay Hill the same retainer and claim they cannot justify such a substantial portion of their budget for one driver who has yet to score a point and convince them he is all he was cracked up to be. This, too, is part of the posturing, of course, but there is a suspicion they might actually prefer him to take umbrage and walk out on them. The whisper is the hand of Bernie could be involved here.

Retirement is an option Hill has considered, although that might have had more to do with the nagging pace of Ralf Schumacher than the doubtful performance of the Jordan. Humiliation at the hands of a whippersnapper is more than he could bear and again, of late, the German has been upstaging him, scoring points in consecutive races. One thing is clear: this is a big race for the Englishman.

Whispers are everywhere. The whispering huddle between these transporters reckons both drivers are staying; the whispering huddle over there won't be surprised if they lose both. Eddie Jordan is adamant: 'That definitely won't happen.'

The whispers around McLaren have to be embarrassing for Coulthard. First the team try for Schumacher, then Villeneuve. The Scot is apparently getting the vote by a process of elimination. He confronts this strange kind of endorsement with admirable outward restraint. His inner irritation can only be guessed at.

'It's not something that has concerned me in the least,' he maintains. 'All I know is what I have been told by Ron and Norbert [Haug] and I don't believe they have lied to me. I don't feel any uncertainty it will be the same drivers next year. But sure, I'll be glad when it's all confirmed and I can focus on the racing.'

German interest is focused on the latest twists in the troubled life of Frentzen. What, for instance, can he make of Head's now widely publicised castigation?

'It's not my cup of tea to talk like that,' he replies with an amiable countenance and ironic manipulation of a quaint old English idiom. 'It's not my character. I don't think it's the way to speak.'

Then how about that not so quaint old rivalry with Schumacher? The great man is not well pleased with him after their skirmish at Zeltweg.

'I can't understand why Michael is upset with me,' he says, sustaining the amiable countenance throughout.

The travails elsewhere must seem as nothing to Dr Harvey Postlethwaite, who found himself holding not so much the baby as the corpse at Tyrrell when Ken Tyrrell walked away. Postlethwaite is one of the more engaging characters in the paddock, a ray of eccentric individuality: loud, irreverent, sardonic, funny, deeply knowledgeable, articulate. He also happens to be the man who designed the last Ferrari that won a Championship, the constructors' title of 1983.

'I feel like the executor of somebody's will,' says Tyrrell's senior official. But, undaunted, he adds, 'In seventeen or eighteen years I've had two teams and I still love it. When I wake up in the morning my first thought is of motor racing. When I go to sleep at night my second last thought is of motor racing.'

It has been a curious kind of motor racing at Tyrrell this year – going through the motions, fulfilling a commitment, marking time until the old team is no more and the new team, BAR, rises in its place. He is not expected to be part of that new team but yes, he intends to stay in Formula One. Some say he is joining the other new team, Honda, others that he will have a job with FIA. Before that, the last rites at Tyrrell. Sitting in the corner of the Tyrrell hospitality area, which seems already to have been cast adrift, situated as it is separate from the other team motorhomes, he says:

Yes, it is a little bit sad that Tyrrell is dying, but a large bit not sad. The death of the Tyrrell team is probably a sign of the health of Formula One. The Tyrrell operation could not continue the way it was set up. It had to change. That change took place and as is so often the case when these things happen, it meant the Tyrrell family finally lost control and in a very short space of time ended up having nothing more to do with the team, which I suppose is an inevitability.

But it's far better that the team slot is occupied by somebody with a lot of money, with a lot of ideas who can bring a lot of new things to Formula One. Frankly the Tyrrell team was occupying that space but finding it almost impossible to survive against a level of budget and technological means and partnerships that were just leaving the team behind, year by year. So ultimately I think it was good and healthy. I have no sentimentality for it at all.

The best bits have been the most successful bits. We had a reasonable year at Tyrrell in '94. We had a wonderful period in the early nineties with Alesi. That was absolutely superb.

That earlier period at Tyrrell followed his earlier period with Ferrari, whom he joined in 1981 and where he worked with, among others, Gilles Villeneuve, father of Jacques, who was killed at Zolder, Belgium, in 1982. Postlethwaite's face lights up as he recalls:

> There is no doubt those years, '82, '83, '84, '85, were fantastic with Villeneuve and then Patrick Tambay and Mario Andretti, and then Michele Alboreto. That was a super period because we were competitive. We were up there and that's what gives you the buzz. And beyond that, Wolf and Hesketh, wonderful times. My enjoyment is allied to the competitiveness of the cars. And it was a period when drivers were your friends. James Hunt was a terrific guy. I loved him. I think the last driver I felt I had a friendship with was Jody Scheckter, and we're still friends. Very few drivers since then.
>
> The problems always with drivers, and particularly if you are an engineer, designing cars, is that it's very rare in this, as in any other sport, that you go out on a high. When a driver leaves it's always because he is dissatisfied with you or vice versa, which means ultimately he will blame you for not producing the goods, and you will blame him for not driving properly. So the ultimate relationship with a driver tends to be slightly sour, which is just one of those things.

Unless, of course, the driver is taken from us prematurely.

> I don't know Gilles' son so it's difficult to compare them, but I think the difference is that Jacques is probably very professional and he looks to me to be pretty calculating, whereas Gilles was bubbling with natural talent and just had a huge effervescent desire to drive racing cars. He was professional and concentrated and all that sort of thing, but he was a daredevil. The things he used to get up to in the car were just unbelievable ... [He has to pause

to control his laughter before he can make the rest of his tale intelligible.]

He used to drive out of the pits and go off on the first corner every time at Fiorano [Ferrari's own test track], just to upset Forghieri [Mauro, the long-serving designer/engineer]. The Old Man loved it. Absolutely loved it.

Enzo Ferrari was a very interesting person and the older you get, as somebody said to me the other day, the more you appreciate how clever he was. He was a very skilled user of people, and he always developed quite a good rapport with the people around him. When I look back now it's amazing. I got on with him very well, certainly for a number of years, till he became infirm at the end, which was a very difficult period at Ferrari. That's when the politics got very difficult. But to begin with he was fantastic. Totally dedicated, there all the time. Hardly ever left the office. I'd talk to him two or three times a day, have lunch with him, discussing everything. Mostly girls and cars.

The politics are probably a little over-stated. It's become apocryphal. In any racing operation you've got people who are very single-minded and Mr Ferrari's way of operating was to let people rise to the top. The team was not particularly well organised in the way that an English team is. It was Italian, it had Italian feel, Italian style to it, and therefore there was a certain amount of survival of the fittest about it. There was a certain amount of divide and rule, also, but I've seen some racing teams that were far worse in that respect.

At the end of the day you'd got bags of money, super engines, super working conditions, test track, drawing office. You didn't want for anything. I'd far rather have that and put up with a couple of political problems with a bit of back-biting and a bit of in-fighting than have this wonderfully smooth operation but no facilities and no money. Hell, no, it was fine.

But how about Ferrari today? And the conspiracy theory that Ferrari must win the Championship because Formula One needs them?

It's much easier to talk about Ferrari objectively being here and out of it. The conspiracy theory I regard as a load of cobblers. Ferrari are nowadays under no more pressure to win than any other racing team. What the hell must the pressure be like on Ron at the moment, with Mercedes and all that behind him? The pressure to win is enormous, and I think it's no more or less so at Ferrari.

I think also it's mythological that the Italian press are particularly difficult or hard-hitting. The whole of the press around the world is putting Formula One under the microscope, and I don't think it's true any longer that Ferrari have to have supper at the hands of the Italian press any more than other teams. Going back fifteen or sixteen years it probably was true they were under a lot more pressure but now, in 1998, I think the pressure is fairly evenly spread across the whole of the leading teams.

Ultimately the pressure comes from within the team and when I worked at Ferrari it had very much the feel of an English team because there was one guy at the top who ran it and his word was law, and the team was relatively small. You could recognise the roles of people whether it was Williams, Ferrari or Wolf Racing. They were the same sort of racing operations. But Ferrari had always been a bit bigger and of course they made the engine, which was the one thing that distinguished the team from all others.

I loved it and would, given the chance, do it all over again. I think if one were to be honest, I might have spent my time better elsewhere . . . [another pause for laughter] but I certainly liked the ambience and I liked to be in Italy. My family lived there and liked it and I still have enormous ties with Italy. I go back there a lot. I've got lots of friends there; I do lots of business there.

I still probably speak the language better technically than I speak English!

Life, in any language, is very different at Tyrrell in 1998. The team have yet to score a point this season.

It's much harder at this end. It's easy to go motor racing when the results come. It's bloody difficult when they don't, because the hours are the same here as they are up there, the effort's the same, the mental torture is the same, and when you don't get the results it's bloody awful, incredibly frustrating. All that pressure comes not from reading the press, or from sponsors necessarily, it's the pressure the team puts on itself to succeed.

Formula One is quite different now from what it was in the early eighties, but I don't want to say it's better or worse. It's just different. Fun is down to the individual. You've got to make your own life and your own style. I mean, four or five of us were coming to the circuit in a car this morning and we were in convulsions of laughter over something stupid. That's still there, and that joke will go on all weekend.

Today Formula One is well funded and I mean, look around, we don't want for anything. Look at the facilities we've got. It's wonderful. Ultimately there's a lot of money washing around and the people who are paying it ask a lot of questions and want to know how it's being spent. Go back to the eighties and the type of sponsorship around was because the MD of the company enjoyed motor racing and wanted to turn up at the odd race. Well, that doesn't happen any more.

Sponsorship now is controlled. Sponsors want to know whether they are reaching the right audience, whether promotion is targeted to the right A or B sector. If anything, that's where the outside pressure comes from, sponsorship and the money side of Formula One, because the money enables us to do all this. Nobody holds a gun to the sponsors' heads, they're in it for a reason and that reason is for exposure, and that means success.

Success has long eluded Tyrrell. Despite the 'wonderful' period of the early nineties, the team last won a race in 1983, and Jackie Stewart had his third and final Championship success with Ken Tyrrell in 1973. The team's drivers in 1998 are the previously untried Takagi and the much-maligned Rosset. About Rosset . . .

It's very difficult to be critical about any Formula One driver because the answer at the end of the day is well, if you're so clever you get in there and do it, and of course you know you'd go off at the first corner. So to be critical of any driver would be wrong. Let's face it, Ricardo brings to this team a large slice of the budget which is allowing us to race this year. If he wasn't doing that it's doubtful whether he would hold his position. However, he is our driver, we have him in the car and we have to do the best possible job we can for him and with him. It's a situation which I am personally very uncomfortable with. It's not of my volition.

Takagi is definitely a talent. He achieves his performance without any difficulty at all. When the laps come, they come with complete ease, which makes me think that in there is something very, very good. It's difficult for him at the moment – it's his first year, his English is not very good, and he's probably still not quite focused enough because it's a bit too easy. He's got a team-mate at the back of the grid. When he's into his second year and he's got a bit more pressure on him, then we'll see how well he goes. But he is undoubtedly a talent and I think he'll get a seat. I wouldn't like to say if Rosset will.

One of the problems we have is just lack of consistency. Takagi has looked very good in practice at the last couple of races, then got it wrong in qualifying or did what he did in the race in Austria, spun up the inside and it's gone. My feeling is there's a pretty strong car there waiting to come out, but we can't put the bits together to make it happen.

Every person in Formula One wonders what Schumacher would do in their car. I think the answer is he'd go a second quicker than any other driver you could put in. The more interesting question is what would happen if you put in Damon Hill, or Ralf Schumacher, or Frentzen or somebody.

Michael Schumacher has to be amongst the very best ever. Some people say he is flawed because he does some pretty harsh things. I don't want to say they're wrong or right. I just think that's the winner in him. At Silverstone, when he was behind Hakkinen, you just knew he was going to win the race. I think what happened at Austria was because he was trying so hard. I think he's worth every penny Ferrari pay him. He's the ingredient they lacked for a decade. You have to be prepared to put the best driver in the car. The Old Man didn't always do that.

How Schumacher rates alongside Senna we never found out. It's probably the thing motor racing has most missed. If Senna was still there it would have been *fantastic*. It's my opinion that the driver to beat Schumacher has yet to come into Formula One.

I'm not particularly enjoying this year because I've ended up having to do something which I wouldn't have chosen to do. It's not pleasant but one is professional and I'll do what's necessary in the best possible way for the people we employ and the people I've worked with over a number of years.

But yes, I want to stick around. The stupid thing is I still get an enormous buzz out of the engineering. To me the engineering of Formula One cars is still absolutely absorbing and interesting, far more so than the drivers. I'm never happier than when I've got my head in a gearbox.

Clearly, it is time to take our leave.

Across the way at Ford's flagship team, Stewart, Alan

Jenkins muses over the prospects of BAR. He and his colleagues have come through the dreams of a new adventure to discover the harshness of reality. He recalls an excited atmosphere within the camp for their first race last season, at Melbourne, the like of which he had never previously experienced, but then he also recalls how the team were worn down by the intensity of the competitiveness in Formula One. Come the second year, it is a hard grind. As teams grow – even the smaller ones now have workforces of 200 plus – so they have greater difficulty recruiting suitable personnel. He contrasts this with his days at McLaren, who won the 1984 Championship with about 80 people. Stewart's workforce is made up of 41 design and technical staff, 120 in operations, which includes the race team, and almost 40 in commercial, finance and administration roles.

Jenkins offers a little more insight into the plight of the unfulfilled Magnussen, who apparently had a slightly complicated private life and would think nothing of taking phone calls from a girlfriend on his mobile in the garage. He would say little at briefings and claim he could not get a word in because Barrichello dominated proceedings. Subsequently invited to contribute, he would recoil. Verstappen has instantly been more confident and assertive. The information is given with sympathy and no little dismay.

From out there in the woods emanate the sounds and smells of campsite festivities. Other troops from Schumi's Army are on the march through the small and usually tranquil town of Hockenheim, well lubricated and in no mood to contemplate retreat.

Saturday bristles with life; bright, optimistic, vibrant. Vehicles decked in red, full of passengers decked in red, turn off the road and disappear into a maize field, bound, they are assured, for some hidden car park. Almost no one trekking over the motorway bridge towards the main entrance of the Hockenheimring is wearing anything other than regulation Schumi gear.

Inside the paddock Villeneuve's purple hair raises regulation smiles as he hurries by; except as someone observes, the dye is fading to expose an ever-thinning problem. It was Irvine who reckoned the Canadian went to the toilet in his helmet so as not to display his bald pate.

Schumacher removes his helmet earlier than scheduled in morning practice, pulling over his car out in the country. He watches proceedings from the sidelines, joking with marshals. This, though, is no laughing matter. He has completed only six laps and his programme can be torn up. Rosset spins, returns to the track, then goes off again and this time crashes heavily. Coulthard and Hakkinen are quickest.

Over lunch it is generally accepted Ferrari are in the mire, so we can expect an extra race, on 11 October. Now Estoril has emerged as favourite, rather than Jerez. Then again, perhaps Ferrari will need two extra races, even a third. Yes, throw in Mugello, one of their regular haunts. Cynicism is running wild. Rosset looks like missing out on a third race this season. Prof. Sid Watkins, head of the Formula One medical organisation, has advised the Brazilian not to take part in qualifying and Tyrrell have withdrawn him.

The stadium is almost full, a hum of expectation rising from the mass of humanity. A few Finnish flags sprout defiantly from its midst, a Dutch flag too, but mostly the scene is a restless, anxious red, like a poppy field swaying gently in the breeze. Some fans have Prancing Horse transfers on their shoulders. Those with klaxon horns are tuning up. All are counting down the minutes to one o'clock. Schumacher cranks up the fervour by appearing at the pit wall and saluting his people. Irvine, insouciant, in shades, saunters over to the pit wall and eases into a seat.

Schumacher takes to the circuit and the German roar in the stadium is a tad unnerving. Out there on the circuit, however, Schumacher cannot get close to Hakkinen and Coulthard, and gradually a horror story unfolds as, one by one, another six cars move ahead of him. Villeneuve, third, reaches a top speed of 217.666 mph. Schumacher can take no more when he feels Diniz has held him up and waves his arm in exasperation. Now he isn't so smart.

Takagi, as if retracing his team-mate's fateful steps, has a big shunt and rips off half his car. To the consternation of his embattled team, he comes within a couple of feet of a repeat in the spare car. They are grateful to have one car on the grid for tomorrow's race. The stewards have confirmed that since Rosset has not qualified, he cannot take part.

Hakkinen, who has lowered a pole time of last season for the first time, stands on his seat, then on the pit wall, taking what acclaim he can muster from a largely disenchanted gallery. Coulthard concludes 'it looks as if we've got Schuey on the run' and points out that the German's fit of pique is an unusual departure which perhaps proves the pressure, in front of his own fans, has got to *Der Meister*. 'It is the wrong time and the wrong place to have my worst qualifying position of the season,' Schumacher laments.

Ralf has delivered a consolation of sorts with fourth place, one ahead of Hill. Jordan are buoyant but Hill's solicitor-manager, Michael Breen, stationed at the doorway to one of the team motorhomes, is angry about stories suggesting his client will have to take a substantial pay cut to stay at Jordan. He anticipates a deal within 14 days, and does not expect Hill's salary to be reduced.

Some of Alesi's advisers, including Berger, are presenting his case for a drive at Williams. Of course, the Austrian cautions, they would have to put up with three nuclear explosions a year. Alesi smiles and protests, 'No. Only two.' If he continues to drive for Sauber, surely there can be no way with Herbert?

'Why not?' Well, because of what you said at Silverstone. 'That was three weeks ago,' he says with an expression that indicates no explanation should be necessary.

Formula One bosses, on constant alert for fledgling talent, have an eye on this afternoon's Formula 3000 race as well as their own more immediate business. A downpour at the start fills older witnesses with trepidation and no one is surprised at the first-lap pile-up in the spray. Mercifully, every driver involved walks away unhurt.

When the race has finally run its course and the noise subsided, McLaren and Mercedes announce they have re-signed

David Coulthard and Mika Hakkinen for the 1999 season. Things are looking good for the team in grey. Even the late afternoon skies over Hockenheim seem to acknowledge their dominance.

Sunday morning is still grey and sombre, a reminder to Schumi's Army that nothing miraculous is likely to have happened over night. The sunflowers again have their heads bowed in respectful recognition of their man's predicament. The auguries are not good. Outside the circuit the atmosphere is muted, as if the swell of optimism has been punctured. Hordes of people are still making their way across the bridge, but you sense this is an act of duty rather than faith. Conviction has drained with yesterday's rain. However, since they have paid for their tickets, they might as well see it through.

Richards, chatting outside the Benetton motorhome, is handed a new shirt by a member of his team.

'I'd better change into this before warm-up,' he says. 'My wife obviously can't tell the difference. It should have chevrons on.' Walkinshaw sallies forth, contemplating a better race day for his team. By the way, what *did* he say to his drivers after the Austrian Grand Prix?

'Nothing that's printable,' he growls.

Pople is pushing his Arrows tyre trolley for just about the last time, bracing himself for a ritual send-off.

'I got presented with a picture of the trucks, signed by everybody, and that was nice. I expect I'll get soaked after the race, strapped to the pit wall or something. Then I'll probably have a drink with the lads back at the factory on Tuesday.'

Coulthard is quickest in warm-up, then Ralf, Hakkinen, Villeneuve and Michael. Whatever their aspirations today, there are no obvious clues in the body language as they report for the drivers' briefing, accompanied by their team officials. The Ferrari pair are among the first. They climb the stairs to the control tower, sign in at the door, and melt into the darkness of the room beyond. Coulthard and Hakkinen march up side by side, the Scot with his race-suit rolled down, clutching a mug of tea.

As the drivers are addressed by Charlie Whiting, FIA's race

director and the official starter, the Goodyear crew lighten up with a water fight, to the vociferous approval of their neighbours and rivals at Bridgestone. Some ten minutes after they assembled, the drivers file out to be taken on the showcase lap of the circuit, while the FIA officials go their separate ways. Prof. Watkins, who sits in on the meeting, makes his way to one of the two FIA mobile offices, parked next to Williams. These, too, are painted silver grey.

Prof. Watkins has been Formula One's resident doctor for 20 years and now heads an extensive and highly skilled operation that guarantees drivers in distress the swiftest and best possible attention. The medical centre at each circuit is equipped like a small hospital and, should a driver need to be taken to a proper hospital, a helicopter is on permanent stand-by. The Prof. is a passenger in a fast car that follows the racing cars on the first lap of the Grand Prix, and for the rest of the race sits in the car, waiting in the pit lane to respond to any accident. At this meeting he has also been on duty for the Formula 3000 race.

Prof. Watkins is an eminent neuro-surgeon and although, at the age of 69, retired from the health service, runs his own practice between race meetings. Here he is much more than a doctor. His dry humour and healthy perspective on life are equally remedial. He enjoys a cigar at most times, and in the evening will savour a concomitant Scotch. When he can break from his work, the chances are he will be fishing in Scotland. He is perhaps the most respected individual in this paddock. He looks slightly uncomfortable in his blue, protective overalls but he talks easily and eloquently, with no trace of his Liverpool roots, propping up a partition in the mobile office.

My heart isn't in my mouth any more when I follow the first lap. It used to be, but you get used to it. I've done a lot of first laps now. But we don't like it in the rain because you can't see anything. I think there were thirty-two cars on the grid yesterday, throwing up an enormous amount of spray, and you just don't see anything after the start, until you see the bits and pieces. There were no serious problems, though, yesterday. You really do have to have a very good driver, who is sufficiently cautious but sufficiently quick so that you stay in contact with the situation.

Here he has a German ex-racing driver. Yesterday's incident, you suspect, was an eerie reminder of Pironi's crash.

The rain yesterday wasn't quite as heavy as it was that day with Pironi. That was a very bad accident. The boy was very badly injured. He was in a lot of pain when we arrived, a lot of deformative with the fractures in his legs. We basically put him to sleep in order to extricate him. We had to cut a bit of the car to free his legs. Everything worked pretty well after that, except for the gentleman who came with an umbrella to protect the driver from the rain.

The accident was so bad we brought the helicopter to the scene and when we carried the stretcher to the helicopter he walked into the rotor blades with the top of his umbrella. There was a loud snapping noise as we took off. When we got to the hospital at Heidelberg and landed, the pilot examined the blades and said the helicopter was unserviceable. They had to bring a truck to take it away. So we were lucky to get to the hospital. Just shows how people who are trying to do good can actually create dangerous situations.

There was a lot of criticism in the journals afterwards because it took us a long time to get Pironi straight and there were complaints we hadn't put any protection over him and he was getting wet. But it wasn't doing him any harm because he was in his normal gear and it's quite helpful to be cold if you're in a shock condition. It protects the internal organs.

Pironi's life and limbs were saved but his Formula One career was over and he sought to satisfy his thirst for speed elsewhere. He was killed in a powerboat accident five years later.

That 1982 season claimed the lives of two other drivers, Gilles Villeneuve and a young Italian, Ricardo Paletti. Safety and medical precautions have been constantly revised and improved since. The Prof. also chairs FIA's Advisory Expert Group, which steers scientific safety research and development. Cars now incorporate better protection and serious injuries are increasingly rare.

The facilities in the medical centres everywhere are up to the standards of the best intensive care units, and some of them exceed those standards by adding operating rooms, X-ray machines, laboratory analysis and occasionally a CT scanner. Here, for example, they've got a wonderful X-ray facility. We X-rayed young Rosset's elbow and neck and the quality was such we were confident he hadn't got any bone injury.

He was very shaken. He'd had a big accident; he went in laterally and banged his head very hard on the head and neck protection, and that showed extensive damage from the impact with the helmet. It was quite clear he'd taken a lot of G through his head and although he was not concussed, if he had not had the head and neck protection, I would have expected a serious head injury or neck fracture. The safety precautions worked well. But I felt it would be unwise for him to try again. That was the best advice I could give him and the team. They don't have to follow my advice but they did.

Nelson Piquet famously challenged the Prof.'s judgement after a serious accident at Imola, in 1987. The Brazilian said he was fit to race. The Prof. said he wasn't. The Brazilian protested. The Prof. said if he was fit to race how come he was wearing only one shoe? That suggested he had something wrong with his foot or something wrong with his head. Either way, he wasn't fit to race. He didn't race.

Drivers are fertile ground for medics, physios and the like.

Some drivers have fallen prey to doubtful 'practitioners', acu-
puncturists and dispensers of magic potions. A particularly suspi-
cious 'doctor' was known as 'The Ju-Ju Man'. The Prof. is more
approving of the attention current drivers receive.

> Whenever we get a driver who's had concussion, for
> example, but appears to have laughed off the effects of it,
> and I say I don't think you should drive, the team has
> been very good. Since my role became respectable,
> they've taken the advice seriously. People were wary of
> my role originally. Fortunately, I've never been attached
> to any particular team, and originally I was FOCA, now
> I'm FIA, but I steer an independent course and I think
> have a respectability.
>
> There is a lot of paramedical help, I would phrase it,
> and some of it is entirely appropriate and correct: the
> physiotherapy and the nutritional attention, and the atten-
> tion to proper fluid balance. All these things are abso-
> lutely OK. If the drivers are vulnerable to some people, I
> don't know about it. It's a personal thing between them
> and whoever they've got advising them, and as long as
> they are fulfilling the FIA regulations in terms of health
> and behaviour, then I am happy.

The attention for any driver involved in an accident at a Grand
Prix is assured in moments. Many of the medics are unpaid, as are
the teams of marshals. The Prof. will not necessarily be the first
doctor on the scene.

> In my car we've got a local surgeon, a lady, and the FIA
> anaesthetist, Gary Hartstein, from the University Hospi-
> tal in Liège. In addition there are four intervention
> vehicles around the circuit, staffed by the ONS, which is
> the German safety organisation, with a doctor in each car,
> and there are ambulances around the circuit. We have
> also the spinal teams, who are trained to extricate some-
> body who may have a spinal injury. We have three teams

placed strategically around the circuit. Altogether, apart from the FIA people, there are twenty-five doctors. The chief medical officer is a surgeon, a very experienced motor-racing doctor. The whole organisation makes up a very happy team.

Most of the doctors are voluntary and just get their expenses paid. If you priced this service at x pounds an hour, it would be enormous. They're here from Thursday morning until Sunday night. The exposure on the circuit is very long, particularly when we've got Formula 3000 as well. For example, yesterday I was here at seven o'clock in the morning and left at seven thirty in the evening. I think there are three German neuro-surgeons apart from myself here, so it's a good place if you're brain-damaged. Hakkinen asked me recently if I would like a ride in the two-seater and he would drive it. I said I don't get into cars with brain-damaged drivers.

Johnny Herbert's got a great sense of humour and I had a bit of fun at his expense recently. It was at a golf day the drivers turn up at for the British Brain and Spine Foundation. I was asked to say a few words and talked about a couple of areas where progress had been made, then said we'd made a third fundamental discovery, which was how to grow a brain, and Johnny Herbert was our first example. There was clear evidence of success but the full potential had not yet been reached. He took it well, of course. He's a great chap.

I don't have a problem communicating with the younger drivers. I suppose I haven't grown up yet, either. They look at me in a very fatherly, or grandfatherly, way. Take Rosset yesterday. He wasn't very pleased when I said he shouldn't drive but I said I really had only one function, which was to try and keep him alive. I said I'm actually your father or grandfather in that sense, and he said, 'Yes, I know you are.' I thought that was rather sweet.

With Senna, he had a particularly fond relationship.

I haven't got as close to any other driver. I've got pretty close to Gerhard Berger since the accident, because he was such a good friend of Senna's. He came to the hospital after the accident and he's been on the Advisory Expert Group as the driver representative. He's been enormously helpful, intelligent and practical.

With Senna I think it was just a personality harmony between us. We got on from the first time I saw him in trouble, which I think was in his first year in Formula One. I just liked him and for some reason he liked me. I've not deliberately withdrawn from other drivers since and it wasn't a deliberate thing that I got so friendly with Senna. Had he survived then we would have been very close friends forever.

I didn't want him to race that day, but there was no reason or rational explanation for my preventing him. I was worried about him racing and he thought a lot when I suggested to him he shouldn't race and should even consider giving up altogether. I said to him why don't you give it up. You've been world champion, you're the quickest driver around, you haven't got anything to prove. If you give it up, I'll give it up and we'll go fishing. And then he thought long and hard and said there was no way he couldn't race, he'd got to go on.

My principal regret when I got to the accident and realised how gravely injured he was, that it was going to be a fatal outcome, was that maybe I should really have leaned on him a lot more. Not that he would have taken any notice. I don't think he would have for a moment. There's a limit to what you can do and you have to respect what the other person wants.

He was unique in his interest in the care and treatment of a driver at the scene of an accident, and learned from watching us. It was typical of him to go to Ratzenberger's accident the day before his own. He'd stopped at several other accidents and helped the driver. Erik Comas had an accident at Spa and when I got there Senna had stopped his car, left the engine running, and had taken Comas's helmet off and was holding him correctly by the neck, to make sure his neck was protected. He said he'd also made sure Comas had got an airway and was there any more he could do. I said no, you'd better push off. So he got back in his car. Same with Zanardi's accident at Spa. Senna spun to avoid hitting the marshals and hit the barrier just behind Zanardi's final point of destination, got out of his car and knelt alongside and asked if there was anything he could do.

Schumacher's a great chap but doesn't really show the same interest in this side of things. He's very technical and practical about safety in general, but hasn't shown any great interest in the medical aspects of it. I guess most of them like to shut it out of their minds. I can understand that. But Senna was very analytical.

A lot of people ask me how much longer I'll go on and I really don't know what the answer is. I'm getting on a bit but I do enjoy it enormously. I still enjoy the first lap. It's a question really of agility. As long as I can get in and out of the car and have something to contribute, then I think it's OK. But I do appreciate that many young physicians would like to have my job. They think it's time the old man went, permanently. In the end it's down to Bernie. I say to Bernie, I'll go when you go.

The great bowl of the stadium is full. Out in the forests, too, the spectators have taken their places, 130,000 of them in all. But today something is missing. There isn't the same bravado, the same feeling of destiny in the atmosphere. There is a discernible resignation in the Hockenheimring. Less than half an hour to the start, Schumacher does a lap, returns to the garage and the mechanics swoop on his car in a blur of activity.

On the grid Bernie and family are accompanying this week's VIP guests. Boris Becker is a regular visitor to this race.

Schumacher brings his car into position and now his mechanics are Sellotaping the bodywork. Is his salary such a drain on the budget? He returns from the toilet, waving to the fans, but the cheers are warm rather than fevered. Even a final word from his mother, Elisabeth, a beaming, squat woman in a white jacket, is unlikely to help. That leaves the rain, but a few drops are all the heavens will grant him this time.

He swings around a tardy Wurz at the start and is soon up to seventh, but Hakkinen and Coulthard are away cleanly, first and second, and there they stay. It is formation slaughter. Ralf leads the chase only to be outdone by an ill-advised two-stop strategy. Villeneuve now runs a strong third, Hill fourth, comfortably ahead of Michael, who can advance no further than fifth in the outclassed Ferrari. Ralf is sixth. Takagi finishes 13th.

It has been another wonderful weekend for Hakkinen, who leads the Championship by 16 points, and for McLaren. Villeneuve and Williams have come alive again, and Jordan are up to fifth in the constructors' standings. Hill is rejuvenated. Michael Schumacher gives Hakkinen a congratulatory slap on the arm but the Finn seems scarcely to notice. *Der Meister* could be just another face in the crowd, just another racing driver today. He says he is sorry he could not do better in front of his fans but could not expect a miracle. Things are now difficult yet not impossible. He will not give up. The cynical whisper is Ferrari have been found out, that they were warned of a comprehensive post-race scrutiny and had to make sure their car was legal.

The stadium is empty, the forest silent. And still it is grey and still the sunflowers bow their heads. Perhaps they knew all along.

8

Budapest

PRESSING BUSINESS

The Hungaroring will forever stand as a landmark in Formula One, a roly-poly terrain that welcomed this mobile manifestation of capitalism into the Eastern Bloc. Things have changed since the first Hungarian Grand Prix in 1986, not all for the better, some would argue. The wide-eyed innocence and enthusiasm of the early races have been replaced by hard-nosed opportunism and western decadence. But then who are Formula One people to complain or patronise?

What remains is one of the world's stunning cities, or rather twin cities. Buda rises high above the Danube; Pest stretches across the plain beyond the other bank. Noble buildings, many bearing the scars of history, strike a defiant posture in the maelstrom of modern living. And if the gypsy violins can become a trifle tedious, they provide variation from all those grunting engines.

A 20-minute highway drive out of the city is the circuit, a tame-looking squiggle in and out of the hillocks, which offers little for the purist and still less for the driver with overtaking intentions. Until two years ago the final approach road – make that track – to the circuit was similarly frustrating on race day, snarled up as it was by traffic and further congested by pedestrians. When Bernie Ecclestone, too, was held up, despite the presence of a police outrider, and blew his top, something had to give. Come the next race, guess what? There was a bypass, more than a mile long, for Formula One personnel and guests only. It is called Bernie Avenue.

Some things do not change and this Thursday is as hot as the first Thursday and just about every Thursday since. The combination of temperatures approaching 100°F and 77 laps of this tortuous circuit represents a daunting prospect for the drivers and Finland's hero, Hakkinen, talks of sauna-like conditions and the problems of sweat dripping beneath the visor. Superman Schumacher, never one to miss a psychological points-scoring opportunity, dismissively contends: 'Compared with saloon cars, Formula One cars are air-conditioned.'

An attempt to turn the heat on Schumacher by engaging him in the debate over the legality of the Ferrari stirs the emotions behind the cool front. He maintains he finds it 'silly' that people can imagine he would use an illegal system, because there are too many big players involved in Formula One. For good measure, he reiterates he never used illegal systems, as some suspected, on his way to the 1994 Championship with Benetton, recalling he 'was really upset' by the allegations.

Then how about his prospects for this season? Even his own people have given up on him, he is told. Seventy per cent of those polled by a German publication said they did not now believe he would win the title.

'Public opinion changes,' he responds. 'At the beginning of the season people said I would not be able to win races but I have already won four. We'll wait and see.'

As Rubens Barrichello confirms, he must buy out his contract with Stewart (for a price said to be £2.2 million) if he is to join Williams and contends he is now ready to join a leading team. Schumacher still attracts the photographers' attention by taking a long, deliberate drink from his red bottle. His sponsors just might approve. The consummate professional.

In the shade of the McLaren hospitality area, David Coulthard is emphasising the importance of taking on board fluids before this race. Much has been made in the past of the drink bottle in the car, but Coulthard says: 'You have so little room in the car for a bottle, no more than a mouthful. And in any case if you started with a block of ice, within two or three laps it would be boiling. It's that hot in the car at a place like this.'

Preparation is vital. The team have been testing in similarly stifling conditions at Jerez and he has been training in the heat. Fitness is critical and these days, he contends, Schumacher is not the only driver in excellent physical condition. He has no doubts, for instance, that Hakkinen is fit enough to take on Schumacher if it comes to a head to head in the later stages of this Grand Prix. The cockpit temperature can reach up to 130°F and drivers could lose as much as half a stone in weight.

'Yes, it will be one of the hardest races of the year,' Coulthard says. 'We'll be hot and sweaty and I'd rather be by a pool. But for the last two years we've had the facility at McLaren to test our fitness and we've worked to improve our fitness. You can always be fitter and work even more at it, but I feel as fit as I've ever been.'

Friday morning is cloudy and fresh. The irony is lost on no one sweeping along Bernie Avenue. The man himself arrives in a dark limo which glides through the paddock, headed by a police outrider, and pulls up outside his bus. Bernie's on-site office has been given particular attention here. A light-grey carpet, bordered by potted plants, creates a patio effect in front of the bus. It could be a display at a garden centre. Alongside, red carpets and drapes, and white conical-shaped canopies cannot quite disguise the fact the FIA offices are flimsy sheds. The sleek grey mobile units stand contemptuously across the way.

Within the community they talk of this as a 'Bernie race', referring to his promotional rights. But then they will tell you he has a finger in many if not most of the Grand Prix pies. He is renowned for making governments and conglomerates part with their money. Although much has been made of his digital TV 'gamble', sources close to him suggest he charmed the television companies into funding the venture.

Despite the domestic skirmishes over the share of television fees, you would be hard-pressed to find anyone here who questions that Ecclestone has made Formula One the business and spectacle it is today, to the benefit of everyone involved in it. He has found money for struggling teams and supported individuals in need. He rules and protects his own like a Godfather, and picks up £1 million a week for his efforts. The long-planned flotation of Formula One should make him a billionaire. And yet he retains the accent and hustle of a London barrowboy. According to motor-racing lore, he put his business acumen on track on the back of the 1963 Great Train Robbery. He fields that theory with impish relish: 'There wasn't enough money on that train for me.'

His wheeling-dealing began in his schooldays, buying and selling cakes and pens. He graduated to second-hand motorbikes and cars and developed a parallel love for racing and competition.

'He wasn't brilliant but he wasn't bad and you didn't want to get in his way,' a contemporary says. Ecclestone was always a man on the move and advanced to running teams and drivers, eventually buying Brabham. He united and fought the teams' cause as president of the Formula One Constructors' Association, and now also dons the Establishment hat as vice-president (marketing) of FIA, the governing body. Max Mosley, president of FIA, is the political head of Formula One, but Bernie runs the show.

At the age of 67 he retains an insatiable appetite for the sport and the work. He is fastidiously hands-on and obsessive about order and discipline. He constantly pounds the paddock, a blur of white shirt and dark slacks, scarcely checking his momentum to accommodate a beseeching team member or journalist. Another blur and he is gone, lost behind the darkened windows of his grey bus. The interior, too, is grey, and simple and functional. Not everyone feels comfortable knocking on his door and that probably suits him – 'It's nice to have five minutes' peace now and then.' He rejects any notion he rules by fear, yet admits there has been some dissension in the ranks.

> People don't need to be intimidated by me. I've got an affectionate, sort of Godfather image here. What I try to do is be fair with people. And strict. Because if you let these guys do what they want to do, God knows what would happen. Looking after the little details is important. We are really like a McDonald's franchise: so many chips, so many this, so many that.

People sometimes say I make too much money. I don't know how you can say what anyone's worth, but I'm probably not worth it. I make what I earn, which is what is agreed. Is Schumacher worth what he's allegedly getting? Maybe there's loads of people who can do the job better. People get rewarded on their performance, no matter what they are. If you run a race team you know on the Sunday whether you've done the job right or wrong. I have to wait till the end of the year, when the balance sheets tell me if I've got it right.

People who make that sort of money really and truthfully don't need it and I don't. It's a way of keeping score, to see if you've done a good job. That's the way I see it. I'll never be able to spend what I've earned. I don't spend more than the average man. I don't spend any money on myself. I have a plane, but I couldn't do what I do unless I had my own plane. Sometimes I do three countries in a day.

The biggest problem is we've all come up together. I've been on all sides of the street – team owner, race promoter – so I know everybody's problems. When there's no money involved the family's united. As soon as there's money, members of the family start to think, 'I should have more.' People get a little bit jealous and complain, and it gets a bit more difficult. I've tried to help teams over the years but it's like somebody drowning and screaming for help. You throw the lifebelt to them, then when they get to the shore they say, 'You idiot, you hit me on the head with the lifebelt.' Life is like that.

Any paranoia over Ferrari is understandable. A complicated formula for allocating prize money and funding is based on past as well as present performances and, in recognition of the Italian marque's historical status, they receive what amounts to a support levy from the other teams. Ecclestone makes no bones about acknowledging the importance of Ferrari to Formula One, but this is purely a fiscal consideration and should not be confused with sentiment. Ferrari are still winning races, they are still the biggest draw in the business. Other once mighty teams have faded and disappeared, including Brabham and Lotus and now Tyrrell. Only the strong and commercially viable are welcome. Ecclestone says:

> Teams get rewarded on their performance no matter who they are. If Ferrari are winning they get more than Minardi, and if Minardi happens to win and Ferrari don't then Minardi would get more. It's been difficult to get some motivated enough to get off their backsides. I honestly can't understand why some teams who haven't won in twenty years come to a race with absolutely zero chance of success. They are delighted when they finish. Then there's another group who are delighted when they are in the top ten, and another lot happy to be in the top six. I couldn't run a team like that. I'd rather stop.

Ecclestone's life makes little concession to breaks or holidays. His children Tamara, 14, and Petra, nine, have been more regular visitors to Grands Prix this season.

> I'm always going to take a holiday but I've always got so much to do, so I never take a proper one. I spend any spare time with my kids. Tamara was close to Senna. He would phone up and so on. After he left us, she sort of lost interest in Formula One for a while.

Ecclestone has been accused of insensitivity to the tragedies that have blighted his sport and he found himself at the centre of controversy when he talked of the 'natural culling' of drivers. Those who know him best counter that his unsentimental manner and uncomplicated delivery mask a softer, caring being. Some might refer you to Tony Blair! His generosity apparently did not extend to willingly handing over his wife's £600,000 ring to muggers as they returned home one evening a couple of years ago and he was beaten up.

★ ★ ★

I don't live in fear but when something like that happens to you then you become more cautious. I was a little laid-back before. Now we've put in more security at home. I don't have personal bodyguards. In different countries, yes, you take certain precautions, but normally I don't.

We live in a violent society. In the old days a burglar would come in the house when you weren't there and disappear. Now they want to come with you in the house and they don't care what they do to you. It's not the old-fashioned thief any more. It's a whole different breed. Most of these people are opportunists, snatching handbags and watches, and beating up old ladies of ninety for twenty quid.

The risks of the job he can cope with.

It's exciting. There's always so much to do, new things to do. I still get just as much of a buzz out of it, and what the public want we have to sell. I didn't envisage Formula One becoming as big as it is now. Anybody who sits back and says he predicted this would happen is not really telling the truth. Maybe I got lucky.

I keep saying I'm going to pack in. I'm always going to pack in next year. Next year we'll see. But if I stopped doing what I do I would probably drop dead. I'd die of boredom. I think whoever follows me certainly won't do the job in the same way I'm doing it. I'm an entrepreneur. I fly by the seat of my pants all the time. I'm hands-on all the time. Maybe what will happen is that three or four guys would do what I do in a much more managerial way. There'll be different levels of operating. Maybe it will be better.

Few in Formula One are prepared to bet on that. A control freak he may be, but he is not alone in enjoying luxurious travel and hotel accommodation. The 'working classes' are thankful, too, for jobs and the chance to be part of the show.

Hill, one of the better-paid drivers, is reaffirming his conviction he will be driving for Jordan next season. 'I think they're just waiting to sort out Ralf so they can announce both drivers,' he says. Hill urges Eddie Jordan to keep them together next season, maintaining they are good for each other and the team.

Ralf Schumacher is in the other Jordan motorhome area, trying to fathom his boss's bellowed messages and hand signals. He smiles politely back to the near motorhome. A few minutes later, a plate of muesli is placed in front of Eddie.

'For you Mr Jordan.' Eddie thanks 'Ralf's man' and dutifully wades in.

'It's actually very good. Try some. No, honestly, please.' Unbeknown to 'Ralf's man', Eddie has just devoured a late fry-up, toast and tea. 'Ralf's man' beams from the other side of the rail and Eddie raises his spoon in a gesture of appreciation. The things a team owner has to do. Now he has to talk to Michael Breen, Hill's solicitor, who pulls him just when he's had a stomach full. Another course of negotiations he could probably manage without right now.

At least Eddie's team are on the up. Next door, Alain Prost is solemnly confronting his interviewer, explaining he always said it was going to be difficult, that the team needed time and he is confident improvements will be achieved. Prost are one of only three teams without a point this season. John Barnard is expected to join them and head their design team, but first the Englishman has a legal dispute with Arrows on his hands. Further along the paddock Rosset is assuring anyone interested he is fit to resume. A more sympathetic team member lets it be known the Brazilian visited handicapped children on his arrival here yesterday.

Rain falls on the morning practice session and Michael Schumacher is among those who spin, although he performs a 360 degree pirouette and carries on as if nothing had happened. Hakkinen and Coulthard are fastest, Schumacher is third, Rosset 20th. In the afternoon the track is dry and this time the order at the top is Coulthard, Hakkinen, Schumacher. Rosset is 21st.

Coulthard, Formula One's Man Friday, declares his intention

to sustain his form this weekend but effectively promises to move over, should he be required to, for his team-mate.

'I don't think it would be strange, or unfair, if the team asked me to support Mika, given the position in the Championship,' the Scot acknowledges wistfully. 'Looking at it from the team's point of view, it makes sense. They want a one–two, and they would prefer the one to be Mika.'

Hill has put Jordan in the top six again and Eddie, his marathon breakfast digested, is buoyant. Just the man, perhaps, to confront with the frustrations of those locked outside the cage, the many who pine for closer contact with their idols. EJ acknowledges the problem but points out things have changed since Graham Hill's days. The scale of Formula One now makes it impossible to please everybody all of the time. That said, there should be give and take and it is important to satisfy the ordinary fans.

Ross Brawn, Ferrari's technical director, takes over from Schumacher to contest allegations of cheating.

'You can't defend yourself against an accusation like that, so it's a very nasty, malicious thing to say. If someone says you have a fantastic system that no one can detect, how can you prove them wrong?'

Schumacher, relieved of diplomatic duty this afternoon, is chatting inside the Ferrari compound with his new buddy, Alesi. Soon they are joined by Ralf. Up and down the paddock, little gossip packs are leaning on trucks, sets of tyres and awning supports, exchanging news, views and theories. Down at Alesi's team, Sauber, team-mate Herbert admits he feels he has to move on. He can take no more of the Sauber–Alesi combo. He has given up on Williams so he is pinning his hopes on Stewart.

Formula One folk like to make a fuss over birthdays, espe-cially their drivers' and bosses', and this evening Arrows' staff wheel out the cake and candles for Tom Walkinshaw. The nor-mally laconic Scot, who couldn't repeat what he said to his drivers after their coming together in Austria, is now gleefully relating their latest embarrassment.

It was in Germany, where the drivers had Volvo road cars

equipped with talking navigation gadgets. Salo and Diniz set off from a dinner in Heidelberg for their hotel in Walldorf, some 15 minutes away. An hour later team members were becoming worried. The drivers eventually turned up after an hour and a half. They had dialled into the instrument Waldorf with one 'l' and had been instructed to head in the other direction along the motorway. 'Drivers, heh?' is the burly Walkinshaw's final, taunting comment as Salo and Diniz stare sheepishly into their laps.

Walkinshaw and the drivers depart, leaving the motorhome staff and a few other team members and guests to sing in a new day. Graham, armed with electric guitar, and Tracey Ogden wander down from Ford. Half a dozen from Sauber turn up. One or two others, from Prost and Minardi, take an inquisitive peep as rock classics are given a fearful but enthusiastic mauling. The breakfast cornflakes go flying, the vac is whipped out to remove the evidence and the bopping continues.

'And out there in one of those garages,' someone reminds whoever cares to listen, 'some mechanic is telling his mate to just go up a touch on the settings . . .'

The temperature is up a touch on Saturday morning, although flaky clouds are still defying the sun. On the hills and in the stands, Finnish flags are to be seen in profusion as never before. This is about as close as it gets to a local race for these fans and their man is homing in on the title. The dust won't bother them but shoe-shine boys are on duty to pamper the posh punters of the Paddock Club.

Hakkinen cheers all his followers with fastest time in morning practice, ahead of Coulthard and Schumacher. Hill is sixth and his team-mate, after three spins, is eighth. Rosset is 22nd and last.

Bernie has Stallone on his doorstep again and gets away with a brief encounter. The movie man struts his stuff through the paddock to markedly diminishing interest. Is he *passé*? 'No, just boring,' a presiding judge concludes. Down at Prost they are more concerned with lunch. In keeping with tradition, the tables here always seem to fill up quicker than elsewhere. In the early eighties, long before Ligier became Prost, when the team were up there with Williams, Alan Jones expressed the opinion that if they spent a little less time on their eating and a little more on their racing they might do better.

But even the Brits have to eat and invited guests from Fleet Street, the BBC and specialist magazines turn up at Winfield to find that man Stallone and company occupying their table. Er, excuse me Sly. Huh? Yes, I'm afraid you can't sit there. Huh? Off you go, there's a good chap. Huh? And off he goes. His ego is buffed up again when Alesi comes along to see him and they chat in the front of the Winfield bus. They emerge with matching smiles and handshakes, Stallone wearing Alesi's cap. So that's Alesi in the film then? You could see him as a mini version of Stallone.

Out in the pit lane, minutes before qualifying, it's Hill's turn to be interviewed by Stallone. Presumably Stallone knows his name now. Villeneuve swaggers on to the scene already wearing his helmet. Perhaps he wants to avoid Stallone, or maybe he's just been to the toilet, or could it be he's not happy with his latest hair colouring? It's a sort of auburn, a normal kind of hue.

Out in the stands and along the banks, the blue-and-white flags are fluttering in high expectation. At 13.00 hours the official time screens declare the pit lane open, the signal qualifying can begin. At 13.07 and with no car yet on the track the message reads: the pit lane is definitely open. No one is in a hurry to go out as sweeper on a notoriously dusty track. Fisichella eventually takes the plunge and slides off. Coulthard sets the early pace but Hakkinen outstrips him. Schumacher and Coulthard retaliate and again Hakkinen responds. They will line up: Hakkinen, Coulthard, Michael Schumacher, Hill.

Hakkinen is prepared to go 'flat out' and Schumacher feels he will be strong enough, wet or dry. He is less convincing when challenged by an experienced British freelance journalist, Mike Doodson, over an escapade the previous morning. Doodson has learned Schumacher 'raced' Villeneuve to the circuit, weaving in and out of the traffic, and wonders if such behaviour is compatible with his position as FIA's representative on road safety. The German is boxed in.

'I don't know what you are talking about to be honest,' he mutters. 'For sure, when you go to the circuit you try to sneak through the traffic. I don't think I did anything unreasonable. Were you there? Did you see it?' Doodson wasn't there but his source is sound. 'You see, there is too much gossip around. I don't know who spread this story,' Schumacher comes back. However, he is bright enough to know that won't do. 'It's true that Jacques and I left the hotel at the same time and we arrived at the circuit at the same time. But I don't think we drive exceptionally different from the way the Hungarian people do here anyway.'

That raises a laugh and he is sort of in the clear. There was a time when racing drivers felt they had arrived at the circuit improperly dressed if they hadn't driven in like maniacs. Villeneuve's father, Gilles, would challenge his contemporaries to a hire-car race from hotel to track, and lay down one rule: the accelerator pedal must be flat to the boards for the entire journey. Red lights, traffic queues, little old ladies on pedestrian crossings – no excuse. They would scramble through ditches, up banks and along central reservations, and somehow make it to the circuit in one piece.

In this politically correct day and age and for Schumacher especially, of course, it is a prickly subject. He and Doodson resume their discussion in the paddock and the waspish Schumacher invites his irritant to ride in with him the following morning. Doodson, not a man to look a gift horse in the mouth, accepts.

Hill is revelling in his best qualifying position of the season. This track, he says, provides Jordan with the acid test and today's performance is an indication of the progress made. He doesn't know why this is such a good track for him – he had his maiden victory here in 1993, and has had another win and three second places since – but he cannot expect to be on top of the podium this time. Any place on the podium would be an exceptional result.

Rosset is 22nd and misses the cut for the third time. Now he complains Tyrrell are giving him insufficient attention and concentrating their efforts on Takagi.

And still the Ferrari 'cheating' controversy rumbles on. Ron

Dennis explains McLaren's suspicions centred on Ferrari's braking system rather than any 'traction control' device but mud sticks and the Italian camp are still anxiously engaged in a damage-limitation exercise. Selected journalists are invited into the Ferrari compound to be assured nothing untoward has been going on here. This rather strange departure serves only to deepen cynicism among some in the media centre.

Unlike the majority of national journalists covering Formula One – sportswriters who happened to find themselves here through force of circumstance and may never have seen a Grand Prix before they were sent on this job – most members of the press corps are motor-racing fans, even frustrated drivers. Many have had no formal journalistic training but took up the pen for the vicarious thrill.

Gerard 'Jabby' Crombac has been around longer than anyone. The pipe-smoking 69-year-old still trawls the pit lane for information, which he feeds into the FIA news bulletin and the Japanese market. He has had a number of roles within racing over the past 50 years. He was a friend and confidant of Colin Chapman and Jim Clark, and became recognised as something of an Anglophile. His command of English shames some of the British-born in the paddock. But is he Swiss or French?

I'm Swiss but I consider myself a political refugee in France because Switzerland banned motor racing following the Le Mans crash in '55. Switzerland is ruled by referendum and the people voted against circuit racing. There are only hill-climbs. So I'm in France. I started in motor racing in '48 but not as a journalist. I was doing lap charts in the pits. In '49 I was a trainee racing mechanic, sweeping the floor. Then in '50 the World Championship started and I became *Autosport's* continental correspondent. I also did a few things for a French magazine called *Automobile* and was freelancing for a long time. Then in '62 I started my own magazine, *Sport Auto*.

I keep writing because I love motor racing. Journalism is only a way for me to be in the wake of racing cars. I've done everything in motor racing. I've been an organiser, I've been assistant team manager on several occasions, as well as a journalist, and having tied knots in my career enables me to keep going to race meetings and watching the cars go by. I find that if I stay at home and watch a race not knowing who's got the right tyres and so forth, it's not my cup of tea. And especially if you listen to the commentaries, you find that often they are . . . not very enlightening.

The press side of Formula One has certainly become more competitive but I would say that is simply a reflection of the number of people involved. The more people there are, the more competitive it is. It's the same with drivers. In my starting days, for a driver to be in Formula One he had had, previous to that, to buy himself a sportscar and show he was good enough. Finally he had to buy himself a Formula One car or find a team who would give him a ride. There was no short cut. There were no freebies from karting and so forth. Therefore, these guys were all affluent. The plateau on which you could choose was so much narrower that the quality was lower. Obviously there were some exceptions, the Fangios and the Clarks. But you have a larger choice now, and it's obvious the larger the choice the better is the end product.

Less is written about the actual motor racing nowadays, and for two reasons. One is that a lot of people prefer human stories which are not necessarily related to motor racing. The other reason is that you don't get at the cars any more. In the early days there were no bodyguards at the entrance to the garage, so you'd go in, have a look at the cars, and as there were so few of us you could talk to the engineers and they would say yes, see, I've done this and that this morning, and you could discuss it with them.

Nowadays it's all secretive and you can't get at the car. You can only see the car moving, which is a great disappointment for me. Even when a new car is being introduced, there are clouds of smoke and things, but you don't get close to it. You can't look at it. So, as a result, the new generation of journalists has nowhere to learn and knows nothing about the car. It's frustrating for me. I wish I could look at all the cars, I wish I could talk to the engineers and they would answer my questions, because for me the car is more important than the driver.

I was close to Jimmy [Clark] and to Graham Hill and to Jochen Rindt and to many others because they were my friends. It's not because they were drivers. I can be as close to some journalists because we are in a world living together, sharing cars to go to the circuit, going to the same hotels, the same restaurants. It was the same with Jimmy, with Graham and with Jochen.

It's very difficult now. There are several drivers here to whom I've never spoken, because you can talk to a driver only if you need to do an interview and then you have to go and see his PR people and make an appointment. Now, as I don't do so many driver interviews – I prefer to interview engineers – I don't talk to them. They don't know who I am and to tell the truth I see some drivers and wonder is this Tuero, is this Rosset? It is a completely different world.

I would say there are many things that are better, many things that are worse. This is the pinnacle and now we have the comfort of the press room and you can see the time each lap. In my early days I was doing my own lap chart. At the end of the race you had no press release, you had to go and talk to every driver, every team manager, to find out what happened. It did sort out the men from the boys, I must admit. It's obviously more comfortable now. But what you have lost is the conviviality, talking to the guys, getting close to the cars. It was a very small world and everybody knew each other.

The evenings at the Kyalami Ranch, where everybody was staying in South Africa, were fabulous. Each team had its own table and we were all there. Now they are staying at different hotels and even if they are in the same hotel there's not a party where everybody will have their own table and will be throwing buns at each other, or even live trout from the fish tank as we did at the Hotel de la Ville in Monza. That doesn't exist any more. It was a pleasant atmosphere, which has gone. On the other hand, it's much more comfortable now with much more remuneration.

The commercial scale has not been driven by someone, it is a by-product of television, which has rendered Formula One the most important show in the world. The only audiences that can top it are for the soccer World Cup and the Olympics, which are every four years only. Formula One has fewer viewers but it is on each year. That has created so much interest it is bound to become what it is now. And this is what has created the good and the bad.

It is true there is a feeling sometimes that FIA is trying to have the Championship decided in the last race. I'm not saying they are favouring someone in particular, though maybe they have a weak spot for Ferrari because this is the team which attracts the most interest worldwide. It is the only team that started in '50, not in the first Grand Prix but in the second. It's a by-product of that, and it can't be helped.

I don't say I enjoy it but I don't say I will hold it against anyone. It's normal, considering the amount of money involved. Even the teams which are complaining are heavily funded, and the reason they are so heavily funded is that Formula One has become a tremendous show. If the show was not interesting . . .

I remember when Jimmy won the World Championship at the German Grand Prix. It was August. If it had been the same this year, with Mika becoming world champion at Hockenheim, the rest of the season would have petered out. Television would not have been interested, half the journalists wouldn't have turned up, and therefore the clout of Formula One would have been lessened and the teams which are complaining of manipulation would have fewer sponsors for next year. So we are all rowing the same boat.

Members of the British media with a footballing bent find conviviality at a Budapest restaurant that evening as they herald the start of the season. The barmy army, including ITV's Jim Rosenthal decked in his Oxford United replica shirt, apply the 'we'll hum it – you play it' method to coax the traditional musicians into a rendering of the BBC's *Match of the Day* theme tune, much to the bewilderment of other diners. But then this 104-year-old eclectic establishment survived an attack from Soviet tanks, so they should not be unduly concerned.

Race day and the morning sun is again struggling to penetrate a cloudy resistance. Mika's merry men in blue and white contemplate no such trouble for their leader. The McLaren camp, if not so exuberant, appear equally self-assured.

Doodson has turned up at the media centre a little later than he had anticipated. His lift was booked for 7.45 but the driver didn't show until 7.53. Doodson sat in the back and, he says, appeared to surprise Schumacher by fastening his seat belt. Also in the Alfa Romeo 156 was Schumacher's Indian trainer, Balbir Singh. Doodson reports: 'Of all the world champions I have been driven by – and there have been many – I have to say Schumacher is the most disappointing.'

By that, of course, he means Schumacher conducted himself impeccably. The atmosphere in the car was a mite fresh, if not frosty, and Schumacher told Doodson he felt the press needed to be controlled. He sought to expose the unscrupulous nature of the media by revealing another journalist had informed him that Doodson had lost his driving licence. Doodson said that was not true. Schumacher banked a point. When they arrived at the circuit, Doodson noted Schumacher had been passed by Hakkinen.

The mood at Jordan is decidedly up-beat, although that might have something to do with the photo-shoot being orchestrated before warm-up, as well as Hill's grid position. Model Melinda Messenger is changing into her working clothes in the bus as commercial director Ian Phillips receives assurance everything is ready in the pits.

Phillips, a former reporter and editor of *Autosport*, crossed to the 'other side' with the March team and helped put together the Leyton House Formula One operation. On 2 January 1991, he set out with Eddie Jordan on his Grand Prix adventure.

I realised when I got to this side how little I'd known as a journalist. There's so much that goes on, a lot of which is pure nonsense to be honest because we're all trying to mislead each other. But there is an awful lot going on that just never surfaces, or if it does it's six weeks after it's actually happened.

As far as money is concerned the press are enormously off the mark. We would expect them to be adding noughts because it's good copy but they are over the top with contracts and yes, they are over the top with Damon. [So much for the £5 million man, then.]

The money side is one thing teams do guard and we are constantly reminded by Bernie that Formula One finances have been secret for a long while and that's the way they should remain. A lot of people say it's curious and ask why we don't publish prize funds and this, that and the other, but it's part of the whole mystique of Formula One. That's why the public are kept far away from it, if you like. The few people we bring into a circuit are given access they can't otherwise readily get, which means the value of what we've got goes up.

It does Formula One absolutely no harm if the press give inflated figures but there are occasions when negotiations are very delicate and things get out. I'd love to be able to say honesty is the best policy, but can you actually say to the guys, because of x, y, z this has got to be off the record? I don't think you can. Journalists are in a competitive business and they may feel they have to write about what you've said, but it can be enormously embarrassing when speculative pieces appear in the press.

It can be embarrassing also when a driver publicly airs his dissatisfaction with his car, engine or team.

That certainly doesn't help in any way. You're always under pressure from sponsors and we never like publicly to slag off any of our suppliers. That's an internal matter, it's not for public debate, and I would subscribe to the idea that no team member, from the drivers to the most junior mechanic, should slag off any of our suppliers. Everybody's doing their best. We all make mistakes and public criticism isn't helpful at all, because we're talking about a lot of money from all those people, and their goodwill.

In this paddock you're probably looking at budgets of up to a hundred and thirty million dollars or even as high as a hundred and fifty million dollars at Ferrari – and with Michael Schumacher on board it would need to be that high – and a lowest of about twenty-five million dollars. You'd be hard pressed to do it for less than that. We're in the lower-middle bracket; between forty and fifty million dollars is what we have to achieve.

The biggest drawback for us is that we haven't got to the level where we can go out and play the driver market for both drivers. We're still in the position of having to have a young guy we don't pay anything to, but then if you discover a good guy the problem is you are fighting to keep him. That's the situation we are in and we don't have the financial muscle yet. We're working towards it but you can't spend money you haven't got.

We believe we have to invest in research and development, the design team and the factory. If you've not got performance there's no point in paying for a good driver, so as we've got more money we've put the emphasis on trying to find the performance and strengthening that side of the company. The next step is to make sure we're fully competitive in the driver market.

All of this won't cave in when cigarette money goes. It's fairly inevitable budgets will be reduced but to the outside world nothing will change. I think by that time we will have got to testing bans and things like that and more races. More races means chances to earn more money. You go testing and all you do is tear up hundred pound notes. If it costs ten thousand pounds a mile to run and you run two hundred miles a day, four days a week, it's an awful lot of money. At least when you go racing you are earning.

This side of the fence still fascinates me . . .

He trails off as Melinda Messenger, now just about in a latex outfit in the team sponsor's colours, trips through on her way to the shoot with Hill.

'There's a bit of a wrinkle at the side,' he points out.

'No, there's a rip.'

'Oh,' he says as the shiny curves make for the garage. 'She's such a gorgeous girl. The job does have its perks. Anyway, where were we?

I think the whole negotiating and scheming side of things is fascinating and this goes unseen by outsiders, like planting rumours to upset people or to destabilise them. And the wonderful thing is, you've got Mr Ecclestone, who is as mischievous as anybody but is probably the biggest fan of motor racing, still. I find after thirty years that I wouldn't be too upset if I had to miss a race or two, but that man is an absolute, out-and-out enthusiast.

Nobody should quarrel with how much money he makes out of it. Every single person working in this paddock is earning a living they couldn't get in a normal line of business without him. When I think back to my days as a journalist, you probably had to travel five miles to find a telephone line. There was nothing. Sometimes you had to wait until Tuesday for the results to come out. Now you've got beautiful air-conditioned press rooms and an information flow and all the rest of it. He has made everybody's life easier. And he's very good at getting governments to part with money!

At the end of a race meeting, whatever the result, I find I am absolutely drained. There's so much emotion involved, building up over a period of three or four days. All your emotions are tackled at some stage or another. The two-hour race is just the climax.

First of all you've got to make sure the drivers are happy, and ensure they achieve the balance between what they've got to do on the track and what they've got to do for the sponsors, meeting guests and all the rest of it. Every aspect of it you get involved in. You've got to be alert to the needs of the sponsors and their guests, and so has everybody else in the team.

The mechanics have to be aware of who the important guests are because inevitably they are going to come to the garage and be in the way. But it's part of what we do – sell them the opportunity of a lifetime to go and stand in the garage. You may have a panic on but you can't afford to have a mechanic turn round and push a visitor out of the way or be rude to him, which in the heat of the moment could happen . . .

He is distracted again as the shiny curves come back into view.

'Have we got a little problem here?'

'They're splitting. Damon just put his hand there.'

'Oh, right,' Phillips says and chuckles approvingly.

Phillips and Eddie Jordan operate as a double act in pursuit of sponsorship, and results improve their powers of persuasion.

It is very competitive out there and at the end of the day it's performances that count. Eddie and I have a telepathic

understanding of dealing with situations and presenta-
tions. The business side is almost straightforward. None
of that will work if the human relationship isn't right and I
think our strength is Eddie's ability to charm the birds out
of the trees, then I go in and make it work, basically. I
make sure the nuts and bolts are tight on the deal.

I think there is a certain buzz here in our team and
we're proud of it. I hope we never lose it. I think we've
become . . . I don't want to say more serious because
we've always been serious about wanting to succeed. But
we've matured and added a bit more professionalism to
what we do without, I think, losing any of the company's
charm in doing so. I guarantee as long as Eddie Jordan
owns the company it won't change because that's his
character. The responsibility may fall on others of us to be
a little tougher on occasion, but there will still be Eddie
everybody can go to.

EJ is also perceived as a man who likes money and may not have
quite the focus to reach the top of the Formula One league.

Yes, he has a certain reputation, but people have short
memories. They forget that the people who brought him
success in the eighties, before he came into Formula One,
like Johnny Herbert, Jean Alesi, Martin Donnelly, hadn't
got a bean. Now, he might have robbed a man from Outer
Mongolia who was never going to achieve anything,
persuading him to pay double for the pleasure of racing in
the British Formula Three Championship but by doing
that Eddie was able to make Herbert the champion. There
isn't anything wrong with that. He's quite happy to say to
him 'I robbed you' and the guy never complained.

To say he likes the money too much, well. To set up
this company, Jordan Grand Prix, in the middle of 1990
to go racing in 1991, in the midst of the deepest recession
the world has probably ever known, he put up every
penny, every bit of brick and mortar he and his family

owned. The bank owned his home. It took four and a half years for him to get that back. That's a risk a lot of people wouldn't take. He was quite comfortable, he could have carried on the way he was, but he had an ambition. He risked everything.

If he was to reinvest his original stake in the company, it would be swallowed up in three months. So what's wrong with him having his money back and earning a living? Unfortunately the myth of Eddie Jordan gets confused with what is the reality at Jordan Grand Prix as a serious company. He doesn't do anything to dispel the myth, but the reality is he could have cashed up and gone away and left us a long time ago. He could cash it in and retire. He's got a good company which is probably worth a few quid now.

But Eddie still wants to succeed. He is driven on by the fact he wants to succeed. We're in our eighth year of Formula One. Remember it took Williams eleven years to win a race. Benetton won two races in twelve years. We've built a solid company, as Frank did over a period of time, as Benetton, evolving out of the ashes of Toleman, did. It takes time. We've seen the super teams come and go, open chequebook racing and all the rest of it. They all disappeared in the space of three years. During the time Jordan have been in Formula One, sixteen teams have disappeared.

Eddie is the last true privateer who will survive in Formula One. No individual will be able to put down his worldly goods of two and a quarter million or whatever it was and enter Formula One. It just isn't possible any more. He's the last guy. Sauber have come in since and survived, but for three years they were bankrolled by Mercedes. It wasn't the same deal at all. Jackie Stewart had the backing of Ford. We had nothing. We paid for everything.

I think if we're patient we can go all the way. It is down to money. But we make a little money go a long way. If we get to within twenty-five per cent of the sort of money McLaren or Ferrari would spend, we could do the job. I've no doubt about that at all.

Phillips moves to the next table and greets two more of his team's 'important guests'. While mechanics and engineers prepare their cars for the track, the business activity continues back here. Along at Ford, Martin Whitaker, head of the company's European motorsport operation, has a visit from Benetton boss David Richards. Benetton have been linked with Ford on and off all season and Richards' Subaru rally team recently lost Colin McRae to Whitaker's camp. The latest theory is Benetton will be powered by Ford in the year 2000.

Another visitor to the Ford compound raises eyebrows all round. The black figure must be seven feet tall and asks for Jackie Stewart. The wee Scot peers up from his caller's navel. A diligent journalist asks the woman accompanying the mystery man who he is. 'That's my son,' she declares. He is, in fact, Brian Williams, a basketball player with Detroit Pistons. Colin Jackson, in Budapest to go for gold in the European Athletics Champion-ships, is a guest at McLaren. Merlene Ottey, here in an ambassa-dorial capacity, has evidently developed an appetite for Formula One and lunches at Sauber. Presumably there are no vacant places at Prost.

Hill is among the first to park his car on the grid and he whiles away the time sitting on the wall with Jackson. A crescendo of cheers and jeers and horns signals Hakkinen's arrival. He cuts his engine and has to be pushed by his mechanics through the mêlée. An even noisier mixed reception warns of Schumacher's approach. He, too, turns off the power but judges his freewheeling momen-tum perfectly to carry him into his slot unaided.

Stallone, still wearing Alesi's cap, is playing photographer, and for the photographers. The smile slides from his face when someone calls out: 'Hey, Slyvester.' The din of a kasbah seems a more appropriate soundtrack for this chaotic scene than the funereal strains of the Hungarian national anthem, now being piped into the atmosphere.

Hakkinen and Coulthard conduct a familiar refrain at the start of the race. Schumacher is in tune but misses a beat after his first pit stop and finds himself behind Villeneuve. Schumacher makes an early and brief second stop, Coulthard is sent in to cover but McLaren have been outwitted. When Hakkinen emerges from his second call the Ferrari is in front. Worse still for Hakkinen, he begins to slow. Coulthard takes up the chase but Schumacher is streaking away. Even a minor off at the last corner cannot prevent the German from making time and more for a third stop. One of his greatest victories is secure. Hakkinen nurses his sick car in sixth.

Fans spill on to the track and Schumacher tells of how they tapped his emotions. He dreamed of something like this but thought it could only be a dream. He reveals how Ross Brawn improvised with a three-stop strategy and instructed him to open a gap of 25 seconds in 19 laps. 'I said thank you,' he grins. The astonishing effort has reduced the Championship deficit to seven points and he has not a bead of sweat to show for it. Coulthard looks devastated physically and psychologically. Hill admits his drive to fourth place has left him exhausted. Frentzen, troubled by a virus all weekend and badly dehydrated after finishing fifth, is on his way to hospital.

It is a sultry late afternoon and the blue-and-white flags have disappeared beyond the horizon. Hakkinen, after a shower and soothing words from his boss and his wife, puts on a philosophical front.

'You have your ups and downs in motor racing . . . One point is better than no points because at the end of the season that could be important . . . This result has made the Championship more exciting.'

No one is more aware of that than Bernie. His bus is on the road again. He is not at the wheel, it can be confirmed.

9

Spa-Francorchamps

BEAUTY OF THE BEAST

It is simply the greatest circuit of them all, perhaps the last real circuit; a throwback to the days of road circuits and cars with no wings. If the old Nurburgring, just over the border in Germany, was the biggest and most ferocious beast, the original Spa wasn't far behind; and unlike the new Nurburgring, the modern version of Spa, although barely half its former length, has retained its characteristic claws. At 4.3 miles, it is still the longest on the current tour.

The approach to Spa and the village of Francorchamps prepares no one for the beast lying in wait. Belgium is generally an underrated country and the Ardennes a largely undiscovered gem of dark forests and green valleys. Immaculately maintained stone houses and gardens give off an air of dignity and hard-earned comfort. The nation's reputation for chips and chocolate is justified yet the wider gastronomic delights may surprise the first-time visitor. Spa itself is teeming with restaurants as well as water and the finest of all is L'Auberge. Minardi may not have the resources of Italy's premier Formula One team, but they know their food and they stay here every year for the Belgian Grand Prix.

The nearest point of the circuit is some ten minutes away, on the edge of Francorchamps. From there it carves through the forests and sweeps into the valleys. Its beauty and challenge are unsurpassed. The high-speed corners are awe-inspiring in the best of conditions, terrifying in the worst. Eau Rouge is the most fabled and feared of them all. The cars plunge down a hill, flick left, then flick right and make the steep climb up out the other side – at 180 mph. What makes Spa still more daunting is the capricious nature of the climate, its propensity for change from brilliant sunshine to torrential rain and back again in minutes, or from one section of the circuit to another. Low cloud can shroud the higher parts, reducing visibility to a few yards. The elements of intimidation serve merely to enhance the mystique.

This Thursday offers a typical meteorological mix and the campers in the fields and in the forests have come prepared. Huge plastic sheets are suspended over barbecues and tables. Spectators and team personnel alike are wrapped in gear more familiar at rallies than Grands Prix. Martin Pople, the truckie-tyreman-rig designer who moved from Arrows to BAR, is wearing jacket and tie for his fact-finding mission. He and his party are particularly interested in the new West motorhome, a double-decker monster to match McLaren's. The conventional Mercedes bus, parked between them, is dwarfed.

The top teams have chosen central pitches in this paddock, thereby reducing the walk to the steps which lead up to the elevated pits area. Jordan are at one end, which perhaps suits them this weekend. It has emerged they are involved in a legal dispute with Ralf Schumacher. The team contend they have a valid contract for his services next year; he and his management maintain he is free to leave and join Williams. The case has gone to the High Court.

A member of the Ferrari staff is trying to fathom the weather. 'When I arrived here yesterday,' he is telling a later arrival, 'it was blue. After an hour it was black, absolutely black.' Johnny Herbert, an ever more regular visitor to Ford, has turned up in an anorak with the flag of the Union emblazoned on the back.

Mika Hakkinen, now defending a seven-point lead, has learned since Hungary that the front anti-roll bar of his car came adrift in that race, jamming one of the suspension pushrods. The most important thing, he stresses, is that he still has the advantage. Spa? It's fantastic to drive, of course. Damon Hill willingly joins the fan club. Everybody gets excited coming to Spa, he says. But what about the weather?

'You have to have a good weather forecaster,' Hill advises,

tongue in cheek. 'I first raced here in Formula Three in 1986 and it's rained every time I've been here. Last year we nearly got away with it. Then, when we were sitting on the grid – bang. Down it came. The truth is no one seems to know what the weather is going to do here. I think the best thing is to use seaweed.'

Hill is in good heart, a reflection of his form on the track of late. However, he and all-comers are upstaged by Heinz-Harald Frentzen, now recovered to tell the tale of his moving experience in Hungary. In graphic detail.

'I had to go to the Williams toilet every five minutes,' he says. 'I had to take my mobile with me. We did some analysis in the toilet and it did not look very nice. I made the decision to go to the hospital after the race. Afterwards we discovered I had some salmonella.'

Who says the Germans have no sense of humour? Michael Schumacher, reduced to near convulsions of laughter, cannot resist getting in on the act and has a weather experience to relate. His team's forecaster said it would be fine, and it rained . . . Stick to the driving, Michael. He has a more serious offering on his brother's situation, maintaining, 'Ralf has several options and will take the one that is right for him,' while acknowledging the credentials of a 'very experienced' Williams. He is caught off-guard when asked about Ferrari's 600th race. He clearly is under the impression that landmark is to be reached at Monza, not here. The celebrations, appropriately, are to be held at the Italian Grand Prix, but this is the actual 600th, he is assured.

Schumacher prefers to regard the anniversary as motivation rather than pressure. In any case, this is his spiritual racing home, a short trip from the family base in Kerpen. It is the scene of his debut, his maiden win and wins in the last three years. He was first across the line in 1994 also, but disqualified because his Benetton was deemed illegal.

'In certain years I have had a lot of luck and fantastic races and things have come together,' he says.

Things are coming together in the paddock, now that the rain has receded. Bernie Ecclestone nips through almost unnoticed, dressed in civvies of checked shirt and light, casual trousers.

Philippe Streiff's presence in a wheelchair is a reminder of the price some pay in pursuit of their dreams. The amiable Frenchman broke his neck in a crash during pre-1989 season testing. He greets every glance with a warm smile as he is guided towards the Williams motorhome.

The awning is unzipped on a boisterous scene. The focus of the noisy attention is the latest French edition of *Playboy*, which features a regulation female and an apparently enthusiastic new playmate, Jacques Villeneuve, the latter respectably attired of course in his working gear. He even took his car along for the shoot. Couldn't have had anything to do with the sponsors, could it? The Canadian sits at a table, protesting, 'It's a tough job.'

At the far end of the hospitality area Frank Williams is in his stand-up harness, telephone headset on, talking to someone back at the factory. No one should doubt he is still on top of the job, and the job is going well after a torpid start to the season. He looks better, too. But then self-pity has never been on Williams' agenda. He put his fateful accident down to driver error. Never could resist a corner. Now get on with it. Today's message is the same.

'We're getting back to where we'd like to be because the car's faster,' he says in a matter of fact way that renders all else irrelevant. He does, however, go on: 'We made modifications to the car before Magny-Cours and we've made some very good progress in the last couple of races,' which represents the best kind of response to early season criticism of the team. 'We don't respond to criticism,' he maintains sharply. 'It doesn't hurt me because I never read it. The guys are all grown men, they know they are there to do the very best job they can and that's what they try to do. Sometimes we are successful at it; sometimes we're not. It's called competition. Talk is cheap. The only thing that really matters is action: achievement and progress, or the opposite.'

It is widely held that Williams' lack of achievement this year is due in no small measure to the defection of Adrian Newey to McLaren.

'That was a long time ago. People perhaps forget that despite

Adrian's absence from the previous November, of '96, we won two titles last year. I guess people only see what they want to see.'

People see a team with a propensity for losing their world champions, and perceive that talent drain as mismanagement or misjudgement which besmirches Williams' reputation. Nelson Piquet, Nigel Mansell, Alain Prost and Damon Hill all departed, for various reasons, as title holders. At least Villeneuve has stuck around for another season. Frank's ire suggests a contradictory view.

'That's an extraordinary . . . We've not lost Jacques. People decide to do their own thing. Think of all the Championships we've won. That's what we should be talking about rather than . . . Oh dear, give me the gun, Hamish . . .' Hamish, his nurse, catches the mood.

'We've had to take his shoelaces away,' he says dryly.

Frank resumes: 'People can say what they like. We just do our business, doing the best for the team. Sometimes we keep these guys, sometimes they decide to go, or we decide we'd rather go somewhere else. This is what competition or business is all about.

'Jacques is leaving us, we're disappointed, but there's no hard feelings or bitterness. We made him an offer which was clearly not the offer he was looking for, and he chose to go elsewhere for his own reasons, and I respect those reasons. He's a racer. He's a fantastic competitor and we love him. He's very welcome back at this motorhome any time he likes. And that's how it should be.'

Relations were patently less cordial when Hill was sacked as he closed in on the 1996 Championship, and both parties acknowledge they are unlikely to join forces again. But Williams now proffers an olive branch.

'There's probably no prospect of Damon driving for us again in the near future. But whilst we had a bit of a hiccup at the end of '96, which left him feeling very disappointed, human beings work out things and as time goes by enmity or any acrimony tends to disappear. I don't see much of Damon but there's no bad feelings on our side and I hope there isn't on his. We'd never let emotion get in the way of good judgement.'

Williams' disability is said to have undermined his position with engine partners Honda and ultimately led to their separation at the end of 1987. Others have found strength and inspiration in Williams' determination to carry on his racing life and achieve still further success. Wayne Rainey, the former world motorcycle champion, paralysed in 1993, has told of the motivating influence Williams had on his new challenge as a team owner.

'Wayne, bless him, was probably exaggerating. I don't know if I was an inspiration but it's a nice compliment. All I said to him was this will be your problem, the first year or two is always the most difficult, but it will get better, easier. It was just inside-track information for a man new to walking down this particular road.'

Even given Williams' resources, the best of care and a racing obsession to cling to, his plight is unimaginable to any able-bodied being. However, he vehemently refutes any notion it was a fight he was not willing to take on.

'No way did I get depressed. Never, ever. Over my dead body. Fortunately I'm too busy and I'm still loving it. I enjoy everything about it, the paddock life, the chat, the lot. If I didn't I'd get Hamish to put a little tent around me, zip it up and not let anybody in. My job is to try and represent the team in a straightforward and evasive manner,' a grin now appearing on his face. 'But I never give misinformation.'

Then what's the latest on the driver front?

'We're still looking to September. We want to announce both drivers at the same time. There are a number of drivers, including Heinz-Harald, who are possibilities.'

The rain has returned but the forecasters say it will be gone by race day. No one is convinced.

A cool, damp Friday morning discourages early activity in the forest camp sites. A 'Parking Full' sign confirms Schumi's Army are here in strength, but they are not quite ready to venture forth. The paddock is similarly docile, easing into the day and the gossip. Renewed speculation about Stewart's future is helping raise the temperature around the tartan camp. Jackie is adamant he is not about to sell his team to Ford or anyone else.

'I hear I'm rich but it's not so. I'm building up a business here;

it's going to be Paul's. I'm not interested in selling. There's no drama. I'm here to stay for some time yet. What we are doing is having more involvement with Ford and some of their people are working with us. But that's as it should be.'

He reiterates, for good measure: 'There's no chance of Benetton getting Ford's best engines in 2000. If Benetton do a deal for that year they would have to have '99 engines.'

Whatever his prospects for a factory deal, David Richards has secured some ties with Ford by winning the contract for his Prodrive operation to run the company's British Touring Car Championship campaign. As for Ford's ambitions to take over a team, an insider argues they would be better advised to look elsewhere. They have, indeed, been linked also with Benetton and Jordan.

Ralf's man is on the move again, plate of muesli topped with slices of strawberries in hand. This time he has the long walk from the Jordan motorhome to the pits, where Schumacher is presumably locked in a technical meeting with his engineers.

The opening meeting with the beast passes without serious incident. Hakkinen has a spin but a gentle landing and is fastest in the session. Hill returns to base for a break with a photographer frantically back-pedalling in front of him, firing his camera barely six inches from the driver's nose. Hill never flinches nor checks his progress and maintains his momentum in the afternoon session, finishing fourth behind Michael Schumacher, Hakkinen and Coulthard. Sixth is Villeneuve, despite a spectacular off attempting to take Eau Rouge flat. He loses control on the rise at 180 mph and ploughs into a tyre-cushioned barrier.

'That had to be my best shunt since I came into Formula One,' a smiling and unhurt Villeneuve says at the back of the Williams garage. 'It was down to me. You can take the corner flat, or just about, if you get it right. This time I didn't get it right. As I went into the barrier I thought, "Ooh, this is going to hurt." But I'm OK.'

Along at Jordan, Hill believes it is no longer possible, or at any rate sensible, to take Eau Rouge flat.

'Jacques tried it and look what happened to him. He's a lucky boy. I knew he'd be proud of that. You have to take this track by the throat and it's difficult because these cars are sliding around so much.'

Jean Alesi, likening Villeneuve's accident to Alex Zanardi's here in 1993, and Michael Schumacher commend the safety measures that have protected the Canadian.

Martin Whitaker has Ford's reputation to guard and stresses complacency at Stewart will not be tolerated. However, as much as he would welcome a second front-line team, his hands are tied for another two years.

'It's not a question of our pushing them,' Whitaker says. 'They need to push themselves. The leadership of Stewart Grand Prix knows well enough what it has to do. I believe there are advantages in having two teams, somewhere down the line. Internal competition is good. But right now we don't have that intention.'

After an uncertain and unsmiling start to the season, Alesi is winning his internal competition with Herbert. The sparkle is back in those blue eyes and, between the eruptions, he again radiates his boyish charm. Like Hill, he is enjoying every facet of his renaissance. He obliges a couple of Sauber guests by signing their caps as he talks.

For me it was extremely difficult at the start of the season because I didn't test and with a new team there are always problems. But race by race we have made improvements and we should have a minimum of five points more – from the races at Monte Carlo and Silverstone. I feel more motivated now but it is a team that gives you motivation because they are nice, nice people. When I am not making points here I am so sorry because they deserve points.

I asked about the situation at Ferrari but it was probably not the right moment and they are fighting for the Championship and don't want to change anything. But it's not true I could not get on with Todt. He is a very intelligent person and he forgives me for what I said. Every time I see him I say, 'Sorry, Jean,' because I know I was not right with him, but when it happened it was not a good moment for him or for me. For him because he told the team we had to change everybody and he still found things difficult, and with me because I believed so much in him I asked too much, and then we fight.

For sure I am more mature now but still the same person inside and it's because I drive with passion. I need that. I have this passion for the good results and also the bad results. When something is bad for me I suffer, but when it's good I feel so much better.

As his bust-up with Herbert and subsequent withdrawal of the 'him or me' ultimatum illustrated?

Exactly. Because the race after that I went to Sauber and said sorry. I did say that and it was in the newspapers and it made trouble for Sauber. I said that was what I felt at the time but now it's past. With a team-mate it cannot be a dream non-stop. There are good moments and bad moments. I was extremely unhappy about Silverstone, but if Johnny is my team-mate next year I will be happy. I have no problem.

Of course Berger grew accustomed to the 'nuclear explosions'. Alesi laughs and acknowledges his old partner's observation.

Yes, but you know ever since I have been doing my job my father said to me, always when you go to work, leave your character at home. Just go and be professional. It was not so easy. But always when I have my nuclear explosion, like Gerhard said, it starts from something. It doesn't start because I didn't make love the night before!

Alesi is French by place of birth and speaks Italian with a distinct French accent, but that character his father warned about is the pure Sicilian of his parents. His Christian name is actually Giovanni. Alesi, 34, now lives near Geneva with his Japanese wife and their child, but he has roots old and new in Avignon;

such as his precious collection of cars, including a 1932 Rolls-Royce Phantom II, a vineyard and his latest venture, an olive grove.

I became Jean when I was eight or ten because at school it was difficult. Now it's not a problem but twenty years ago the people were . . . not racist, but it was French people, France, Italian people, Italy. When you crossed the border it was quite something, and now it's nothing. I was born in Avignon and of the Alesi family only my brother and sister were also born in France. All the others in the Alesi family are Sicilian.

Usually with my cars I say OK, I have some fun then I sell it, but there is one car I will have forever, if God wants. That is my first car, which I have had since I was seventeen, my Fiat 500.

The vineyard is going well. Before coming here I stopped there to check the grapes. I think it is going to be a good wine. But you have to wait because you never know in this business. It is so interesting. You can change the quality of the wine so much if you do your job well. The other thing I will do is olive oil. I have a hundred and twenty trees of fifty to seventy years. I think it will be very good oil.

This will be part of my future, with racing. One day I will have to stop driving but I want to stay in racing in some way. I don't think it will be running a Formula One team. Alain is having a bad experience! But for sure I have a few more years racing. I really believe in the quality of the work. If I work as I am doing I think it will pay off. I train more than ever and I am happy with my driving. I want to continue working hard and improving the Sauber next year.

But you cannot predict far ahead in Formula One. I still dream and maybe I should be at the front. I think some people misunderstand me. For sure some have a wrong opinion of me because they hear wrong things about me and because when I was with Ferrari the team was not like the team is now. When I was there they were rebuilding everything, and the problems I had were unbelievable. Now it is completely different. They have the reliability and are probably the best team.

Schumacher is booked for a series of interviews with an international array of television companies this afternoon and the crews queue patiently outside the Ferrari media bus for their turn. An opportunistic German hijacks Hill on his scooter and bags a two-minute bonus. Schumacher agrees to give a final, unscheduled interview on the hoof as he makes for the garage to see the troops. It is six thirty.

Saturday morning is cold and drizzle hangs in the air. Enterprising locals are beckoning cars into carefully taped off parking areas in their fields and backyards. According to the temperature read-out on the circuit tower it is 13°C. The works must have frozen. It can scarcely be 3°C.

Practice generates a little warmth and from Minardi at one end to Williams at the other, technicians are staring at screens at the back of the garages, monitoring the heartbeat of their cars. A small but unequivocal message discourages casual visitors to Prost: 'Accès Sur Invitation'. Jordan and McLaren have canopies suspended between their trucks, covering their tyres. In Hungary they provided shelter from the heat; here they provide shelter from the rain. McLaren have a doorman who might have stepped straight from Jaeger's shop window. A staffman in an anorak, loitering behind the FIA weighbridge, cannot stifle a yawn.

Late in the second half of unofficial practice the sun at last makes a partial appearance, just in time to illuminate another spectacular accident at Eau Rouge. Mika Salo goes off further down the hill than Villeneuve, thumps the barrier, and bounces out into the middle of the circuit, where the car rotates wildly. Again, remarkably and mercifully, the driver walks away from the wreckage.

Other drivers watch the pictures, expressionless, from their cars, as Prof. Watkins and his crew arrive on the scene and have Salo taken to the medical centre. From there he is sent to hospital for a brain scan and observation. Charlie Whiting, the race director, leads the inspection of the scene. The five rows of tyres are re-positioned in front of the barrier and the road is swept. The trackside and car-safety precautions have passed the test again. The drivers resume practice as if nothing has happened. Ville-neuve is actually racing Ralf Schumacher through Eau Rouge. A more circumspect Hill is still third fastest behind the McLarens.

At lunchtime Prof. Watkins reports: 'Salo's just got a head-ache. We've sent him to hospital to see if there's a clot inside as well as outside.' He knows he can afford to joke. But for the car's head restraints, which are reduced to powder, the Finn would have broken his neck or worse.

Eddie Jordan is obviously pleased with himself, relating a *tête-à-tête* he had with Michael Schumacher the previous evening. Schumacher was reported recently as not only reiterating his belief that Ralf's career would be better served by moving to Williams, but also echoing the popular contention that Jordan is a mite too fond of the money to achieve ultimate success.

'I went over to Michael in the restaurant and had a right go at him,' Jordan says. 'The Schumachers are the last people who should be calling me a money-grabber. We gave both of them their chance in Formula One. I told Michael he should keep out of Ralf's business. He may say he's been misquoted but he didn't have it in him to come over to me and apologise. Things are sorted now though and are a hundred per cent OK with him.'

Things with Ralf are clearly not 100 per cent and Eddie is considering his options. Takagi is on the market, complete with in-built Japanese link to suit Mugen-Honda. However, it is thought he could take Herbert's place at Sauber, and the word is Diniz, armed with his father's supermarket millions, could be top of EJ's shopping list.

All this hustling is a thing of the past for the tall figure exchanging warm greetings with Alesi. Ken Tyrrell is making a rare appearance in the paddock and has no shortage of fussing attendants. As yet he has not been sighted with Craig Pollock.

'It was all a bit sad the way it ended because they promised to fund the team properly in its last year,' he says. 'It's not good for them to take a pay driver, and everyone knows Rosset's record.'

Tyrrell is here as a fan, with his wife Nora, watching from a stand overlooking Eau Rouge.

'It's frightening. All those years stuck up on the pit wall you've no idea what it's like out on the circuit. Even the cars coming straight out of the pits go through Eau Rouge at an unbelievable speed. Salo's accident was very strange, to go off where he did.'

The latest paddock wildfire story has BAR on the trail of Nigel Mansell, who is now 45. Apparently it was lit by a mischievous journalist. But then anyone can drop a match here and be caught up by the flames before too long. It is a game many delight in playing.

Celebrities are scarce here. Hardly surprising given the inclement weather. It would take someone nuts – on racing that is – to brave the elements. Isn't that Mr Bean over there? Graham Ogden, in short-sleeved shirt, is grateful for the autumnal nip.

'It's nice to get out here for a minute and cool down,' he says, standing at the front of the Ford bus.

Ken Tyrrell is in position to see qualifying and here no one is playing games. The familiar trio lead the way and even Ville-neuve's extravagant effort cannot make an impression on them, although it does meet with the nodding approval of his boss. Any change in the order will have to be achieved on the final run. Hakkinen stays in front, Coulthard second and now Schumacher has to fend off Hill for third. They jockey for track position, neither wanting to be compromised. Schumacher gets his clear lap, so does Hill, and it's the Jordan that finds the crucial extra pace on the last sector to go third. Hill and Jordan are still in the ascendancy. Salo, cleared to drive, qualifies 18th and Rosset is 20th.

Hakkinen makes a show of taking his hat off to Hill, whose mood is still reflecting his driving. He says, without a trace of arrogance, he is driving beautifully, and he is. Beating Schumacher makes it all the more satisfying.

'He is the acknowledged expert around Spa so it's good to outqualify him,' says Hill, who ruffled a few feathers by publicly agitating for improvements to the car and engine. Now he feels vindicated. 'I've had experience of good cars and was able to tell them what was wrong, and at last the penny's dropped.' Tomorrow he confronts not only the top men in the Championship but also the beast of Spa.

'It's a big boys' track. it tests your nerve and always at the back of your mind is that it's not a place to trifle with. You can't take liberties. There's a macho thing about being the fastest man through the world's most dangerous corner, but the most important thing is the overall lap time and winning the race. I'm not going out for a Sunday afternoon's drive. We've given ourselves a good opportunity of making the podium and there's always a chance of getting something better.'

Schumacher is subsequently stripped of his best time for not observing a yellow warning flag but the starting order is unchanged. While Schumacher and company have been going about their business on the track, security officers have been about theirs off it. A bomb threat, ostensibly by Moslem extremists bent on retaliation against recent US attacks, is not causing deep concern. More police, many of them plain-clothed, and dogs are being deployed but the head of security is content to let it be known he has brought his family to the circuit.

Salo has survived death threats, the stigma of a drink-drive offence, a running feud with his hometown adversary, Hakkinen, and myriad setbacks in his career, so you would expect him to take a brush with Eau Rouge in his stride. He is dining at L'Auberge with a small party that includes his Japanese girlfriend and his British manager, Mike Greasley. He has a bit of a headache, yes, and little wonder. He must have been dizzy. But what about that shunt?

'I've not seen it yet but it was better than Jacques', wasn't it? When the car stopped spinning I noticed red on my glove, up my arm, and it was also on my helmet. It was from the painted tyres.'

You can only imagine the fright that gave the rescue crew. Salo has the bravado of most drivers yet strikes you as a regular

sort of guy. There is nothing regular about starting your Formula
One career in defiance of warnings that it could cost you your life,
and we are not talking accidents here. Salo revealed this bizarre
scenario to his closest confidants and was convinced of a link with
another driver. That episode is now consigned to a dark and
distant past. More recent intelligence suggests he could be in the
frame at Williams, should Schumacher elude them.

Fine weather was promised for race day but the telltale swisssh
of cars passing L'Auberge greets the Minardi crew down to
breakfast. Esteban Tuero sits at the table like a tortoise, his
head peeping out of his anorak just far enough to munch a
croissant. 'Lucky it's not raining,' one of his team says with
heavy sarcasm, waiting for a colleague to bring their car to the
door of the hotel.

The locals really have got this car-parking business sorted.
The parks are numbered and a bus service has been laid on to
some of the more remote outposts, an especially good deal on a
morning like this. A patchwork of umbrellas stretches across the
open stands and hillsides. The Dekraheads – the in-house term of
contempt for Schumi fans wearing the cap of his long-standing
sponsor – are wallowing in the wet. This is playing right into the
hands of their man.

A Dekrahead with an air-raid siren warns of approaching
cars, about to swoop down the hill towards Eau Rouge at the start
of warm-up. In a moment they are climbing up the other side and
disappearing in the spray and fog. Coulthard fails to complete the
half-hour session, and seems none too upset to abandon his car in
a tyre barrier. Schumacher is fastest.

Persistent drizzle is like a wet blanket thrown over the
paddock. Two Jordan girls emerge from the row of zipped-up
awnings with a supermarket trolley of provisions. They cover it
with a plastic bag and make for the pits. Another batch of the
team's 'important guests' bound into the hospitality area and
spread themselves across most of the tables and chairs.

Also here is Michael Breen, Hill's solicitor-manager, steering
the driver through what he maintains is the formality of

confirming his employment with Jordan for another year. Belfast-born Breen is a partner in a firm of solicitors in Gray's Inn Road, London, and has represented Hill since the early days of their respective careers. Mark Blundell, now competing in the CART series, was another of 36-year-old Breen's clients.

At the time I was doing Mark's and Damon's contracts it looked like Mark was going to be the force in Formula One and Damon perhaps not. But I think it's just the roll of the dice and the drives people get in motor sport. I do a lot of sports law generally. My firm acts for the British Cycling Federation, and I've done work for rugby clubs and other well-known sports personalities like Linford Christie, Colin Jackson, Sally Gunnell and Lennox Lewis.

Formula One is significantly different in one way. There are large sums of money involved with which there isn't any comparison in other sports. The amount of money involved in rowing, for instance, is pitiful. I've also been trying to advise Steve Redgrave and his management with regard to getting more revenue. He's a four times Olympic gold medallist but he's never really got paid for it.

Because there's more money involved in Formula One people do become, shall I say, more tenacious to fight their corner. I wouldn't say it's distasteful but I have become resigned to the fact that other people's code of practice is 'all's fair in love, war and business' and that's the way it works. As long as you appreciate that, whilst you don't have to go about things the way they do, you should weather the storm.

There's an awful lot made of the different team owners and their approaches, but it depends who the team owner is and who the team owner is negotiating with. Obviously if the balance of a bargaining position is very heavily weighted on their side, they'll take advantage of it. Who wouldn't?

If an owner's taking an option on a test driver, as Frank did with Damon, and also with David, then he's going to say, 'I want to get you on the hook for the next four or five years.' It was interesting that Frank came unstuck with David. He took options for, I think, five years and when it became the subject of litigation, the Contracts Recognition Board held that to be unreasonable and unduly long, given the length of career of your average Formula One driver. Frank lost out because what he should have done was taken options for, say, two years. But he couldn't help himself because he was in such a strong bargaining position.

The irony was that once David saw that, he used the argument to free himself from his relationship with IMG [International Management Group, Coulthard's former agent]. They advised him on the contract with Williams and David woke up to the fact that his contract with IMG was unreasonable because it was for even longer. They came to an out-of-court settlement.

I certainly don't consider myself to be the typical agent, in particular the typical football type of agent. I can't generalise because I met one at a race four weeks ago, a guest of Jordan, who was a very professional guy with fifty-three players on his books. But there are some football agents whom I don't consider act necessarily in the best interests of their players, and they give agents generally a bad name.

I think some agents take advantage. They sign up young sportsmen and think nothing of taking a half or a quarter of their earnings for their entire career, for little or no investment. Again, those contracts would be unenforceable. It springs to mind there is on-going litigation in Germany between a journalist and Michael [Schumacher]. He had a deal with Michael for, I think, fifty per cent. Anyone who wants to take fifty per cent of a sportsman's or woman's earnings is being absolutely outrageous.

Breen has been accused of not acting in the best interests of Hill, of perhaps being motivated by the big money rather than the best drive.

I have had some bad criticism but there seems to be an assumption I am paid a percentage of Damon's retainer. I'm not. My remuneration is calculated on the basis of an hourly rate. If you're on a percentage you get into difficulties. It might be thought that you're pushing a particular team that are offering a particular sum of money because you're going to get a particular percentage of it, so you're doing it for your own reasons.

Twenty-twenty hindsight is a wonderful thing and I wish I had it. I think the criticism of me first came to the fore following Damon not being retained by Williams. It was said, or rumoured, the reason Frank didn't retain Damon was because he had asked for too much money, which obviously upset Damon enormously. I had asked for a pay increase for Damon over what he was paid in 1996 for his retainer, but it was by no stretch of the imagination out of proportion with what he was paid in 1996, and it was only on the basis of, if you like, a bonus to reflect the fact he had become world champion. So that's the reality.

It wasn't a huge pay increase at all, and I'm totally convinced that rumour was put out deliberately by Frank as a smokescreen, to hide the fact he'd signed Frentzen in September 1995 because of BMW. It's interesting that Frentzen's now likely to leave Williams and they're possibly going to sign another German driver, again to keep BMW sweet.

We were in negotiation with McLaren in 1997 for a 1998 drive, but if you've got to the top of your profession and were being paid a sum of money, would you take a job for significantly less at another team which clearly favours – this was my view – one driver over the other, where the deal was structured on a win-bonus basis, when it's very easy in Formula One to ensure that you don't win? If Damon had gone to McLaren for little or no retainer, and ended up not winning many races, and let's say being told to pull over and let Mika win, would I not be a bigger mug for advising him to take the drive?

How many team owners say they do it for the love of the sport and are happy not to be paid very much money? None. Zero. No one does it exclusively for the love of racing. Damon had two other offers which were way, way over what he was offered here, double and treble the money, which he didn't take. Damon is an intelligent man, and I don't say to him, 'I think you should do this,' and he says, 'OK, we'll do that then.' We have many, many discussions and we talk it through and it's more of a joint decision. It certainly isn't my decision. I advise him.

We can spend our whole lives criticising other people and that's fine, my shoulders are broad enough. I don't lose any sleep over it, no matter who says what, but the basis on which I'm paid doesn't make one jot of difference to where Damon goes, or for whom he drives. It's deliberately dealt with in that way so he can always feel comfortable with it. The advice I give him is wholly independent and I'm not sure there's another manager in the pit lane who's in a position to say that.

Different people have different approaches in negotiations. Tom Walkinshaw is obviously a skilled business negotiator. He works out what approach suits the particular individual and situation. Maybe the negotiations we had were helped by the fact he's from the North of Scotland and I'm from Northern Ireland . . .

And maybe because Eddie's from the Republic of Ireland? Breen just smiles and continues.

Tom says tell me what you want, I tell him, and he says that's fine, that's not fine, bish-bosh, deal done. There are two types of negotiation. One is a lot more time-consuming than the other. You can say I'm going to start high, you're going to start low, there'll be a huge amount of haggling and somewhere down the line we'll have to reach a compromise because we both want to do the deal. Alternatively I can try to short circuit all of that nonsense and say plainly what my client is prepared to accept, save us both an enormous amount of grief, aggravation and hassle, and lessen the chance of souring the relationship in that process. The problem is, if you do that and set out your stall, saying not a penny less, not a penny more, and the other person cannot get it into their head this is what you mean, you can end up with no deal.

I was explaining to someone yesterday that the problem over announcing Damon's deal for next year is not with me, which Eddie overheard and took to be an attack on him and he wanted to know what I meant by that. I said what I meant by that is the problem is not with us, that if you want to make a joint announcement you have a severe difficulty doing that not because of Damon Hill but because of Ralf Schumacher. He said, 'Oh, that's correct.' He also said there would be an announcement at Monza.

I see it that way but I don't want to be perceived as one of those disingenuous guys who deliberately misleads people all the time, because there are a number of people in Formula One who do that. Formula One changes so regularly, it's not within my control, and therefore when Damon's asked the question whether he's staying he says it's ninety-five per cent certain or ninety-nine per cent certain because I say you've always got to leave that one per cent chance.

There's definitely a clique or an exclusive club in Formula One. You have to have been coming to races for a long time before you get to know everyone and people get to know your name and you're accepted. When I first came people would just blank me. I wasn't really bothered about the fact it was unfriendly. I could see it for what it was and my view of it hasn't really changed.

That's not meant as a criticism, it's more something of human nature. It is a bit of a cocoon. You can have a nuclear holocaust in Russia or America or some other place we don't race, and on a Grand Prix weekend no one would really pay any attention. They're more interested in what's happening with the weather and whether it's going to be a wet race, which I think is a bit unreal.

I think sometimes people do deliberately try to score points. There's a lot of one-upmanship, which again is fine if that's the way people want to operate, but I think it's unnecessary. It just makes me chuckle sometimes. It makes me frustrated if it affects Damon, but you've got to accept that's part and parcel of it, that's the nature of the business.

There are also some good, friendly people. A lot is said about Jacques Villeneuve but I have to say one of my abiding memories of the day Damon won the Championship at Suzuka was when Jacques sat on his lap, slapped him on the head and said, 'Well done, Champ, you deserve it.' I thought that was great.

Breen admits he and Hill have not always sat so comfortably with a constant barrage of press speculation and probing. Now Hill's rich vein of form is being used against him by some of his critics – in the pit lane as well as in the media – who contend he is motivated by the need to secure a new contract and that, unlike Michael Schumacher, for example, he cannot drive around a problem. He had only one exceptional race for Arrows and earlier in the season, when Jordan were not so good, he was consistently outpaced by his team-mate.

It's interesting with the press. They want to know what is going on, how much is this guy getting paid and so on. I think sometimes there is pressure on journalists, through their editors, to do a story which other journalists don't have. Around Silverstone particularly it's all whipped up into a frenzy, and invariably it's a storm in a teacup. I think this is the first year we've finally got used to that.

Damon wouldn't want to continue if he was in a car that he couldn't ever perceive giving him a chance of getting on the podium or winning the race because he would think that was a waste of his talent. You have to inject a certain amount of realism. Ferrari have always been a front-running team, but in an Arrows you can't drive around the problem if the thing breaks down or is not competitive, which it wasn't, and the Jordan was not competitive at the start of the season.

You have to have a basic package in order to do that. I would guess Ralf was more comfortable with the car than Damon was. I think the older drivers are like that. Damon's happy and comfortable now he's back up there. The team have done a fantastic job. I have to say I didn't think it was going to happen because it would have been much easier for Eddie to say, 'The car's a dog, we've thrown good money after bad, I could spend ten million dollars and it could get me two tenths,' but he did not take that approach. They do have some good people in there and they have done an incredible job. There is no other sport where it can all change over the course of a weekend. Look at Michael in Hockenheim and then in Hungary.

Breen, father of two-year-old twins, intends to spend fewer hours at the track from next season but sees a future for himself in Formula One, again with Hill, although in the meantime, his client has some unfinished business.

I'd like to go on in this when Damon stops racing. I could see us working together on driver management or maybe something bigger. He obviously has an insight into how a driver thinks, attitude and perception, that I can never have. Martin Brundle is working on that with David, though how far he gets with Ron is a different issue! He's a sounding board, a guy David knows has done it all before. I'm much happier having people in the business who do a good job and you have respect for. It's good for the sport and the drivers.

There are definitely more wins in Damon. I think when he's decided there are no more wins left he'll hang up his crash helmet because he doesn't want to do it just for the money. He doesn't need it. I believe the team have responded and produced a better car, and he has responded by putting in better performances.

Out in the paddock the talk is of the weather and whether it will be a wet race, nuclear holocaust notwithstanding. It was, after all, supposed to be a getting better kind of day. Ecclestone steps from what would be a handsome house anywhere else but here is the circuit office. His only concession to the rain is a large umbrella. The white shirt and dark slacks are rarely hidden beneath a coat. One of his henchmen has no compunction about zipping up his anorak.

'This is what we want,' he says, looking to the heavens. To keep the Championship contest alive, of course.

Hakkinen's good start is not what the Championship wanted but within a few, mind-blowing seconds, that is academic. Irvine's Ferrari touches Coulthard's McLaren, which veers sharp right to the wall, then left, triggering mayhem and terror on the slope to Eau Rouge. Cars at the back of the grid round La Source hairpin blind to the unfolding chaos and ram the wall of wreckage. Wheels are flung into the air and down the hill like bouncing bombs. Thirteen cars fail to complete the first lap. Veteran correspondents reckon it is the biggest pile-up in 25 years.

When at last the scene is still, drivers uncoil and climb free. Irvine hobbles away and has ice applied to his knee. Astonishingly, no one else seems to be remotely hurt. Some instinctively run back up to the pits to claim the spare car. Four of them – Barrichello, Panis, Salo and Rosset – find there is no spare car for them.

For Salo a traumatic weekend is over – well, almost. The stewards refuse him permission to leave the circuit pending inquiries over the crash. He storms out, leaving them with a piece of his mind. He returns in more contrite mood, apologises, and is allowed to go. For the Arrows crew the day just grows longer. They were here at three o'clock this morning, working to ensure the team had a full complement of three cars. Diniz will drive the one car left.

Schumacher and Hakkinen are among the first ready for the restart. As the fire brigade wash the track, team personnel debate the procedure at the original start. Alain Prost says it was 'ridiculous' not to start behind the safety car. Ecclestone is engaged in earnest conversation with the starter, Charlie Whiting, then retorts: 'Why do we need the safety car? We've started in worse than this and we've lost only three or four cars.'

In truth, it is not raining hard. It is also a safe bet the spectacular mass shunt will get maximum global coverage, and the safety measures have again come through with flying colours. Almost an hour after they first lined up, Whiting sends them off again. Hill jumps in front, leaving Hakkinen and Schumacher to jockey for position at the hairpin. The McLaren spins, is hit by Herbert's Sauber and is out of the race. Schumacher wriggles away and pursues his old adversary. Now the safety car is sent out but ironically the rain has relented. They are released again and into the eighth lap Hill is fending off the Ferrari. However, Schumacher will not be resisted. The rain returns and as they approach the Bus Stop chicane the master of Spa takes over once more. In one lap he opens a gap of five seconds. At the midway point he has a half-minute advantage.

On the 25th of the 44 laps Schumacher shapes to lap Coulthard. Instead, he runs into the back of the Scot, the impact wrenching off the front right wheel of the Ferrari. In his despair and fury, the German drives on in his three-wheeler at near racing speed. He turns into the pits, followed by Coulthard. Schumacher leaps from his car, pulls off his helmet and marches towards the McLaren garage, shrugging off attempts by Ferrari engineers to restrain him. He confronts Coulthard, also now out of his car but still wearing his helmet, hurling abuse and accusations before he is hauled away.

Repairs are carried out on Coulthard's car and he drives back into the race, five laps adrift but in hope of salvaging a point, such is the casualty rate. Fisichella does a Schumacher, smashing into the back of Nakano's Minardi, and runs clear of a blazing Benetton. With Irvine out of the race also, Ferrari's hierarchy concentrate their efforts on a protest to the stewards, claiming Coulthard deliberately slowed in front of Schumacher.

On the track, meanwhile, Hill is leading, only to be challenged by the younger Schumacher after another intervention by the safety car. The Englishman fights him off and the team order their drivers to hold station. Jordan are on course for not merely their maiden win in this, their 127th Grand Prix, but a remarkable one–two success even Eddie could not have blagged from the Almighty. Alesi threatens to complicate matters, but Hill and Schumacher inject a little more pace and the Sauber is seen off. Hill has his 22nd victory and his first since winning the Championship almost two years ago. Frentzen is fourth, Diniz rewards Arrows with fifth, and Trulli's sixth place gives Prost their first point of the year. Coulthard is seventh.

Jordan, welcomed to the Piranha Club, Formula One's coterie of winners, by Ron Dennis, does a jig. Hill does a Schumacher, jumping high above the podium. Ralf is conspicuously subdued. He cannot pretend he is happy to be second but accepts the wisdom of the team's instructions and concedes his partner deserved the victory. This result has not changed his mind about wanting to leave, although it has very nearly lifted Jordan to the fourth place that would, it is understood, have kicked in their option on the 23-year-old. The stage is Hill's.

'I'm so happy for Jordan,' he says. 'They try and try. It's never happened for them before. I've won twenty-two. I would never say I wasn't lucky but we'd put ourselves in a position to be able to win. This is special because it's the first win I've had in a car other than a Williams, and it's nice to show I can do it in another car.'

The flags of the Union and Germany are draped across the back of the Jordan bus as photographers clamour for pictures of Eddie and his drivers.

'I knew this would come but I thought it would take a lot longer,' he tells journalists hustling to meet their deadlines. 'I . . . I . . . oh, you know what I want to say, you can say it . . .' and he's dragged off to the photo shoot.

There can be no such licence for the media pack covering the escalating Schumacher–Coulthard row. Both have been called to the stewards. So has Irvine, although he and Coulthard are content to hear their involvement in the early pile-up has been dismissed as a racing incident. The stewards deliberate for more than two hours over the Coulthard–Schumacher collision. McLaren provide telemetry data which they say proves no foul play on their driver's part.

Coulthard is jeered by a group of Schumacher fans as he leaves the meeting. Schumacher beats the stair rail in a show of anger and indignation, his grim-faced expression unaltered from the moment he climbed out of his car. Todt trails him to the team motorhome. Schumacher will make no statement until he has heard the stewards' verdict.

Outside the McLaren camp, Coulthard is speaking.

'He came into the garage like an animal, saying I tried to kill him. I find his behaviour absolutely disgusting. If he wants to discuss it quietly, man to man, then fine, but his attitude is totally unacceptable. Any allegations he's made are completely untrue and the video evidence will prove it.'

The stewards find Coulthard has no case to answer, deciding the collision was another 'racing incident'. Schumacher now issues his statement.

'Lifting on the straight like he did when I hit him is very dangerous. He has the experience to know you do not slow down on a straight like that without giving warning. So one could think he did it deliberately. It is very disappointing to still be seven points behind in the Championship when I could have left Spa with a three-point lead.'

Formula One leaves Spa with a new controversy that is likely to run all the way through testing this coming week at Monza to the Italian Grand Prix in a fortnight. Eddie Jordan and Damon Hill leave to join their families in Oxford and Spain, respectively. The celebrating, too, could run and run.

10
Monza

CLASS DISTINCTION

Whatever your creed or prejudice in sport, you would have to count the home of the Italian Grand Prix as one of the most atmospheric and inspiring arenas in the world. A royal park, with its profusion of imperious trees and tranquil walks, is an improbable setting for a race circuit that generates the urban fervour of the more intimidating football stadia. Monza is Imola with attitude; it brings an added dimension to commitment and passion. This is the cathedral of the Ferrari faithful.

In more recent times the congregation has been joined by Schumi's disciples and the familiar, Germanic figures are already in evidence this hot Thursday lunchtime, establishing their familiar camps in the woods and making their presence felt with familiar boisterousness. Local exuberance requires no artificial additives and radiates its compelling charms along the park roads and at every chaotic checkpoint. Huge squads of volunteer stewards serve merely to compound the confusion. Half of Milan, and their cousins from Palermo, must be here in official bibs. Police officers look on with benign indifference as those without the necessary credentials try to argue their way in and cause the inevitable jam. This is authentic Monza.

There had been much newspaper talk of tightened security, armed police, guard dogs and personal protection for the McLaren team following events at Spa and a hostile reception from some fans for David Coulthard at last week's test here. One banner condemned him as a killer. Michael Schumacher let it be known he wanted to meet Coulthard in private and make his peace, although he still held the Scot responsible for the fateful collision. But as team personnel arrive they find no cordon of heavies and the only canine recruit is a docile-looking mongrel that has to be a steward's family pet.

Much has happened since Spa. Johnny Herbert has signed for Stewart Ford and is now taking some good-natured ribbing from team members at Sauber.

'They've kicked me out,' he says laughing and seeking compassion among future colleagues. 'They've even thrown my stuff out of my little corner in the motorhome.'

Jordan announced Gary Anderson, the technical director linked with Arrows, was leaving and overnight that Damon Hill would be partnered next season by Heinz-Harald Frentzen. This followed an out-of-court settlement brokered by Bernie Ecclestone, releasing Ralf Schumacher to join Williams. The word is Eddie Jordan negotiated sufficient compensation to pay for the more experienced German. 'We will see who has made the better move,' Frentzen tells the media here.

The focus of greater attention, however, is the Winfield motorhome, the neutral territory agreed by Schumacher and Coulthard for their much-trumpeted meeting. Amid the doorstepping photographers and journalists is Schumacher's trainer, Balbir Singh, whose anxiety is apparent when it is suggested Karl-Heinz will be dispensing his traditional cure for all evils. It could be a long vigil.

Eddie Jordan arrives at his motorhome to pick up a bonus for his victory in Belgium – a pristine 1,000 DM note. He bet a Swiss journalist, at 10–1, his team would win the race. 'The money just keeps rolling in,' he says out of the corner of his mouth.

Alexander Wurz is keeping an especially interested watch on the Winfield motorhome. It transpires the young but alarmingly responsible Austrian helped bring his co-spokesmen for the Grand Prix Drivers' Association together.

'It is not easy for one to go to the other and say sorry, so I spoke to both of them and tried last week to arrange a meeting. It was not possible then but I hope they now shake hands because this is not good for the sport.'

After talking for almost an hour and a half, Schumacher and

Coulthard do shake hands and go their separate ways, the German putting on more of a smile as he heads for the Ferrari motorhome. Along at McLaren, Coulthard gives his guarded version of the meeting.

'We have cleared the air and discussed a number of matters regarding overtaking in the wet, which we intend to put to the other drivers and the FIA. I saw things differently from him and what he said at the time was hurtful because it questions your integrity. But I'm thick-skinned. I'm a big boy. It's not a war; it's a sport. I'm happy to fight wheel to wheel with him on the track as I have done in the past and I'm sure it will be fair. I don't want to say too much about what we discussed because it was private. Mind you, it depends what he says . . .'

Schumacher has his turn and is patently uncomfortable. The Bill Clinton resemblance is particularly appropriate this week. Although the American President has a rather more embarrassing affair to grapple with, the Ferrari driver nervously adjusts and readjusts the collar of his shirt.

'It's clear he did nothing wrong at Spa,' Schumacher now says of Coulthard. 'Initially it was not so clear. After looking at it, it was an unfortunate situation but I wouldn't say again he did it purposely to get me out of the race. It was the idea of both of us to have this meeting because it was not good to leave it. I know David quite well and there was no point in keeping this going. It was just a question of the right opportunity and I'm happy it is now sorted out.

'I can't remember ever before losing control in that way and I hope it will never happen again. It was a natural reaction in the circumstances. But I never would have hit him. I have never hit anyone. We wanted to make sure this will not happen in the future. You calm down and become more realistic about it.'

Schumacher bridles when he is asked if he apologised for his reaction to the crash. 'Do you want me to make this a comedy, a theatre? I have already said enough.'

Eddie Jordan cannot say enough about the 'fantasy' that has become reality for his team. He is equally effusive about signing

Frentzen, a driver he wanted two years ago, and what he maintains is the ideal line-up.

'I don't want to be a kindergarten any more,' he says. 'You can't buy experience.' Hill sitting alongside, chips in.

'You can.'

Jordan attempts to cover his *faux pas* by muttering about fog in Oxford. It is an ineffective smokescreen. Hill is irrepressible. He wants it to be known Jordan 'is not a retirement home for ex-Williams drivers' and appears to relish the prospect of partnering a man who took his old job. He gives Frentzen a generous reference and points out that some drivers flourish in certain environments and promises he will help all he can.

At the back of the Ferrari garage, Ross Brawn is preoccupied with matters more imminent.

'For all the testing we've done we've got a long list of things to get through this weekend and that's all we're concerned with now. We stopped thinking and talking about Spa last week. It's gone. No point in worrying about it now. We should be OK. Michael is fine, absolutely fine.'

Even Brawn must be hard-pressed to maintain his composure here this weekend. Another false step now and the Championship is gone and such a scenario will not be well received out there. He does at least make one concession to the pressures. 'My wife isn't coming to this race. Too much going on.' He smiles and excuses himself to get on with it.

The sky has changed colour from blue to grey but the captivating kaleidoscope of chaos outside the circuit is unaltered this Friday morning. Somehow the paddock personnel negotiate the human slalom without undue delay and arrive inside the metal cage unscathed physically or mentally. The paddock here has been laid out differently this year, creating the blocks of a small town. The leading teams line main street, bustling and brimming with self-importance. The more humble are consigned to one backstreet, the tyre companies to another. Class distinction is established and a neat, orderly aerial shot assured.

Ferrari have a prime position at the top of main street,

opposite Williams and close to the pits. The other Italian team, Minardi, are on the other side of the block, of course, although a corner site, at the pits end of the row, affords them a little recognition on home ground. Overdue respect, too, they might tell you, but then they are generally perceived as the classic backstreet team. Born losers. The butt of paddock jokes. It is, after all, almost three years since they scored a point.

This morning Minardi are holding a press conference in a small marquee attached to a restaurant just outside the paddock. 'What are we doing here?' an early arrival asks wearily. The turnout is boosted by Italians with masses of space to fill because this is their home race, and the inevitable battalion of Japanese. Shinji Nakano is one of the team's drivers.

The announcement, however, is not about drivers but engines. Minardi have signed a new deal with Ford, who will have only one other team, Stewart, next year. Stewart have an exclusive contract for the best engines but Minardi are promised an improved unit. Ford are anxious it should no longer be given the disparaging term of 'customer' engine but 'officially supported' engine. Minardi take the opportunity to name their new sporting director as Cesare Fiorio, once of Ferrari, lately of Prost.

Gian Carlo Minardi, the team's founder, conscious of the 'Hollywood' nickname Fiorio's apparent craving of the limelight has earned him, responds tersely when asked if this is a gimmick to get the team in the papers: 'He is not coming here to make movies but to make the team work.' Gabriele Rumi, who bought control of Minardi, is equally indignant: 'We are a small team trying to grow. There are two ways of looking at it. One is to minimise it, the other is to see what we can do.'

The press conference breaks up and journalists head back to the paddock to cast for bigger fish. Minardi might be Italian for minnow. The team are relieved they did not have to face rows of empty seats. All eyes are on main street and here, in particular, they are on Ferrari. Minardi's motorhome is an oasis of calm compared with the constant toing and froing at their uptown compatriots' base. At Minardi they like to consider themselves still a family, with family values and cares. Gian Carlo Minardi, chairman of Faenza's football club, makes sure the mechanics phone home when they are in distant lands. The girl in the kitchen makes her own pasta every day. Visitors are treated royally. Young drivers are given a chance. Fisichella and Trulli began their Formula One careers here.

Rumi, creator of Fondmetal, producers of alloy wheels, shares Minardi's passion for motor racing and the dream that one day they will not be the laughing stock of the Formula One community but respected citizens. Rumi's earlier venture with his own team, bought as Osella and renamed Fondmetal, was short-lived yet did not quell the crusading zeal. Minardi offered another means for the same cause. Rumi is a 59-year-old father of two, bald and bespectacled. Those around him insist his severe countenance masks an altogether more gentle and sympathetic man. It's just that getting the world to take Minardi seriously is a tough business, as he explains in the privacy of his motorhome.

The real problem of Formula One is that the complex mechanism makes you remain the last. There are a lot of difficulties. That is why I reacted the way I did at the press conference to an offensive question. They do not take us seriously. Their attitude is that the team is small and will remain small, but it doesn't matter what I do. We are doing our best to become bigger but we have obstacles, which is this way of thinking. All Italy and all the Italian press are totally dedicated to Ferrari. It is more difficult for the last to become second last than the second to become first.

I have been in Formula One since 1989, when I bought Osella, and I returned to Formula One for the same reason – the challenge. It did not work out the first time but I believe that in three years we will be a team in a stable position in the Championship. Of course I know it is a difficult challenge, but I know also we will improve next year because we will have a really good car. We have good staff, a good team, good facilities, and this new deal with Ford means we will have an engine prepared for us.

This is our programme. We lack only a driver from the top level, and that we will have only when we have demonstrated we have a competitive car. The likes of Ralf Schumacher, for example, will not go to the bottom team. But with this plan we have, we shall eventually be able to attract drivers of this type.

Minardi's seemingly hopeless plight has appealed to the typically perverse British sense of humour in deepest Sussex, where the West Lavington Association of Minardi Supporters has come into being. The team's factory, at Faenza, is on the mailing list for the group's fanzine, *Sempre Minardi*. Rumi is a successful businessman so you have to wonder if his friends regard him as crazy for pursuing this obsession. Rumi drops his mask as he talks of the fans and his family.

Yes, there are Minardi fans, because there will always be those who support the smallest. This is our fascination. They give us sympathy and we hope to give them a better team to support.

Fiorio has seen our programme and has joined our challenge. He knows that in a few years we are going to be stronger, that we have a bright future. He is coming in a critical role, as sporting director. It may not be nice for those already working in the team to bring in someone from outside, but the team wants to go up the grid and we need his kind of experience. He has the fame and that means he is taking a risk with his reputation, but he is willing to accept that.

We have a staff of a hundred and ten at the moment but that will go up. It is not possible to bring in a lot of new people at the same time. This is a transitional period and I am here waiting for when it changes. If I thought it would always be like this I would not be here, I would stay at home.

I don't have friends, I have only my family, and my wife is always here with me. Yes, the Rumis have been successful in business for three generations, but to realise the dream here will be even more satisfying for me. It is a challenge against myself. When you are successful in business it is difficult to start like this because you are not used to being the last and being very badly treated, so it was hard at the beginning in Formula One.

I am getting used to it now but it is difficult to handle, to understand the mentality of these people. They just care about money and don't care about people. We don't exist for them. But we will show them and prove we can do it. In business there is competition but not a direct fight like this, where you have a test every fortnight.

I speak to Jean Todt at Ferrari, but I only hear the views of the other team directors at our meetings. In the paddock they talk among themselves but not to me. They don't see me. I think they don't even know I'm here.

Fans with pit-lane walkabout passes are inexorably drawn to the front of the Ferrari garage. Another popular attraction is Prof. Watkins, sitting back in the front passenger seat of his souped-up Mercedes medical car, casually drawing on his cigar. Youngsters lean on his door as their friends record the moment on camera. Practice is almost half an hour away. The Prof. has time to reflect on Spa.

'The safety precautions worked and generally we've got to be satisfied. But we still need to do more. The tyres came away more than we would like so that's one area we're looking at, and we also need to tether the wheels.'

The grandstand opposite the pits is almost full for the first practice session. A couple of banners direct insults at Coulthard but they are relatively mild and almost lost in the display of devotion to Ferrari and Schumacher – or Schumi, or Schumy, or Schummy. One of the few others to merit mention is Johnny Herbert, and there is a 'Go, Go' message for Hill, which is presumably supportive rather than dismissive.

Ferrari put down their marker before the break on this high-speed circuit that has retained much of its character despite the insertion of chicanes. The old banked section, alas, has long been defunct. Irvine outpaces his team-mate before the rain falls and persists through the rest of the afternoon session. The order is: Irvine, Schumacher, Coulthard, Villeneuve, Hakkinen.

The Finn rushes from the garage to the motorhome to dry off and change; and, no doubt, to maintain his low profile. The Schumacher–Coulthard controversy has presented him with a convenient shield and he has no desire to cast it aside. When at last he re-emerges he affords the waiting media only a brief, innocuous comment. After anxious consideration, on his way from the McLaren motorhome to the West motorhome, he will not even acknowledge the deflection of attention may have been to his advantage. No, he doesn't want to say anything about that. And now he finds sanctuary again.

Irvine has a little more to say *en route* from a late lunch to a de-briefing.

'I don't know how it affected Michael but I don't think it has made the team any more determined to win here because we are at it all the time. We're flat out. He will have learned from it. He is not Mr Perfect, but then who is? Everyone will have learned from it. I would say it's now fifty fifty for the Championship. It can go either way.'

Hakkinen's elusive strategy will have the approval – and perhaps the guidance – of his boss. Ron Dennis is prepared to do the talking.

'I don't think it gets to the team,' he says. 'We are resilient to most things. We build a psychological wall around the team and concentrate on doing the job. We have to be cool and calm, and not get caught up in the hype between ourselves and Ferrari. It will be a cool head that wins the Championship. We have experienced people concentrating on doing their job and if they do it well we will achieve our goal. Mika knows he cannot allow himself to get into the mental arithmetic of what can and cannot be done.'

Dennis has contributed to the hype around his team and Ferrari this season by engaging in a crossfire of allegations about the legality of the scarlet car and is adamant he will not shirk from demanding McLaren's rights if he suspects any foul play in the closing stages of the campaign.

'We are desperately keen to finish the Championship in the right atmosphere, but I won't sit and say nothing if we feel we are being steamrollered. I'll stand up and never run away from a fight. But if everything is equal and balanced, the Championship will have a good ending.'

The mood in the McLaren Mercedes camp is significantly lighter by evening, when Hakkinen and Coulthard share centre stage at West's Paddock Club party with . . . other Hakkinens and other Coulthards. The look-alike competition appears to prove Hakkinen's features are more common than Coulthard's. The winning Mika is a dead ringer and causes pandemonium when he goes for dinner. The restaurateur – and fans clamouring for autographs – are convinced he is the Championship leader. The British press pack create their usual pandemonium at the Mercedes motorhome, trading taunts with the ever-inquisitive Eddie Jordan as he leaves the paddock.

If the locals have been praying for rain they obviously went over the top. It has rained for Ferrari and all Italy overnight and still the heavens are responding into Saturday morning. Schumacher goes on a reconnaissance lap, to the vociferous approval of the fans, but returns to the cover of the garage. He knows what to do in these conditions, anyway. No matter that he is bottom on the time sheet. A quick burst towards the end of the session lifts him to 10th. Clearing skies suggest a drying track for qualifying.

The sun is good for pit-lane business. A group of well-connected guests are ushered through the tape at the front of the Ferrari garage to have their picture taken alongside the scarlet bodywork. One snap and they are led back to the other side of the tape. Next. The sun also breathes new life into the paddock. People hover, pose and chat rather than scurry for shelter, and no nationality hovers, poses or chats like Italians.

Drivers are hovering long after the official start of qualifying, knowing the fastest times will be available late in the session, when the track has dried. The monitor shows puddles lurking still. Schumacher is engaged in seemingly idle banter with Gerhard Berger at the back of his garage, then wanders out to the pit wall. He waves, brandishes the thumbs-up sign, and then blows a kiss towards the grandstand. Irvine, ever insouciant, ever in shades, leans back in one of the pit-wall seats.

One thirty and still no sign of a car on the track. Most of the drivers are now strapped in, but they wait for those puddles to go, or someone else to make a move. At 1.34 Takagi makes the move, soon followed by Hill. And then, at 1.40, a minor landmark – Rosset is top. He has a new engineer, a car more to his liking and an expression that says, 'Told you so.'

The Brazilian enjoys his 15 seconds of fame before the heavy mob takes over. Nineteen of the 22 cars are out on the circuit as Schumacher goes fastest. The lead changes in the blink of an eye: Fisichella, Coulthard, Hakkinen, Alesi, Hakkinen again, Coulthard again. The crucial lap, however, is produced by Schumacher. Significantly, too, Villeneuve is second, ahead of Hakkinen, Coulthard and Irvine. Rosset is 18th and Nakano and Tuero give Minardi the dubious distinction of both places on the back row.

Schumacher, on pole for the first time in more than a year, leaps on to the pit wall to take the acclaim of the gallery and blow more kisses.

'This is a dream result,' he says. 'It's time I had pole. I'm proud and happy to do this, especially at Monza. You should never discount us. We will always be there and we will be there tomorrow, don't worry.'

Hakkinen says he was not prepared to take too many risks today but will not compromise in the race: 'I don't perform to be second.'

There is more fighting talk from Villeneuve, and this will concern the Championship protagonists. He has nothing to lose, they have. 'They are fighting for the Championship, I'm fighting for a win,' the Canadian says. 'I'll be going for it.' And, with a hint of mischief, he expresses his surprise to see Ferrari on pole. The conspiracy theory is never more rampant than when the show comes to Monza. It's good for business to have Ferrari at the front, you see.

Down on main street, in the Mercedes motorhome, Norbert Haug is graciously congratulating Ferrari and looking forward to 'a better race than Spa'. Dennis is less gracious, saying he feels 'cheated' after all the work his team have put in. But they'll be fine in the race, he is adamant.

Main street is out of vision for the fans pressed up against the paddock cage. They have to content themselves with a view of the backstreet. Tuero and Diniz are evidently the big draw here. 'Esteban I Love You' proclaims one banner, 'Good Luck Pedro' another. Even those on main street will need luck tomorrow.

A sunny, vibrant morning. Monza is in its pomp for race day. Campers are arming themselves with their scarves and banners, the hordes on duty at the checkpoints are piling on the drama, the atmosphere tingles with excitement. This is the genuine Italian Grand Prix tapestry. The paddock, too, has an unrivalled vitality. Expectations are spiralling. Can Ferrari deliver? Warm-up is not encouraging. Coulthard and Hakkinen lead the way. Schumacher is 1.3 seconds off the pace.

As the crowd re-assess Schumacher's chances and the drivers have their own de-briefing with their engineers, girls in shiny red two-piece outfits march out onto the track to practise their gridboard routine. The girl in the Minardi kitchen is going through her well-practised pasta rolling and cutting routine. A French TV crew is trying to clear a space in the middle of main street so that their man can begin the build-up to the race. A few yards away, at Prost, team personnel cast a critical eye on the transmission.

Up in the control tower, Charlie Whiting and Herbie Blash, returned from the drivers' briefing, go through their own check-list of final preparations for the race. Whiting was once chief mechanic with Bernie Ecclestone's Championship-winning Brabham, Blash was team manager. Today Whiting is FIA race director and safety delegate. His responsibilities include starting the race, and sometimes stopping it. Blash's title is FIA observer, his role to work alongside Whiting. On the face of it these are jobs for the boys. But these boys have been around in Formula One a long time, Blash for 30 years, Whiting for 22. They are trusted by Ecclestone and Mosley, respected by the teams. They know the tricks of the trade. They are the classic examples of poacher turned gamekeeper.

This weekend has so far been a relatively comfortable ride for the pair. They have had no Formula 3000 race to contend with and today's fine weather holds out the prospect of an altogether easier race than the one they had at Spa. There were no unforeseen problems at the briefing. Whiting, who has appropriately coloured hair and a repertoire of jokes to turn the complexion red in convulsions, runs through a familiar list of reminders to the drivers, who have detailed instructions before them in Document 17. Whiting says:

> We would actually prefer to move the briefing to Friday morning because there are more things to say then, but we just run through a few things and ask them if they have any questions. Sometimes drivers ask difficult questions but usually it's a relatively lighthearted affair. We run through things like what would happen at the start if a car stalled. But they are given notes and there's no point going through the same things every time. Sometimes we'll take up on a particular incident at the previous race, but Michael didn't say anything about Spa. He did suggest the speed limit in the pit lane should start a bit earlier.
>
> The race director's job is to try and ensure consistency in enforcing regulations and the running of the race, all the way through the Championship. The clerk of the course is different in every country. He runs the race on a day-to-day basis – marshals, communications, things like that. We have overriding authority in important matters such as the deployment of the safety car, red flags and so on.
>
> We're bringing on much more equipment and systems. Now we have equipment for jump-start detection, pit speeds, start lights. We have a positioning system so we can see where all the cars are on the circuit at any

time. All that information comes into race control. We bring a greater level of sophistication to how we can run the race. It's not infallible, but it helps a great deal. This has all come along in the last couple of years or so.

Here I start the race from the other side of the circuit. The mechanism is linked with the jump-start system. First of all, we programme it all to the particular race time, usually two o'clock. Then it's automatic, although we can stop it at any time and follow the abort procedure. The pit exit light will go green at half past one. When they have all left the grid on the formation lap the jump-start system becomes active. Today it will show twenty-two cars out of position on the display. As the cars come up into the correct grid positions, the names of the last six out of position come up. In theory, they should be the last six on the grid.

From there it's up to me. It's manual. Once the cars are in position I press a button to initiate the countdown procedure. The five red lights come on, one at a time. If, during that period, we need to stop it – someone stalls, that sort of thing – I press the abort button and the orange flashing lights will come on. Then we have a five-minute delay. When all the red lights are on and everything is OK, I press the button to start and the lights go out. That used to be automatic but we changed it after Magny-Cours, where I pressed the abort button as the lights were going out. It registered as race stopped because I pressed it nought point three of a second after, although I'd made the decision before. [The cars launched themselves from the grid at the French Grand Prix and had to be called back for a new start.]

I have mixed emotions at the start. One is the exhilaration because the start of a Grand Prix has to be one of the greatest spectacles. But also, we both get nervous. Herbie is arguably in the worst place in race control because he has to sort out any first-corner incident, for example.

Herbie Blash takes up the point:

> We are on a landline link because what we are saying is
> highly confidential, and I inform Charlie what's going on.
> He can see only his little monitor. I have a bank of
> monitors and all the information. In Argentina a couple of
> years ago, Schumacher had a shunt and we had to bring
> out the safety car immediately. Sometimes I will have to
> make a decision without speaking to Charlie because he's
> maybe on his way over from the start or involved with
> something else. But normally I do it with Charlie. We'll
> either stop the race or bring out the safety car. We have to
> assess the situation very quickly because the race is still
> going on and you have to concentrate on the rest of the
> circuit, so it gets the heart pumping very rapidly. And, of
> course, we're in a no-win situation.

Whiting agrees:

> That's right. If a race runs completely smoothly, no one
> comes up and says, 'Nice job'. We're like referees.
> Recently one of the hardest parts of the job has been
> coming to terms with the paranoia in the pit lane. Particu-
> larly between the leading teams. They all think each other
> is at it. Trying to ignore all the stupid things that are
> written is also tiresome.
>
> Things have certainly changed since I left a team and
> became technical delegate, back in '88. But Herbie and I
> have been around a long time and we have a pretty good
> understanding of what goes on. People from teams come
> up to you and say so-and-so, and you think, 'What a load
> of rubbish.' They are just trying it on.
>
> A certain team principal whose cars were well posi-
> tioned on the grid at Spa came to me and said one of his
> drivers thought the conditions out there were dreadful,
> that there were puddles everywhere. It just wasn't true.
> We know where he's coming from. That's the sort of thing

we get. We got stick over that first-lap shunt at Spa for not starting with the safety car but I think if Coulthard had spun in the same way on the first lap after a safety car the same accident would have happened. Our opinion was the conditions were such we did not need a safety car. If you started that race behind a safety car you'd have to start every wet race behind a safety car, and that's not what it's for.

Racing in the wet will always be more difficult than racing in the dry. I wouldn't want to do it. But you've heard it for years: visibility is zero in the wet. What's changed?

Prompted by Whiting discussing the difficulties of the job, Blash turns to the hours they put in.

Over a four-day period we're talking forty to fifty hours, especially when we have a Formula 3000 race as well. it's tiring because you have to concentrate very hard. Come Sunday night you are finished. And Charlie goes to every circuit before the race meeting to check everything from the safety aspect.

Charlie nods and takes it up again:

The most exciting races for the spectators and viewers, such as Canada and Spa this year, are the hardest for us. And yes, I have to make sure everything is in place before the race weekend. I go to some places, like Hockenheim, Nurburgring, Silverstone, A1-Ring, and it's pretty easy. They're cooperative and everything runs smoothly. But Brazil and Argentina, it's hard work to get them to do anything we want done. I'll go to both circuits this winter. I'll probably go to Brazil twice.

I'm also in charge of the technical department and you really do have to keep on top of the situation there which is becoming increasingly difficult. A normal day would be a constant stream of people coming to see us about this and that. They will try every trick in the book.

Blash interjects to stress: 'You are dealing with the best technical people around here. They don't get any better than these guys.'
Whiting resumes:

The Ferrari thing is obviously there at us all the time, but you just have to ignore it. From a technical point of view, when you hear McLaren are doing this, or Ferrari are doing that, we know they're not. But sometimes it's written up in *Autosport* or something like that. There was an article last week about McLaren's front suspension – complete rubbish. We know it is.

The cars are constantly scrutineered, but if people put their minds to it anything is possible. We have to realise that. You can make a bank impregnable but if someone really wanted to find a way in they probably could. We're in the same position. We're the police and we make things as difficult as possible. We are four people in the FIA technical department and there are all those out there trying to get as close to the line as possible. I don't think anyone these days has got the bottle to cheat deliberately in a big way because the stakes are too high, but they'll certainly go as close to the line as they can.

Maybe we're being a little naïve in thinking no one would do it. But if you were in, let's say, Ron Dennis's position, I don't think you would deliberately go out to cheat. If you did anything in the software, for example, it would have to be so well hidden from us not to see it that if we did find it, it would be obvious it was done on purpose. You saw what happened to Toyota in the World Rally Championship; they were given a long ban when they were found out. It just isn't worth it.

There were rumours last year that a leading team had augmented their permitted allocation of tyres by applying an appropriately coloured marker. Whiting doubts the story because of the chemicals and re-agents used in the scrutinising procedure. However, tyres are now bar-coded.

Much has changed since Whiting and Blash were on the other side of the line. Everything was less sophisticated then, including the cheating. This is, of course, a slightly sensitive area for present-day upholders of the law, but they do concede they were conscious of dubious practices at the time. Whiting says:

> I remember one very windy day, in Montreal I think it was, and everybody's bodywork was blowing around, but the Williams engine cover was standing bolt upright. Somebody went over to Frank Williams and told him he'd better have a word with his guys because it must have been a bit heavy. We knew what they were doing. They were running the car light in practice, then changing the bodywork when they came in. The cars weren't weighed during practice in those days, just selected at random at the end.
>
> I'm not saying Brabham weren't aware of a few tricks. We often had to run ballast because the car was a bit light, but obviously ballast was in place at all times!

His tongue appears to be lodged in his cheek and it is a convenient moment to excuse himself so that he might have a word with a man from Bridgestone, patiently waiting outside. Over to his smiling partner:

> I like to think we were very smart and knew what everybody was doing to remain competitive. The teams were actually against the governing body as well as each other. There was lots of, shall we say, honest cheating going on. I believe some teams used leaded seats and solid lead rear wings. Teams would go out and do their quick times in qualifying, come in, and put on the really heavy wing, nose and seat. Most of the going quick was done in qualifying, although the water-tank trick was for the race.

Didn't you start that? A smirking Herbie confirms:

I think we did start that. But everyone knew the score then. The water tank was only ballast. You were allowed to top up your fluids after the race, so on the formation lap you would dump fifteen gallons of water. By the time you got to the grid you were nice and light, you'd go and do your race, and at the end you'd top up with water and you were perfectly legal.

There was a lot of fun then but it's still very enjoyable because it's still very exciting, especially in our position. Before the race the legs are going up and down and the pressure's on. That's adrenalin you can't go to the shop and buy. If you are working for a team, you go away from a race meeting on a high or a low. You've achieved something and people see that. But what we achieve nobody sees, so it's down to personal feelings and satisfactions. You know if you've done a good job or a bad job.

The job does have its unforeseen complications. In Australia we had a threat from the Greens and we had a microlight coming towards us just as the race was about to start. So we were dealing with the police, Air Force, all sorts of people to make sure he didn't disrupt the race. They also had people hitting tennis balls onto the circuit just before the start, people hanging from bridges, tree climbers, all sorts, so it was a bit of a scramble to deal with that.

At the end of the race in Hungary this year, fans decided to invade the track after the leading car had gone by. So we were involved in that, helping the officials look after the safety of the drivers as well as the spectators. There are all sorts of problems people don't get to know about. We get the odd bomb scare which the general public and even the people in the pits don't always know about.

Whiting, returned to the office, joins in:

We had a streaker at Silverstone. We also had an example

of how things can go horribly wrong at Silverstone. On the morning of race day there was a total power failure. If you've got no timing, no televisions in race control, you can't go on. Fortunately, it came back, but that was a bit of a nightmare.

I still enjoy the life but less so. We're not really treated any differently on this side but in our position we have to be more and more on our guard. If I'm seen having a cup of coffee at Ferrari, Ron might stick his nose in and want to know what's going on. That's why the only place we accept hospitality is in the Winfield motorhome because it's generally accepted to be neutral territory. We often get asked to go for lunch here, there and everywhere, but we don't.

We are absolutely, totally impartial, and sometimes that's difficult to get across. If we'd had to put a safety car out in Hungary, when Schuey was getting that time up, we would have done so. End of story. But some people are a bit cynical about that sort of thing. Everyone seems to think Ferrari can do what they like. Well, believe me, they can't. We'll put the safety car out when the track's unsafe and that's it.

[Whiting's attention is diverted by a demonstration 'race' of Ferraris from down the years, a celebration of the marque's 600 Grands Prix.]

Look at those. Unfortunately, that wouldn't do anything for a lot of people involved in Formula One nowadays. Sad, isn't it? And John Surtees has won. Blimey, you wouldn't believe it, would you? An old car like that.

I think Formula One's very healthy today. Everyone's under scrutiny more and more, and tiny improvements in performance, tiny advantages on the track, seem to be sought more and more. If they can find a hundredth of a second, they're happy. All those little bits add up. Fifteen years ago, if doing something on the car wasn't worth a second a lap it wasn't worth doing. They're looking for advantages everywhere now, which shows the level the sport has reached, and we try to keep up.

The same goes for monitoring things on the track. That's why we try to develop more sophisticated systems which will be more in line with current Formula One. Unfortunately, it all costs money. You could never have envisaged it on this scale. The cars now are the most wonderful things. Ten and fifteen years ago, when you had thirty-eight or thirty-nine cars, some of them were garbage, really primitive things. Now, people may laugh about Minardi but the car is superb, beautifully engineered. They all are. Some obviously better than others, but the engineering is just fantastic.

Blash emphasises the point:

We'll never again have teams in Formula One that shouldn't be here. New teams have to be able to meet certain criteria and give financial guarantees, so you're not going to get rubbish coming in.

When the season is over Whiting will be off on his tour of inspection, visiting not only Brazil and Argentina but also a new circuit in Malaysia and the Kyalami track in South Africa, which may be restored to the calendar. Blash, a part-time FIA official, will return to his research, development and manufacturing company at Brabham's former factory, and his roving role with Yamaha. They plan to switch off over Christmas and the New Year.

After switching off the start lights this afternoon, Whiting will make his way from trackside to race control. He will sit alongside Blash and the clerk of the course. Chiefs of fire, police and medical operations, and other FIA personnel will be on hand. The group will number about ten.

Whiting has a small lap-top display which tells him the position of every car on the track. This technology alerts officials to, among other things, the need for blue flags, which indicate a car is about to be lapped. The entire race can be played back in the case of dispute. Another development will duplicate the trackside flags system with coloured lights in the cockpit. Whiting's crew have gadgets for almost every conceivable purpose and eventuality.

'We can send messages to the monitors,' Charlie says, 'such as yesterday when the cars weren't out during qualifying. We said rain is forecast. They took no notice. These lights show us the status of the start lights and under that is the button to stop the race or practice. It stops all the timing and indicates red flags.' It is a red button covered by a protective flap. Beyond the instruments and equipment within arm's length is the bank of screens beaming pictures from fixed cameras positioned strategically around the circuit.

'There are thirty-five to forty monitors to look at in all,' Blash says, 'so you can imagine the concentration required. We have to keep an eye on the blue-flag situation. It's particularly complicated with all the pit stops now. The days of leaving it to the marshals are gone.'

'We probably follow the race closer than most because we have to,' Charlie adds. 'But we can still enjoy it. We've had some great races this year.'

It is rush hour on main street. The place is a whirl of movement and conversation. A girl with platinum-coloured hair, whom you might expect to be a Page Three pin-up but is said to be a top Finnish violinist, is pulling a few heartstrings. The appearance of Elizabeth Murdoch, daughter of Rupert, the media tycoon in the process of buying Manchester United, triggers inevitable conjecture about Formula One's television future. Paddock shuttle buses compete with people for space, adding to the scene's unmistakably Italian feel. And across it wafts the smell of Minardi's pasta sauce.

The girls in red – now also wearing red wigs – are in position with their boards. It is perhaps judicious to note this is not another indication of bias towards Ferrari but part of a sponsorship deal with Campari. Irvine's red car launches from the pit lane, closely followed by Schumacher's. Hakkinen practises his start at the end of the pit lane. A frenzied commentator announces Schumacher's approach to the grid. Coulthard steers his car into position and joins the usual driver trek to the toilet. Mechanics will tell you that last visit does not always suffice to the end of the race. Nelson Piquet took a perverse delight in leaving a trademark wet seat.

In Coulthard's absence, his car has been stripped of wheels, nose and front wing, and most of its bodywork. There seem to be as many people working on the McLaren as there are cruising the grid. Star-spotters have ticked off a squad of *Serie A* footballers, including the German striker Oliver Bierhoff, who scored twice for his new club Milan last night. Bernie provides a personal escort to Mick Jagger. Stallone is almost knocked over in the scramble to snap the Rolling Stone. Ralf Schumacher's crew are more concerned with mopping up a fuel spill.

Brother Michael has some cleaning up to do after a sloppy start relegates him from first to fifth. Hakkinen swings into the lead, covered by Coulthard. Irvine is third, Villeneuve fourth. The German takes the Canadian halfway around the first lap and Irvine on the third. He closes on the McLarens but it is clear the fastest man on the circuit is Coulthard, who is allowed to go past Hakkinen. However, on the 17th lap the Scot's engine blows and he pulls off the road.

Hakkinen and Schumacher plunge into the trailing clouds and anxiously dart this way and that. The Ferrari attacks at the chicane, the McLaren resists only to lose momentum in the process and cannot match Schumacher's acceleration on the exit. Schumacher's course seems straightforward enough, yet Hakkinen retaliates after their pit stops. With eight laps remaining he has closed the gap to 2.6 seconds. He pushes a little too hard and spins off. He manages to keep his engine running and his race alive but now, with failing brakes, his objective is survival rather than victory. He is passed by Irvine, then Ralf Schumacher, before making it to the line in fourth place. Alesi is fifth and Hill completes another good day for Jordan with sixth.

This, though, is Ferrari's day and an exultant mosaic of humanity soon stretches along the track as far as the eye can see, at its heart a huge, shimmering banner bearing the Prancing Horse. It is Ferrari's first one–two success here for a decade and lifts the team to within ten points of McLaren in the Constructors' Championship. More importantly, Schumacher is now level on points and wins with Hakkinen. With two Grands Prix remaining, the Finn holds on to his lead only because he has two second places to Schumacher's one.

'My grandmother said if it was unfair what happened at Spa, it will be equalised at Monza, and she was right,' Schumacher says. 'She is seventy-four years old but she is clever. At the start it looked like I wanted to go for a walk instead of a race. It was terrible. Now we'll keep Mika under pressure. I'm not saying he is going to crack, but it was easier for him earlier in the season. He's been a good racing driver this season but we will see how he handles it with two races left.' The off-track test of nerve is already under way.

'We've noticed every time we've put McLaren under pressure it's gone well for us,' Todt says. 'Emotions here mean nothing. We have to live with reality and the reality is that Michael has six wins. I don't know when that was last done in a season by a Ferrari driver.'

The answer is 1952, the driver Alberto Ascari. But McLaren, devastated though they look in the immediate aftermath of this defeat, and 'nervous' though Hakkinen concedes he feels, are given a rallying call by Dennis, who knows his team have again let in Schumacher.

'If you can't take the heat you shouldn't be in the sport,' he defiantly pronounces. 'We're not wimps. Neither of our drivers is and we're going to fight all the way and put pressure on them.'

Schumacher is content to leave the sparring to the bosses. He celebrates with his mechanics – restored to a full complement after one was knocked down in the post-race stampede by over-exuberant fans – then moves on for the customary tipple with Karl-Heinz; or at least that is what his ever-watchful trainer is being told.

Whiting and Blash appear to have come out of the race unscathed, which probably means they have done another good job. They have also had to contend with more jibes about Ferrari bribes. Yes, they owned up, they'd each been offered a 355 model. Trouble was, they were yellow. Couldn't have them. Got to be red. At that moment Dennis, wearing his earphones, looked up towards the control tower.

'You'd have sworn he could hear us,' Whiting laughs.

Ferrari's win this time can be attributed to neither favouritism nor the elements. The fragile calm of the day's weather has now been broken by driving crosswinds and rain, which sweep the litter from the stands. Minardi would have required a more drastic act of God to get among the points, but Tuero has finished the race, albeit in 11th place and two laps down on Schumacher, and this Italian team, too, go home in good heart.

11

Nurburgring

HOME RUN

Late September in the Eifel region of Germany, counterpart of Belgium's Ardennes, is an ominous appointment for the squeamish, even if the modern Nurburgring bears no spiritual or aesthetic resemblance to its great ancestor. The climate is perceived as providing further potential assistance to Michael Schumacher's cause on another home track. The Luxembourg Grand Prix has been created here to dodge tobacco advertising restrictions and provide Schumi's Army with a convenient means of spending more money.

The opposition camp, however, also lay claim to home comforts – or home pressures. Mercedes are anxious to recover self-esteem after the shambles of Monza, and Norbert Haug, who fits the stereotype of the stout Mine Host at the local Gasthof, remains the consummately hospitable and candid head of the company's racing operation. Far from cowering in the glare of the inquisition, he is up front, prepared to take any flak thrown his way. This Thursday he has also brought with him his GT racing drivers, to give guests a taste of the real Nurburgring, the Nordschleife.

A lap of the old circuit with Bernd Schneider – who happens to be not only an excellent GT driver but also Oliver Bierhoff's brother-in-law – is an experience to ignite the senses and fill you with admiration for the men who raced Grand Prix cars around here. It is the ultimate roller-coaster ride, a screeching switchback made all the more exhilarating by dew still sheltered from an unseasonable sun, which highlights the first golden splashes of autumn this gorgeous morning.

'That's where Niki Lauda had his big accident,' Schneider says casually. The crash, in 1976, almost killed the Austrian and sounded the death knell for the old Ring as a Formula One venue.

Haug demonstrates he is no mean driver, either. Journalism and touring car competition feature on his impressive CV. He manages to keep Schneider in his sights until he is interrupted by a call on his mobile. It is Ron Dennis, seemingly lost in Koblenz. He must have been lumbered with Salo's navigation gismo. Eventually the Mercedes' brakes cry 'enough' and Haug pulls in.

The flirtation with nostalgia is over. Time to confront the realities of modern Formula One. The situation is close, tense, and no one can ignore the possibility of another unsavoury climax to the Championship. Schumacher was stripped of his second place after colliding with Jacques Villeneuve at Jerez last year. Haug envisages a wholesome finale this time – for the sport and for his team.

Last year's finish was not good for Formula One but it was not good for Schumacher either, and I do not expect a similar end to this Championship. Nobody can afford that. The sport learnt from that situation. It is certainly never our way to go motor racing. Having said that, I think it was a reflex action by Michael. Nobody should think we are pussycats or the sweethearts of the starting grid. We are fighting and there is no doubt that we can attack as well. But I do not want to see wheel banging and stuff like that.

If you become world champion by using a team-mate to block other competitors you might as well throw the World Championship away, because it is worth nothing. I don't say Irvine is doing anything. If somebody intends to kick us out of the race he probably can do that. But the Championship that has been gained fair and square is a worthy Championship.

Who is qualified to say Mika can't stand the pressure as well as Michael? You saw what he could do in Austria. If you are confident you don't make a lot of noise about it.

That is a rule of life. Those who make a noise are just nervous and trying to cover up.

Down at the new, anaesthetised circuit, the regulation trappings are in place, although someone has been charged with taping off a gap by Bernie's bus lest it should become a thoroughfare. The door at the other side is blacked out. Ross Brawn is wheeling between two of his team's transporters *en route* to the pits, understandably content with life. There was a time when the euphoria of a Ferrari win, especially in Italy, would have distracted the team for weeks. Not this team.

'I've told everybody not to get carried away with Monza,' Brawn says. 'This is going to be tough, like all the others. But they're level-headed. Michael's in good form, he's very calm. He's got a good chance here but I've given up trying to say which circuit is best for us.'

Hakkinen is said to be less calm. According to paddock gossip he was reluctant to test last week and when he did turn up he was melancholy, his body language giving mechanics the message: 'I can do my job, you do yours and make sure I have a car to win.' The official line is that he had been told he could rest and did not have to test. He turned up because he chose to.

He looks calm enough as he and Schumacher stroll into the media centre for a pre-Grand Prix joust, each aware the other – and the world's press – will be analysing every word, expression, gesture and nuance. Schumacher, smiling broadly and evidently finishing his lunch, leads the way, a couple of paces ahead of the Finn, then turns and offers his hand as they reach two chairs. Photographers ask them to do it again. Still smiling, Schumacher tells them they are not quick enough. 'This is not the movies.' He relents and poses greeting a compliant Hakkinen. They sit and the Championship leader is given the honour of speaking first.

Hakkinen: 'We're still very competitive and have the fastest car. We have a strong, powerful engine – forget the last race! The tyres are good, the team have experience, they're really motivated and all committed to win. They are definitely one of the best, if not the best team.'

Schumacher: 'Our strongest point is reliability. Right now our package is close to the top. We have won and been competitive on most types of circuit. I believe I have a fifty fifty chance of winning the Championship.'

Hakkinen: 'We have been giving too many presents this year. If the reliability goes it is very difficult for the driver to react. But you can't go into a race thinking something can go wrong. You have to race flat out to win.'

Schumacher: 'The pressure comes from outside, what people around us feel. I'm never nervous in the car. I'm pretty confident. Any feeling in the stomach is usually before the race. I feel more nervous when I play football.'

Hakkinen: 'I've been in Formula One a long time and there's always pressure. It is something you have to handle. In the car I am confident with my ability. If you allow the pressure to get to you, then you can make mistakes. I'd be wrong to say there is not pressure, but you have to make it positive pressure.'

He plays down the implied threat rain would bring, insisting that, while he prefers a dry race, he has no problem with a wet one. Schumacher says he is of like mind. Hakkinen talks of a routine build-up: training, relaxing, keeping a cool head. Schumacher is more extravagant, revealing he organised a karting romp for his mechanics and engineers last evening. Alitalia rescheduled flights to get Ferrari team members to Germany for the event, such is the influence of the man and the Prancing Horse. Brawn, Schumacher is amused to relate, did not have the stomach for it and pulled out after a couple of laps.

This image of fun and togetherness is doubtless meant to contrast with the perception of a beleaguered McLaren camp. Hakkinen counters by maintaining he is excited by the prospect of their showdown and would not be requiring any unfair contribution from David Coulthard.

'Certainly I would never think of getting my team-mate to

take the other driver off,' Hakkinen says. So would Schumacher ask anything of Irvine?

'The only thing I would ask my team-mate is to stay away from my daughter when she gets to the age,' Schumacher says to raucous laughter.

Each driver is invited to give his assessment of the other and Hakkinen responds with a glowing tribute, citing Schumacher's extreme pace and his two Championships. He is less forthcoming about the German's weaknesses, offering only a tantalising clue: 'It would be uncomfortable for me to start explaining.'

Schumacher presents a generous endorsement of Hakkinen's talents, his speed and consistency, which means the German's satisfaction will be all the greater for beating him. The beaming McLaren driver calls for 'more'.

'How much?' Schumacher asks before delivering a less sugary encore. 'The rest we will see. It is the first time for him fighting for the Championship. It is a new situation for him. I am confident and hope to fulfil the expectations of the people.' But has his grandmother given him a pointer for this race? 'She has said something but I'll tell you after the race.'

Another family matter Schumacher does not wish to divulge is whether his wife, Corinna, is expecting their second child, as reported in Germany.

Hakkinen makes his way back to the McLaren compound, where he will be available for more television, radio and press interviews. Coulthard, too, is on parade for an hour this afternoon. For the rest of the weekend the team want them to be left in peace to get on with their work. Coulthard is palpably irritated when the opening question seeks his evaluation of the Championship protagonists, rationalising he cannot know how they are feeling. His tone mellows, especially when he has the opportunity to talk about his own season.

'I think we have the same atmosphere in our team. I don't sense anxiety or nerves. Mika has proved he can win and I'm confident he can win. It's not been a waste of a season for me. You gain experience. I've made fewer mistakes, I feel I'm still improving and although I'm disappointed I'm not in the Championship battle this year my thoughts are already on next year.

'I can understand why people think Michael is tougher than Mika, but Michael has had more incidents and he always says it's the other guy's fault. I don't believe Mika will give an inch because he wants the Championship and if it comes down to the last corner he won't be found wanting. I think Mika deserves to win the Championship. His race wins have been very clean. Not all of Michael's have. His win in Argentina, for instance, was not sporting. Given this is a sport, may the best sportsman win. Michael appears to have made more mistakes this year. Whether he is getting older or closer to the edge I don't know.'

Mmm. On the road from the circuit, in villages of crooked, half-timbered houses straight out of toy-land, some of Schumacher's younger fans wave Ferrari flags to passing cars. They question neither his age nor his integrity. He is simply their hero.

Overnight rain has given way to a fine if sharp Friday morning. An English voice heard on the approach to the circuit reflects the scale of this sporting event. 'Who's got tickets?' he demands repeatedly. This might be Old Trafford or Wembley. Bernie, still declining to cover his white shirt while most of the paddock personnel are wearing anoraks, checks in at 8.45, presumably satisfied he will not have to endure a stream of people passing his door.

At the other end of the paddock, Stewart Ford are holding a press conference to confirm Rubens Barrichello will be staying with the team next year to partner Johnny Herbert. The Brazilian had hoped to join Williams but he was effectively shackled by a compensation clause and earlier this week Frank Williams named Alex Zanardi and Ralf Schumacher as his pairing for 1999. Barrichello says that in spite of 'a lot of rumours' he is happy to be part of the Stewart 'family' and has 'a good feeling' about next year.

Jackie Stewart, aware his team's efforts in this, their second year, have generally been regarded as disappointing, says structural changes within the organisation, as well as a new factory and test team, will enable them to be better prepared for next season. It is known he is competing with Arrows for the services of Gary Anderson, recently released as Jordan's technical director. Inevitably, however, Stewart's views on the main event here are being sought and he obliges.

There's no doubt Schumacher is the best driver in the world today. There is always one dominant driver in an era and he is the driver of this era. He is the man of our time. Mika is a very mature driver now, he's fast and he's done a good job. He has had accidents, such as at Silverstone and Monza, and got out of jail. But I think if you look at the World Championship, clinically and coolly, and what it stands for, it would probably be better for the sport – although Mika and McLaren would not see it this way – for Michael to win it and Mika to be the bridesmaid this year, then win it next year.

Ferrari have not had a Championship winner for nineteen years and Schumacher has done a hell of a job for them this year. So have the team. It's a combination of car and driver. I feel, though, that Schumacher has developed a little over-confidence in executing some of the things he's done. I never had it, nor did Fangio, Clark, Lauda or Prost. Ayrton had it and now Michael has it – a certain arrogance from being number one. It's not healthy and it can have the effect of causing more incidents we would want to avoid, and end in tears.

Ayrton would have grown out of it, with more experience. He had not reached his full potential. The same applies to Michael. I talked to Ayrton about this because I calculated that in an eighteen-month period he had more collisions than the combined total of all the champions since 1951. It was an indication of his aggression and over-confidence. That arrogance is a genuine flaw and there can be an incredible penalty that comes from it. If you had this situation in football with, let's say, Michael

Owen, and he was to get aggressive, then somebody would 'look after' him. In our day we all told anyone who misbehaved to cut it out, and it worked.

I don't know if Mika can do it to Michael and teach him a lesson. Michael always feels it's the other driver's fault. But it can't always be the other party. It's like a marriage. It takes two to tango, and to make a racing accident. I've never thought about speaking to Michael. I'm not sure he would understand and don't think it's my role to force myself on his behaviour pattern. If Ferrari or FIA ask, OK.

If I knew who was going to win I'd make some money. Mika should win, but the way he and McLaren are going they could lose it. They will have made an immense effort. So will Ferrari. They are the two teams with the biggest budgets in history. They are just shovelling money and technology at it. I think the pressure is affecting Mika more. When you haven't won it, then it's quite a big deal. It's not so much when you've got two titles under your belt.

Michael was not expected to win but he has made an exciting Championship out of what seemed like being a dreadful bore. If Michael loses it he will still get credit for being the best and making a contest of it. He is on a big roll now as a man and a driver. I believe he has earned the right to be a triple champion.

Herbert, embarking on his penultimate Grand Prix with Sauber, is evidently demob happy. A pair of pliers, left in the footwell of his car by an errant mechanic, caused his demise at Monza, yet he and his crew had fun with pliers all round when they went karting the other day and he shares the joke with friends. Schumacher is fastest in the first half of today's serious business but Hakkinen is top at the end, followed by Fisichella, Villeneuve, then the Ferrari number one.

The Ferrari number two, sixth today, makes for the motorhome of sponsors Marlboro and attacks a lunch of pasta.

Irvine is unshaven, undaunted by Hakkinen's time and unrelenting in his verbal hounding of the opposition.

There's no way Mika's mentally tougher than Michael. You saw it again at Monza. Michael's a lot tougher. For sure Mika will crack under the pressure. Michael knows he will have another shot at it if he doesn't get it this time. Mika knows this might be his only shot at it and that creates the pressure. He's got to make the most of it.

Hakkinen is not my priority and I'm not going to give him any room, but I'm not going to have him off. I wouldn't do it even if asked. Things can happen by accident, but that's racing. There's a seventy per cent chance of a first-corner coming together. They are constantly saying we have traction control but Ron Dennis must be blind if he says that now. We were struggling as much as anyone today and his car was faster. If he says we're cheating he's mad. It's actually pretty arrogant to say that. If we are cheating, how come their car is still faster?

Michael's certainly made mistakes but he's always made them, gone off and survived. We laugh about it. But he's winning races in an inferior car and driving at a different level from the rest of us. His car is always dancing around; he's always on the edge. It's been an amazing performance by Michael and the team to bring it to this. They don't have team orders at McLaren, we do. If we didn't run team orders Michael wouldn't be in with this chance. If Coulthard had helped Hakkinen more, Hakkinen would be champion already. McLaren are making it hard for themselves.

He pulls down one of the two pairs of shades perched on top of his head and finishes his pasta. But why two pairs?

'These are the first two of this type in Europe. Don't want anyone else wearing them, do I?'

The media pack doorstepping McLaren have a run-in with a

couple of mechanics, who angrily force a path from their garage. We're trying to work, growl the mechanics. So are we, reply the journalists. 'They're definitely twitchy,' a radio man says.

There is a niggly exchange, albeit couched in humour, when the other two German drivers, Heinz-Harald Frentzen and Ralf Schumacher, are brought together for the benefit of the home market. Frentzen, who swaps places with the younger Schumacher next season, says: 'I hope Ralf's seat is not too big for me.'

Ralf is transparently unimpressed and retorts: 'I'm going to have a new seat so I'll not have the same problem as Heinz-Harald.'

Corinna Schumacher, Michael's unassuming wife, is allowed to pursue an apparently urgent mission unhindered. She makes a rare foray down the paddock with a bowl of something presumably edible in her hand. It could prove she is eating for two, somebody suggests. Perhaps it's not edible at all and Michael's done a runner. The popular theory is that she has lost one of her dogs. Whatever the truth of the matter, she returns from a distant corner of the paddock with bowl still in hand and no sign of a dog. Or Michael.

It is probably safe to state Corinna will not find what she is looking for near Bernie's bus. Not only has the tape been extended to seal off the FIA mobile office units as well, but a white garden fence has been erected. All that is needed now is a rose bed.

A final thought for the day is stimulated by graffiti in one of the paddock toilets: 'Don't ever forget the second best driver in the world.'

More overnight rain is taking longer to dry this morning. Schumi's Army, converging from every direction, are more eager to hit the road than their hero, who sits out much of the early session. But then he has a man who does for him and the ever-faithful Irvine is pounding out the laps. Schumacher gets to work in the second half of the unofficial stint and is a whisker short of Hakkinen's time.

The temperature has plummeted since Thursday and groups

standing out in the paddock hunch their shoulders and tap their feet like men waiting for the pub to open. A group chatting outside the Jordan motorhome includes Chris Rea, the singer-songwriter and motor-racing devotee. He has divided loyalties since he is a close friend of Eddie Jordan and, quite naturally for one with Italian blood in his veins, a passionate Ferrari fan.

'It's the first race I've been able to get to this year,' he says. 'I had to do one, didn't I? Ferrari are in with a great chance now, aren't they? It's down to the man. There's only one I might still put in front of him and that's Clark.' Not Senna. I don't think he could sustain it, physically, the way Schumacher can.'

A brief shower before qualifying proves to be of little consequence and the usual suspects are seeking elbowroom at the front of the grid. Hakkinen surges clear, then Schumacher clearer still, to stunned expressions in the McLaren garage. Hakkinen improves but not enough, and now, even worse, he is nudged off the front row by Irvine. Coulthard is stranded in fifth place. The message is written across a landscape of red jubilation: Schumacher, with Irvine in close attendance thanks to the best quali-fying performance of his Formula One career, has wrested the initiative from Hakkinen.

'I was cheering with the rest of the team for Eddie's second place,' Schumacher says. 'Nobody could have imagined Eddie would pull out a lap like that. We have practised our starts so we should get that right this time. Naturally I feel some pressure, particularly in my home country, but I'm excited by the situation and confident for the race.'

Irvine, clean-shaven for his special occasion, says: 'Our number one concern is Michael winning the Championship and that is what we're aiming for. I'm a bit surprised with second place. I think McLaren underperformed. Their performance doesn't make sense. It always makes the start more difficult when there's no one ahead of you to gauge it with, but hopefully I can make one of my usual good starts.'

Hakkinen also expresses surprise: 'We're not as quick as we should have been. I was not a hundred per cent happy with the car. I wasn't able to carry my speed through the corners. This makes it more difficult for me but it's the race that decides the points.'

The public discomfort is prolonged for McLaren and Mercedes at their regular Saturday afternoon press conference. Wolfgang Schattling, Mercedes' press officer, is ready, microphone in hand, to introduce the proceedings and Haug is seated for the scheduled 4.30 start. Next to him is an empty seat, due to be occupied by Ron Dennis. Haug and Schattling exchange embarrassed glances and at 4.35 Haug apologises for the late start. This is not their customary way of doing things.

Nor, indeed, is it Dennis's. He insists on order and discipline, from a pristine garage to the arrangement of the condiment sets on the motorhome tables. He tells against himself the story of his having the gravel on his drive taken away twice a year to be washed. His absence is interpreted as further proof of the tension getting to him. Haug checks his watch again and looks up in relief as Dennis hurries from the adjacent McLaren bus and joins him.

'It seems we are a little slow whatever we do today,' Haug says pointedly. Dennis, scarcely appreciating the quip, throws up his eyes. But now he has his chance to speak.

'If you want a close World Championship, you've got one. We can't lose the Championship here. Our approach is to fight. We can't take anything away from our competition. No one in our team is not giving a hundred per cent. Right now it's not good enough. Tomorrow we just attack it.'

All weekend McLaren have been scrutinised for signs of pressure. The shielding of Hakkinen since Thursday is interpreted by some as evidence of their unease.

'No. We're devoid of these emotions,' Dennis replies. 'This is not an egg and spoon race, it's Formula One. It's tough. It's our approach to give our drivers the opportunity to relax and focus. It's logical team management and supported by everyone in the team and our sponsors.' Haug is adamant this is no Schumifest.

'Don't underestimate the number of people behind us,' he says on Mercedes' behalf. 'I have even been asked to sign number three Dekra caps.'

Dennis acknowledges he could have averted this cliffhanger

by adopting the team orders favoured by Ferrari, yet stands by his policy of democracy.

'That might have won us the Championship already but it's not our style. At one stage this season we were advised [by the FIA] team strategies were not permitted, and that is not a particularly comfortable environment in which to function, but I'm comfortable with our philosophy, and even if we lose the Championship I will have no regrets.

'I'm a terrible loser and it would be uncomfortable to lose a Championship we've led so well. Show me a good loser and I'll show you a loser. Given reliability we would have had both Championships by now. But I'd rather have performance. I'd rather have a sweet taste at the end of the season and you're not looking at losers yet. I certainly don't know if we'll win. We don't have the luxury of emotions.'

Few observers of the backstage drama doubt the emotions are being dragged every which way here. As rain falls the ever-thoughtful and courteous Haug jumps up to organise the distribution of silver Mercedes umbrellas to those standing outside the awning. The meteorological turbulence seems a final, grim augury for Hakkinen's team.

Daybreak is barely discernible as menacing dark grey clouds circle the region like the huge native birds seeking prey in the wooded hills and valleys. Dekraheads are parking on every available piece of grass verge, even several miles from the circuit, and marching on in great red waves. Some who tried their luck closer to the stands will discover later today that their vehicles have been carried off to a police compound. Another English tout vies for business with European counterparts. 'Buy or sell tickets,' is his invitation to treat.

Those in place for warm-up watch anxiously as McLaren improve with the weather. The head of the team is pictured monitoring proceedings on Bernie's digital TV. He is identified as 'Ronnie Dennis'. Probably just an innocent slip, Ron. He is encouraged by the important details of the session. Hakkinen is fastest, Coulthard second, Schumacher third.

In the paddock, however, the consensus is that if the Ferrari pair retain their advantage off the grid, Schumacher must win. Wet or dry. Irvine's role is critical. Two red scooters, standing by a Ferrari transporter, serve as a reminder of who's who around here. One bears the name 'Schumacher', the other bears no name. Schumacher and most of the other drivers obediently follow the detour around Bernie's bus as they return from their briefing. Naughty boys Alesi and Irvine take a short cut through his backyard and vault the fence.

Forty minutes before the race all appears remarkably calm in the pits. Ferrari's garage might be an operating theatre. Schumacher's empty car is positioned beneath a large oval light and technicians lean into it, tinkering with instruments. A man in a McLaren jacket, peering in from the pit lane, takes a keen interest in the activity. Schumacher comes into view to a volley of camera shots, climbs in from the left side, and drives out of the pits.

Hakkinen is in position on the grid before his opponent. Keke Rosberg, his manager and Finland's first and last world champion, 16 years ago, stands at the side of the track, keeping a paternal eye on Hakkinen and casting a wary glance in the direction of Irvine.

'Mika's the least nervous among us,' Rosberg says. 'He's fully occupied. He can do something about it. We can't. He's quick, the car's quick. I just hope they're allowed to race and nothing happens at the other side of the track there. You never know what Irvine's going to do. Having said that, he came out and said Michael was to blame for what happened at Spa, so he was fair then. Mika's going for the win. He's got to.'

Chris de Burgh is in the throng around Schumacher's car, assuring Todt of his support. Schumacher, of course, looks relaxed. He is standing by his car, at the front of the grid, talking to Bernie, who has relented in the autumnal chill and put on a grey jacket. Martin Brundle and his ITV crew move in to pick their thoughts. 'Bernie's idea,' a self-satisfied Brundle says, briskly walking towards the tunnel that takes him under the track and to his commentary position. Herbert is nonchalantly strolling back to the grid from the toilet, hands thrust deep into the pockets of his anorak. He could be on his way home from the pub for his Sunday lunch.

Ten minutes later Herbert and the rest set out on the formation lap. Charlie Whiting is relieved to preside over another clean start. Schumacher loses the lead, but only to Irvine, and the German slips by at the end of the opening lap. It is precisely the scenario Hakkinen feared: Irvine is between him and his rival for the Championship. However, Schumacher is not opening the gap he hoped for. Irvine slows but that puts him at the mercy of Hakkinen. The Ulsterman survives a couple of sideways moments and the Finn's signal indicates his exasperation. At the end of the 14th lap Irvine is outmanoeuvred by the feinting Hakkinen and the race is on. Schumacher leads by 8.5 seconds.

Hakkinen, his progress followed as ever from the pits by his wife, Erja, closes in on the Ferrari, reducing the gap to 5.7 seconds before Schumacher makes his first pit stop. Hakkinen stays out for another four laps, straining every sinew to tilt the balance. His pit stop will tell. Schumacher, presumably watched by Corinna although she is not to be seen, turns into the start/finish straight expecting to regain the lead. To his dismay the McLaren re-emerges in his path. The Ferrari twitches as Schumacher leaves his braking as late as possible, but to no avail. Hakkinen stands his ground.

Schumacher pursues Hakkinen with characteristic verve, and perhaps a touch of indignation. For ten absorbing laps they are separated by less than a second. The effort takes its toll. Schumacher, his tyres shot, his heart pierced, drops back. The McLaren crew execute an impeccable second pit stop and even the heavens decline to intervene on Schumacher's behalf this time. He has to concede defeat and send home his supporters in dismay.

It is a chastening and shattering experience for Schumacher. He is not merely disappointed but bewildered. All the optimism generated at Monza and in qualifying here has evaporated. Hakkinen heads the Championship by four points and needs only second place from the final race, in Japan, to win it. Schumacher graciously, if belatedly, gives Hakkinen the champagne treatment on the podium but he is palpably hurting inside, and it shows on the outside. He faces the prospect of a third consecutive season without the title. With Coulthard finishing third and Irvine fourth, Ferrari virtually concede the Constructors' Championship to McLaren Mercedes.

Hakkinen, who should have a pleasant 30th birthday tomorrow, says with similar understatement: 'This certainly makes my situation a bit different from a couple of hours ago. It was enjoyable at the end, but the race was not so enjoyable. It was very tough. Eddie annoyed me in one moment and it was still quite close when I passed him. Everybody knows Eddie's reputation but he was very fair today.'

Schumacher's words articulate everything his body language has revealed from the moment he climbed from his cockpit.

'I was surprised he was able to get in front of me but overall we weren't fast enough and we have to accept that. I pushed hard, hoping for a little hole to sneak down, and that's why the tyres went off. We will certainly not give up because we can still win in Japan and one word sums up the next four weeks – testing. We're going to work non-stop and go for it. If we don't do it we can still be proud of our achievements.'

McLaren staff are pouring champagne and Dennis is loftily pronouncing this as 'probably the most important race in the history of the company'.

The significance sends Ferrari's hierarchy into a sombre inquest. 'They're all in there scratching their heads,' a team member says. 'They can't understand it. They really thought they'd have enough speed to do it.'

Other members of the team are dismantling the motorhome awnings around a television set, which is showing an Italian football match. Barely a penalty kick along the paddock, a party is in full swing. Haug, an arm around Mario Illien, the man who makes his engines, a hand clutching a pineapple like a microphone, is inevitably leading the karaoke session. The sound of Queen provides a fitting anthem: 'It's a kind of magic . . . one dream, one soul, one prize, one goal . . .'

The goal has come tantalisingly into range and the magic cannot be suppressed. It looks and feels like a Championship celebration. Even Schumacher's fans are gatecrashing the party. Since Hakkinen is not in view they settle for his accommodating wife's signature on their Dekra caps. The plaudits are coming Hakkinen's way at last. Some say this is his greatest race. Rosberg smiles in quiet contentment. His driver has been vindicated.

'People have finally recognised Mika is a great racing driver. Even after his wins in Austria and Monaco people were saying he'd crack under the pressure and that Michael is better than anyone. The trouble is, Michael plays down the car to make himself look better. McLaren drivers are part of a team. If Mika had driven a Ferrari here the church bells would be ringing in Italy.

'Michael now knows what he faces, that Mika is not an easy touch. Michael will probably be praying for rain in Japan, but Mika can win it in snow, rain or sun. It's going to be some fight at Suzuka. It can be just as difficult to be second as it is to win a race.'

Hakkinen is still locked in a compartment of the McLaren motorhome; showered, changed, alone with his thoughts, some scattered gear and a picture given him for his birthday. It is a precious, tranquil opportunity to sit and savour the satisfaction.

I don't exactly feel it was my best race. We've not won here by luck, or somebody going off, we've won because we were fast and had the right tactics. I proved a point and if I win the Championship I will feel I deserve it. But when I am on the track I never think about what people think. I just race for myself. I believe in my abilities. A lot of drivers deserve to win it and have proved they're great drivers. Damon Hill and Jacques Villeneuve had to fight for it in the last couple of years. A driver like Johnny Herbert, who has been racing many years, also deserves it.

I don't see any difference in Michael because of this defeat. He feels bad. Of course he is down, especially because this is in Germany. I would feel the same if it happened to me in Finland. But the last race was a disaster for us and we came back, and Michael will be back tomorrow just the same, lifting his team. We do that because we are both professional. He knows you just have to keep going, and maybe the team will find some improvements in testing.

You have to believe in a team and stick to a team with potential. Keke told me to come to McLaren because they had the record, the history. They have great people, the package and the sponsors, and when you have that you know that if you work, one day you will win. And if we go on winning maybe one day Norbert will learn to sing!

Some of the people here have been through hard times, and they appreciate it more when they win. I know how Ron feels; I know how all of them feel. They're working flat out and they believe in me one hundred per cent. That is one of the reasons I don't want to let them down. It's really weird and hard for me to understand what's going on at the moment. We haven't won it yet.

At the end of the day it is still a sport. I can only give it my best shot. If I lose I lose, if I win I win. To be a good winner you have to learn to lose. It doesn't matter when you win, as long as you get your goal.

That's a kind of magic.

12
Suzuka

WHEN THE BIG WHEEL STOPS

It has come full circle, to the shadow of the symbolic big wheel. No one expected it to, not even Michael Schumacher, yet here he is, at the Japanese Grand Prix, the final round of the Championship, still hounding Mika Hakkinen, still in with a chance of winning his third title. The fast, challenging circuit of Suzuka, its figure-of-eight layout as distinctive as the adjacent fairground landmark, has staged the concluding proceedings in half a dozen Championships, two of them in controversial circumstances. In 1989 Ayrton Senna was mugged by his McLaren team-mate, Alain Prost, at the chicane and then disqualified for taking the wrong route back on to the track. The Frenchman had the title. Twelve months later Senna, determined to exact revenge, speared Prost, now in a Ferrari, at the first corner. The Brazilian had the title.

Schumacher, of course, is no stranger to close encounters of the unacceptable kind in deciding races. He tangled with Damon Hill in 1994 and won; then with Jacques Villeneuve in 1997 and lost. The difference this time is that he goes into the Grand Prix trailing his rival, must win and therefore may be less inclined to take risks. The prospect of foul play has inevitably occupied the minds of participants and observers in the five weeks since the Nurburgring, a purgatory inflicted by the cancellation of the Portuguese Grand Prix. It might not make sense for Schumacher to get physical, but how about his team-mate?

Eddie Irvine arrives here under almost as much pressure as the Championship duellists. Ferrari were dismayed he did not resist Hakkinen beyond the 14th lap at the Luxembourg Grand Prix. Schumacher expressed his 'surprise' the Ulsterman had made it 'quite easy' for the McLaren driver. The Ferrari president, Luca di Montezemolo, said Irvine was 'too gentlemanly'. There was renewed speculation Irvine could lose his job to Jean Alesi, which was interpreted as a calculated means of delivering the message. Directly or indirectly, it was made clear to Irvine more was expected of him in this race.

For general consumption Irvine has been content to pledge his loyalty to his team and partner, while stressing he would not resort to dirty tricks. He has, in any case, good reason to be optimistic here. He spent three seasons competing in the Japanese 3000 series before joining the Formula One circus. Suzuka is his favourite circuit. He contends Ferrari have as good a chance of relegating Hakkinen to third place – which they must do to guarantee Schumacher the Championship – here as anywhere else.

However, behind the reflex bravado lurks resentment and angst. He confides he feels an undue burden of responsibility is being placed on him. Why, he pleads, should he be expected to win the Championship for Schumacher. The dissonance is becoming ever more apparent. He senses he is being set up as the scapegoat. A new seat should at least ensure he is spared his recent back problems.

The testing – much of it at Fiorano, Ferrari's own figure-of-eight track – has been unrelenting. They have filched bits and tweaks scheduled for next year's car, although nothing, Ross Brawn is adamant, that would compromise reliability. They have to go the distance. Tyres could be crucial. Goodyear, eager to bow out of Formula One as winners, have responded to Ferrari's every wish and whim. Thousands of gallons of water have been pumped onto the test circuit in the quest for the ideal wet weather compound. At the end of the programme Schumacher revealed 'a feeling' the Championship was to be his.

McLaren's test schedule has been less intense, Ron Dennis laying emphasis on 'quality rather than quantity'. Their lap times at Barcelona have been hugely impressive. They, too, have put a lot of effort, and water, into their tyre choice. The word is the Bridgestone will take some beating if it is dry, but may not be so effective in the wet. The team, and Hakkinen, profess themselves prepared.

'Fear is a negative emotion and I fear nothing about this race,' the Finn says. 'If I had that sort of attitude I would be half beaten already. I have prepared for this race in exactly the same way as for any other race. Why should we change a winning formula? If we treat this race as something different, that is when the mistakes are likely to happen.'

Hakkinen maintains he will go into the race intent on giving his 'maximum', yet concedes he may adapt his strategy according to the circumstances. He says he has no worries Schumacher will attempt any over-zealous manoeuvre and has no intention of pushing his rival off the road. 'That is not my style. I have never done anything like that and I never will.'

Backstage Hakkinen is generally regarded as the favourite, providing the circuit is dry. Second place, it is thought, should be comfortably within his range. Johnny Herbert, a former team-mate of both Championship protagonists, believes the superiority of the McLaren will carry Hakkinen through.

'I think Mika will be a good champion,' Herbert says. 'He's come back well after his accident and I think that probably did change him for the better. My shunt in '88 definitely changed me. People go on about how I'm always laughing and joking but I wasn't like that before my shunt. I decided the only way to get back was to laugh it off, be lighter, and Mika has probably done the same. He made a good recovery in every sense; the slight effect to his face is the only thing. I'm sure the accident made him see a lot of things differently.'

Herbert is one of the many changing teams after this race. His place at Sauber is to be taken by Pedro Diniz, currently of Arrows. Another Brazilian, Ricardo Zonta, winner of the Formula 3000 International and FIA GT series, has signed for BAR. Gary Anderson has joined Stewart Ford as chief designer, while David Richards is also being linked with a possible role in that camp after quitting Benetton over 'restructuring' policy. His plans did not meet with the approval of the Italian family, who put 29-year-old Rocco Benetton, youngest son of Luciano, in charge.

Leaving Arrows along with Diniz is Ann Bradshaw. In fact she is turning her back on Formula One after 14 years to start a new life in the United States.

Ralf Schumacher's last race with Jordan, before changing places with Williams' Heinz-Harald Frentzen, has been soured somewhat by a squabble over back pay. The German served a writ against Jordan claiming $375,000 in fees, $175,000 in bonuses and $20,000 in interest. This second writ issued by the driver against the team in a matter of weeks was withdrawn after Jordan gave assurances the matter would be resolved.

Contract details in the High Court claim revealed Schumacher's payment for 1998 was to be broken down as follows: $600,000 for racing, $400,000 for testing, $1,000,000 for promotion and advertising. These payments were to be made in four instalments. In addition, he was to be paid $10,000 per point, $150,000, $90,000 and $60,000 respectively for first, second and third places, and $1,000,000, $500,000 and $250,000 respectively for first, second or third place in the Championship.

Brother Michael, Hakkinen and their respective seconds are lined up before the media this Thursday afternoon. All pledge their commitment to fair play, although Coulthard does his best to spice up proceedings by saying: 'I certainly won't make it as easy as Eddie made it for Mika to overtake him at the Nurburgring.'

There is frankly scant enthusiasm for talking. Friday morning practice is as soothing as a dip in a pool. Schumacher picks up any psychological points on offer with the fastest time. Hakkinen is down in fifth position. Ralf Schumacher is second, Frentzen third and Irvine fourth. A lacklustre Coulthard is sixth. Michael, however, is convinced we have not seen the 'whole truth' today, while Hakkinen calmly declares himself pleased with business.

Emotions are similarly restrained after qualifying. Schumacher achieves all he can ask of himself with pole position, his third in succession, but as Hakkinen is alongside him on the front row, Coulthard next and Irvine fourth, the Ferrari No. 1 doubtless fears he is not going to have the cover he requires from his colleague. It is tomorrow that matters, he coolly, almost dismissively, comments, and retreats to his lair to plot a myriad strategic options.

Frentzen and Villeneuve, on the third row, encourage Williams to believe they should hold third place in the constructors' standings, while Ralf Schumacher and Hill qualify ahead of the Benetton pair to give Jordan an excellent chance of seizing a best-ever fourth place. Tyrrell will have only one car in their last race. Rosset has failed to make the cut.

Race day is fine and bright, and Hakkinen will believe another potential obstacle has been removed from his path. Schumacher is again fastest in warm-up, but his rival betrays no sign of foreboding. Out on the grid Hakkinen approaches Schumacher and the pair shake hands. The gesture might not have the psychological effect it perhaps had on Fisichella, back in Austria, but it earns the Finn more marks for sportsmanship.

The Championship contenders look more relaxed than anyone in their respective camps. The crowd here is always huge and engrossed. The ballot for tickets and the weekend queues through the fun fair for unreserved places have been traditional features on a par with the big wheel. And yet the Japanese do not necessarily create a frenzied atmosphere. That ingredient has been added by the klaxon sounds of Schumi's Army, and the bellowing of Hakkinen's flag-waving followers.

Tension reaches a crescendo as the red lights come on, only to be left suspended as the orange lights indicate the start has been aborted. Jarno Trulli has stalled and will be sent to the back of the grid. They try again and at 13.13 local time they are again restrained. Almost unbelievably, the driver indicating his distress is Michael Schumacher. He shakes his head in desolation as he realises his stalled engine means he, too, is to be consigned to the back of the field and almost certainly out of the Championship. Ferrari are stunned.

The cars get away at the third time of asking, Hakkinen protecting his inheritance. He is pursued by Irvine as the out-of-sorts Coulthard drops back to fourth, behind Frentzen. Schumacher slices through the two back rows of the grid even before he reaches his original starting spot and by the end of the first lap has made up nine places to 12th. He is 10th after two laps, seventh after five. It is a magnificently defiant response, an inspiring display of bravura. But now it is checked by his old nemesis Hill, who ignores team advice to give way. This is personal. Schumacher pits and resumes the chase on fresh rubber.

Irvine, on a three-stop strategy, finds renewed vigour in his attempt to apply the pressure and rescue his team-mate's cause. The Ferraris produce a volley of fastest laps. The effort takes Schumacher to the ragged edge. He careers through the chicane and collects a sideways slide. By mid-race he is third.

As Schumacher approaches the chicane for the 31st time, Tuero and Takagi demonstrate how to really make a mess of it, their collision dumping debris across the road. As they continue their finger-wagging argument the Ferrari passes through, but towards the bottom of the sloping start-finish straight its right rear tyre gives way. Within moments it is shredding to nothing, the car disabled. Schumacher pulls off the track, his race run, his challenge over. McLaren call in Hakkinen to change tyres, lest he should pick up a remnant of the Tuero-Takagi debacle. The Finn knows that whatever fate has in store for him in what is left of this Grand Prix, he is world champion.

The McLaren crew cannot contain their jubilation, while Ferrari are ready with a united and philosophical front. Di Montezemolo explains an electronics/clutch gremlin caught out Schumacher on the grid and congratulates their opponents, who have also won the constructors' title. 'The dream is finished but be sure we will be back to win next year,' he says. Cynical Italian chroniclers moan they have heard it all before.

Schumacher draws breath on the sidelines, then makes his way back to base. He offers every member of the team gratitude and consolation. 'I'm not delighted but we can be proud of what we have done. We did what people didn't believe we could, we challenged McLaren. It wasn't just a puncture, the tyre exploded. But I knew the Championship was over on the grid. It was such a tiny problem but it was not funny. At least I had some fun in the first few laps. We did not lose the Championship here, we lost it at the beginning of the season and cannot complain.'

Hakkinen paces himself to the line, sealing his Championship with his eighth win of the season. Irvine is second, Coulthard third and Hill fourth, out-manoeuvring Frentzen at the last corner to add lustre to Jordan's fourth place, behind Williams. Schumacher greets Hakkinen in the *parc fermé* with warm though unostentatious congratulations. Irvine pats the top of his helmet. Hakkinen climbs from his car, hugs Coulthard and tells him 'it's your turn next'. He removes his head gear, tosses his gloves in the direction of converging mechanics and engineers, hugs Dennis, then veers off his designated route to the podium to acknowledge his flag-waving fans in the stands. Dennis concedes some sympathy for Ferrari, 'but not much'.

On the podium Hakkinen seems to be struggling to mouth the words of his national anthem, tears beginning to well in his eyes. So much for the unemotional Finns. His wife, Erja, looking up from the midst of the throng, manages to sing, smile and glow simultaneously. Drenched in Coulthard's and Irvine's champagne, Hakkinen embarks on his round of interviews, reverting to the familiar, deliberating persona.

'I don't know how to start telling my feelings. Since starting in Formula One in 1991 it has been a fight every year to maximise my results. It took quite a long time and now it has happened.'

He thanks the team for their efforts and admits he felt a release of pressure when Schumacher stalled, the twisted grin reappearing on his face. He says his mind began to wander when the victory beckoned, but Dennis ushered him back on course with instructions to stay cool. He is reminded of his accident in Adelaide, which many in the paddock thought had killed him, and the subsequent weeks of recovery. 'It made me change completely. This is a dream come true.'

He is applauded as a worthy champion, an honest, decent man. But then Schumacher, too, has retrieved honour from eventual disappointment. He has rarely been mistaken for a paragon of virtue and many will wallow in his latest demise. Most, however, recognise him as the pre-eminent force and major draw in Formula One, the man who defied the auguries to make a contest of it. The pity is the watching world was denied the climax the Championship demanded on a technicality, the rule that stipulates anyone who stalls on the grid must start at the back. It is something for the authorities to mull over. But Formula One is feeling good about itself again. The tainted cloak of last winter has been cast aside, replaced by the comforting after-glow of an absorbing and ultimately amicable World Championship.

Up and down the pit lane they will be analysing and re-running the race and the season now past. It is a time for celebration and satisfaction, dejection and recrimination, reflections and resolutions. There will be heartfelt inquests, cathartic outpourings and embittered separations. Ahead lie new alliances, new challenges. Not very far ahead for many of them. They will be back at this circuit on Tuesday – to start testing for next season.

1998 Formula One World Championship Results

8 March: Australian Grand Prix (Melbourne)
1. M. Hakkinen
2. D. Coulthard
3. H. Frentzen
4. E. Irvine
5. J. Villeneuve
6. J. Herbert

29 March: Brazilian Grand Prix (Interlagos)
1. M. Hakkinen
2. D. Coulthard
3. M. Schumacher
4. A. Wurz
5. H. Frentzen
6. G. Fisichella

12 April: Argentine Grand Prix (Buenos Aires)
1. M. Schumacher
2. M. Hakkinen
3. E. Irvine
4. A. Wurz
5. J. Alesi
6. D. Coulthard

26 April: San Marino Grand Prix (Imola)
1. D. Coulthard
2. M. Schumacher

3. E. Irvine
4. J. Villeneuve
5. H. Frentzen
6. J. Alesi

10 May: Spanish Grand Prix (Barcelona)

1. M. Hakkinen
2. D. Coulthard
3. M. Schumacher
4. A. Wurz
5. R. Barrichello
6. J. Villeneuve

24 May: Monaco Grand Prix (Monte Carlo)

1. M. Hakkinen
2. G. Fisichella
3. E. Irvine
4. M. Salo
5. J. Villeneuve
6. P. Diniz

7 June: Canadian Grand Prix (Montreal)

1. M. Schumacher
2. G. Fisichella
3. E. Irvine
4. A. Wurz
5. R. Barrichello
6. J. Magnussen

28 June: French Grand Prix (Magny-Cours)

1. M. Schumacher
2. E. Irvine
3. M. Hakkinen
4. J. Villeneuve
5. A. Wurz
6. D. Coulthard

12 July: British Grand Prix (Silverstone)

1. M. Schumacher
2. M. Hakkinen
3. E. Irvine
4. A. Wurz
5. G. Fisichella
6. R. Schumacher

26 July: Austrian Grand Prix (Zeltweg)

1. M. Hakkinen
2. D. Coulthard
3. M. Schumacher
4. E. Irvine
5. R. Schumacher
6. J. Villeneuve

2 August: German Grand Prix (Hockenheim)

1. M. Hakkinen
2. D. Coulthard
3. J. Villeneuve
4. D. Hill
5. M. Schumacher
6. R. Schumacher

16 August: Hungarian Grand Prix (Budapest)

1. M. Schumacher
2. D. Coulthard
3. J. Villeneuve
4. D. Hill
5. H. Frentzen
6. M. Hakkinen

30 August: Belgian Grand Prix (Spa-Francorchamps)

1. D. Hill
2. R. Schumacher
3. J. Alesi

4. H. Frentzen
5. P. Diniz
6. J. Trulli

13 September: Italian Grand Prix (Monza)

1. M. Schumacher
2. E. Irvine
3. R. Schumacher
4. M. Hakkinen
5. J. Alesi
6. D. Hill

27 September: Luxembourg Grand Prix (Nurburgring)

1. M. Hakkinen
2. M. Schumacher
3. D. Coulthard
4. E. Irvine
5. H. Frentzen
6. G. Fisichella

1 November: Japanese Grand Prix (Suzuka)

1. M. Hakkinen
2. E. Irvine
3. D. Coulthard
4. D. Hill
5. H. Frentzen
6. J. Villeneuve

1998 DRIVERS' CHAMPIONSHIP

		Pts
1.	Mika Hakkinen (McLaren Mercedes)	100
2.	Michael Schumacher (Ferrari)	86
3.	David Coulthard (McLaren Mercedes)	56
4.	Eddie Irvine (Ferrari)	47
5.	Jacques Villeneuve (Williams Mecachrome)	21
6.	Damon Hill (Jordan Mugen)	20
7.	Heinz-Harald Frentzen (Williams Mecachrome)	17
8.	Alexander Wurz (Benetton Playlife)	17
9.	Giancarlo Fisichella (Benetton Playlife)	16
10.	Ralf Schumacher (Jordan Mugen)	14
11.	Jean Alesi (Sauber Petronas)	9
12.	Rubens Barrichello (Stewart Ford)	4
13.	Mika Salo (Arrows)	3
14.	Pedro Diniz (Arrows)	3
15.	Johnny Herbert (Sauber Petronas)	1
	Jan Magnussen (Stewart Ford)	1
	Jarno Trulli (Prost Peugeot)	1

Did not score: Olivier Panis (Prost Peugeot), Jos Verstappen (Stewart Ford), Ricardo Rosset (Tyrrell Ford), Toranosuke Takagi (Tyrrell Ford), Shinji Nakano (Minardi Ford), Esteban Tuero (Minardi Ford).

1998 CONSTRUCTORS' CHAMPIONSHIP

1.	McLaren Mercedes	156
2.	Ferrari	133
3.	Williams Mecachrome	38
4.	Jordan Mugen	34
5.	Benetton Playlife	33
6.	Sauber Petronas	10
7.	Arrows	6
8.	Stewart Ford	5
9.	Prost Peugeot	1

Did not score: Tyrrell Ford, Minardi Ford.

APPENDIX

DRIVERS AND TEAM MANAGERS BRIEFING

Event : Italian Grand Prix
Date : 13th September 1998
Document : 17

1) If you cover more than one reconnaissance lap please go through the pit lane at a greatly reduced speed.

2) During the formation lap please keep the formation as tight as possible to avoid any unnecessary delay on the starting grid.

    Passing during the formation lap is only permitted in order to maintain formation and then only if your car was moving when the remaining cars crossed the Line to start their formation lap.

3) Please remember to drive at a greatly reduced speed until clear of all Team personnel beside the track.

4) If your car stalls at the start of the formation lap your Team may attempt to start it. However, marshals will be instructed to push the car to the pit exit approximately 10 seconds after the rest of the cars have left the grid.

5) When you arrive at the grid, line boards showing your race number will be displayed on your left. Please take up your exact position by placing your front wheels between the

front of the grid box and the yellow line on the side of the grid box. The yellow lines are placed on the left and right of the grid boxes.

Any final adjustment to your position should be made before the one second signal, the jump start system becomes active at this point.

6)   If your car stalls at the start it will be pushed to the pit exit where your mechanics may attempt to rectify the problem.

7)   If you have to start the race from the pit lane, you may leave the pits only when the pit exit lights change from red to flashing orange.

8)   Please ensure that no wheel guns are left in the pit lane unless a pit stop is imminent. All wheel guns should be kept inside the inner wheel positions.

9)   If you are involved in a collision or incident please remember that you must get permission from the Stewards to leave the circuit.

10)   Safety Car:

When you see SC boards accompanied by yellow flags please slow down to the pace you would normally expect to drive at when behind the car.

If the Safety Car is deployed and the leader comes into the pits, the next car in line, which may not necessarily be the second placed car, must take up position no more than five car lengths behind the Safety Car.

It should be noted that the leader may dictate the pace once the lights on the car are turned out, and if necessary fall more than five car lengths behind the Safety Car.

You are also reminded that you may only exit the pits at this time when the pit exit lights are flashing orange or green.

If you leave the pits whilst the Safety Car is being used, please drive in the knowledge that there may be more than one incident on the track and that marshals may be on the track at any point.

11) Subject to the consent of the Stewards at the time, if the race has to be stopped and the track is completely blocked, the pit exit will be closed and remain so until the track is clear enough to allow cars through.

Under such circumstances, as soon as the pit lane is opened it will remain open for ten minutes. When it closes there will be at least ten minutes until the start of the new formation lap.

12) After the chequered flag is shown all the cars must proceed directly to the parc fermé which is immediately before the first garage as you enter the pits.

You are reminded that no Team members are permitted in the parc fermé without the express permission of the FIA technical delegate.

All drivers, if asked to do so, must have their weight checked after the race with crash helmet.

Charlie Whiting

FIA Formula One Race Director